Paradigm and Ideology
in Educational Research

Paradigm and Ideology in Educational Research
The Social Functions of the Intellectual

Thomas S. Popkewitz
University of Wisconsin-Madison

 **The Falmer Press**

A member of the Taylor & Francis Group
London and New York

UK   The Falmer Press, Falmer House, Barcombe, Lewes, East Sussex,
              BN8 5DL

USA   The Falmer Press, Taylor & Francis Inc., 242 Cherry Street,
              Philadelphia, PA 19106-1906

First published in 1984

Library of Congress Cataloging in Publication Data

Popkewitz, Thomas S.
  Paradigm and ideology in educational research.

  Includes index.
  1. Education—Research—United States—Philosophy—
Case studies.   2. Education—Research—Soviet Union—
Philosophy—Case studies.   3. Education—Social aspects—
United States—Case studies.   4. Education—Social
aspects—Soviet Union—Case studies.   I. Title.
LB1028.P577   1984   370′.7′8   84-1601
ISBN 0-905273-98-2
ISBN 0-905273-97-4 (U.S.: pbk.)

Phototypeset in 11/13 Garamond by
Imago Publishing Ltd, Thame, Oxon.

Jacket illustration by Kerry Freedman
Jacket design by Leonard Williams

*Printed in Great Britain by Taylor & Francis (Printers) Ltd,
Basingstoke*

Contents

To *H. Millard Clements*
a friend and teacher who helped me
understand the importance of questions
about knowledge and interest

Preface

Over the past decade, disagreement has developed within the scholarly communities about the nature and character of social and educational inquiry. Arguments about the role of social sciences have occurred at professional conventions and new journals have appeared to provide a forum for those men and women who take issue with the present direction of social research. Drawing upon European traditions of the sociology of knowledge, hermeneutics and Marxism, the debates have brought into question some of the basic assumptions by which people have engaged in inquiry. Attention is given to the social processes in which research occurs and the social role of the intellectual, pointing to the social and cultural context of inquiry and the human hopes, values and interests that such processes entail.

We err if we do not consider the debate within the social and educational sciences as substantive rather than procedural. The work of science is a work of people who are striving to understand and improve our social conditions and institutional patterns. The competing assumptions, questions and procedures of research contain values that represent deep divisions within American society about principles of authority, institutional transformation and social order. Embedded in research are issues of epistemology, political and cognitive theory as well as people's responses to their material existence.

Certain social dimensions of research are brought into sharp relief. One is the communal quality of scientific practice. Social inquiry emerges from a communal context in which there are norms, beliefs and patterns of social conduct. These patterns are not static and involve continual debate. The debate evolves around differing assumptions about the nature of social life and the purpose of a science, as there are various intellectual traditions that compete to establish standards of inquiry.

Second is the recognition of the social and cultural location of our research activities. We can think of social science as dialects of language which provide heuristic fictions for supposing the world is this way or that way. These fictions or theories are made to seem neutral by the conventions of science which decontextualizes language and makes knowledge seem transcendent. But scrutiny of the languages and procedures of science compels us to recognize that neither is devoid of human hope and interest. Our methods of research emerge from our involvement in our social conditions and provide a means by which we can seek to resolve the contradictions we feel and the worlds that seem unresolved in our everyday life.

A third important dimension in the work of inquiry is the social role of the intellectual. To talk about school learning, achievement or academic engaged-time is to assume a role in the dynamics of institutional reproduction and transformation. The categories taken by the researcher have been shaped and fashioned in contexts of people who have struggled with the strains and contradictions of our human conditions. The social and educational researcher appropriates, exploits, reformulates and verifies ideas that have their roots in social movements.

The social role of the researcher poses a contradictory character to the work of educational science. The researcher acts as an expert-in-legitimation, creating symbolic canopies that make the interests of few seem the interests of the society as a whole. At the same moment, there is a criticizing and probing attitude towards human society and its particular situations in time and place. These two aspects stand juxtaposed in our sciences.

The purpose of this book is to explore the social location and contradictions of social science. It is to probe how social assumptions, cultural location and political interests become intricately tied to conceptual, procedural and design questions. These issues are given focus through case studies in American and Soviet pedagogical research and evaluation. These research communities provide a specific historical context to consider the larger sociological issues of social science and the social role of the intellectual.

Because of the general and specific focus, the book has different publics. It is directed to professionals, academics and students interested in critical analyses of social institutions. The researcher is considered a social type who is located in the general dynamics and represents interests of society.

This book is also designed as an introductory text for courses in research methods. The focus on paradigms enables a consideration of the interrelation of questions, concepts and data gathering procedures. The discussion illustrates research as a complex process in which particular data collecting techniques assume meaning and significance only in relation to the assumptions of the larger intellectual traditions in which the techniques are applied.

In this respect, I consider research methodology as a subject matter of this book. Its themes and organization are a response to university research and graduate programs which focus only upon the 'how-to-do-it' tasks of data collection and analysis. Research is thought of as a series of techniques in statistics, testing or observation that are practiced independently of questions, assumptions or concepts. Labels such as qualitative or quantitative research, for example, ignore the underlying values and commitments of science which give variation to the use of statistics or field study.

To focus solely on techniques and procedures produces certain limitations to the conduct of inquiry. First, the lack of situating concepts and techniques within their social and philosophical contexts produces knowledge that is often trivial and socially conservative. Second, the social sciences have competing traditions. To consider the various traditions as differences only in techniques is to obscure the assumptions and implications of these traditions. Third, social and educational sciences have a dual function of describing and orienting people to the possibilities of human affairs. To filter out discussion of the social circumstances and cultural location that guide policy option is to mystify social arrangements.

The arguments of this book emerge from my dissertation, begun in 1968. I was concerned with problem-solving in political science and its implications for the tasks of curriculum design. The study, drawn from the sociology of knowledge, focused upon the paradigmatic assumptions, commitments and procedures of political inquiry. Because of the general social and political turmoil of the times, American political scientists were confronting basic questions about the assumptions, implications and consequences of that science. Younger members of the discipline were questioning the hegemony of behavioral political science and arguing that research served as a 'handmaiden' of existing institutions and helped to legitimate social and economic inequities. These men and women formed 'radical caucuses' within the organizations, critiqued existing methods and sought alternative paradigms by drawing upon European critical social sciences.

The themes of conflict, value and historical location that are part of this social science have, I believe, important implications for those who wish to select and organize knowledge in schools. These debates which were initially joined in the late 1960s have been returned to by me over the years and have widened to include issues of the 'nature' of science and the social role of the intellectual. These issues assume great importance in a society in which the knowledge of the scientific expert is made paramount.

As drafts were written and rewritten, I had conversations which helped to clarify further my thoughts and the issues discussed in the book. Among those who I would like to thank for our conversations are Cathy Cornbleth, Kathy Kasten, Kerry Freedman, David Hamilton, Hannah Hill, Henry Giroux, Allan Pitman, Roger Tlusty and Ian Westbury. The participants in the paradigms of educational research seminar helped me over the years, as they responded to the issues interwoven in this book. Also of importance is the University of Wisconsin Graduate Research Committee which provided the support that enabled me to pursue certain themes in this book. Special thanks are given to Carol Newland who has maintained her sense of humor as we worked over the years and who, in an age of technology and word processors, has mastered faulty programs to type this manuscript.

Chapters one, two and four have been rewritten from earlier drafts to provide continuity of theme and argument. These chapters originally appeared in *Theory and Research in Social Education* (Educational Research: Values and Visions of Social Order) Vol. 5, 1978; *Journal of Education* (Paradigms in Educational Science: Different Meanings and Purpose to Theory), Vol. 162, 1980; and *The Study of Schooling, Field Based Methodologies in Educational Research and Evaluation* (Qualitative Research: Some Thoughts About the Relation of Methodology and Social History). Praeger Publishers, 1981.

I wish to thank Kerry Freedman for designing the cover of this book.

Chapter 1

Educational Research: Ideologies and Visions of Social Order

If (these conditions of social science being historically influenced) make trouble for us as social scientists, remember that they are a great advantage to humanity, by leaving men the illusion of choice. I speak of the illusion because I myself believe that what each of us does is absolutely determined (Homans, 1967).

It is often thought and said that what we most need in education is wisdom and broad understanding of the issues that confront us. Not at all. What we need are deeply structured theories in education that drastically reduce, if not eliminate, the need for wisdom (Suppes, 1974).

The above statements are part of more general treatises about the nature of social research. The authors argue for social/psychological sciences which provide explanatory statements about human behavior.[1] They believe the power of the explanations lies in their objective, culture-free quality. Yet, as the quotes suggest, the very search for scientific reasoning reflects commitments which go beyond the coherence of findings or methods. Underlying the practice of social research are assumptions about society. These assumptions refer to the nature of social control, order, and responsibility. Far from being neutral, inquiry is a human activity which involves hopes, values, and unresolved questions about social affairs.

The purpose of this book is to explore the social roots of social science and the central question of the social function of the intellectual. The argument of this chapter orients the discussion by focusing upon social and cultural elements that underlie the process of educational inquiry. To locate the social origins of disciplined knowledge is to consider the potency and limitations of our endeavors to understand and improve social affairs. To consider social science as a human activity is also to provide a way of rethinking the meaning of science to our everyday life.

A theme of this book is that social science is a response to the interaction and conflict among a variety of intellectual traditions. To understand these research traditions and their implications, there must be inquiry into the social, political and epistemological assumptions that shape and fashion the activities and outcomes of research. One of the ironies of contemporary social science is that a particular and narrow conception of science has come to dominate social research. That conception gives emphasis to the procedural logic of research by making statistical and procedural problems paramount to the conduct of research. This view eliminates from scrutiny the social movements and values that underlie research methods and which give definition to the researcher as a particular social type. As a result, the possibilities of social sciences are at best limited, and at worst mystifying of the very human conditions that the methods of science were invented to illuminate.

The particular focus of the analysis is upon the pedagogical research communities in the United States and the Soviet Union. The focus upon these research communities provides a specific historical context to consider larger sociological issues of the social role of the intellectual. Most discussions of the intellectual have been abstract, giving little attention to the actual dynamics within society. Tying our general understanding to concrete historical practices can enable us to consider more adequately the complexities of our social conditions and role of human agency. The 'case' of pedagogy is, I believe, sociologically significant. The central cultural location of schooling makes this occupation an important element in reproduction and transformation. Educators' 'use' of scientific forms provides entrance into the problem of professionalization, the dynamics by which occupations have appropriated scientific procedures to rationalize, control and alter institutional contexts.

Educational Research As a Cultural Imperative

Social research expresses human commitment and value in at least three ways. First, research exists within communities of discourse which maintain and develop standards of inquiry.[2] Second, research may respond to our perceptions of social and cultural conditions. Our studies reflect our deep moral and political concerns and provide possible direction for reconciling social contradictions within our institutional arrangements. Third, research is part of an occupational community that is structurally related to other institutions in society. Social research has a highly valued status in society. Many people believe that political, social, and educational issues require scientific solutions. Deliverance from the domination of nature and from social oppression is believed to require expert knowledge. This privileged status imposes certain contradictions upon the work of social inquiry. In this section, these three cultural dimensions of social research will be explored.

Science As Communities of Discourse and Social Commitment

Much of the sociology of science emphasizes the community aspect of scientific inquiry (Hagstrom, 1965; Storer, 1966). A scientist conducts research within a scientific community, a context which both encourages and controls scientific imagination. Scientific communities involve commitments to certain lines of reasoning and premises for certifying knowledge. Each scientific field has particular constellations of questions, methods and procedures. These constellations provide shared ways of 'seeing' the world, of working, of testing each other's studies. As people are trained to participate in a research community, the learning involves more than the content of the field. Learning the exemplars of a field of inquiry is also to learn how to see, think about and act towards the world. An individual is taught the appropriate expectations, demands and consistent attitudes and emotions that are involved in doing science.

It is within a community context that scientific imagination and creativity occur. While it may seem paradoxical, the procedures, norms and interactions of the scientific community maintain a form of anarchy which encourages individual creativity (see, for example, Storer, 1966). The social organization of science provides and creates the general standards which guide individual pursuits. The individual, however, must interact with the people, events and material of the world. As if living in a large house, individual scientists can do their own 'thing' in the privacy of their own rooms, and every once in a while converse about their ideas, break bread (the 'conventional' way), and do the required, general household chores. Communal recognition requires that the individual provide ideas to the community, and intense competition (and sometimes in-fighting) exists among individuals to provide the 'commodity'.

Socialization into a disciplinary field involves social, emotional and political elements as well as cognitive ones. Kuhn's (1970) analysis of scientific change suggests that the social elements of scientific communities must be accounted for when considering how scientific knowledge progresses. At any one time, Kuhn argues, a discipline has a dominant scientific approach, with interrelated questions, procedures and conceptual perspectives. The dominant or 'normal' science of a period has well established research problems and the task of individual scientists is filling in the puzzle, for example, to provide a more complete picture of the composition of genes or lasers or to provide the missing variables that influence student outcomes in achievement.

Kuhn suggests that at certain times anomalies appear that seem unresolvable by the normal science and new concepts and tools are developed. These challenges to the normal science, which Kuhn called revolutionary science, result in anxiety and debate that is not always resolved by a test of data. The challenge to the existing disciplinary beliefs becomes not only a challenge to the objective questions of the science but to the scientist's basic premises about the organization of reality itself. For example, two competing notions of psychology vied for acceptance in the 1890s — the issue of the debate was not empirical data, but what should be considered legitimate psychological research. The dispute, which began 'rationally' and 'scientifically', degenerated into personal attacks. In such cases, scientific perspectives are part of the scientist's consciousness, involving both emotion and cognition elements.

The importance of social control and conflict in science is evident in the establishment of networks of personal contacts, sometimes called 'the Invisible College' (Crane, 1976). In each field of study, there is often a small group of highly productive and influential scholars who communicate informally about their work. Papers are communicated prior to formal publication, meetings are held and letters exchanged to transmit ideas, and laboratories maintained for scholars to share. These small, often elite, social circles set priorities for research, recruitment and training of new students, and monitor the changing structure of a specific field of knowledge.

But such a social circle poses one of the ironies of scientific communities. Networks resist as well as stimulate new developments. The revolutionary ideas of the young Neils Bohr were resisted by a prominent scientist of his time. Bohr's ideas were contrary to existing dogma held by the scientist who controlled the laboratory. Bohr found it impossible to develop his ideas in that laboratory and was forced to move to a more hospitable scientific environment.

The conflict that underlies scientific work is an important element of science itself. At the cutting edge of science are many different perspectives which compete for acceptance or dominance in a field. If we examine the social sciences, for example, there are differing conceptual and epistemological approaches that continually compete in our attempts to understand and explain. For example, political scientists may describe politics as a 'civic culture', a 'pluralistic democracy', or a 'power elite'. Each conceptual lens orients the researcher towards different types of social phenomena and offers different types of explanation of politics. Recent work in the sociology of sciences indicates that in the forefront of the physical, biological and social sciences are multiple perspectives.

The differences in conceptual lenses in the social sciences often represent deep-seated differences in root assumptions about the nature of the world to be investigated. Behavioral sciences, for example, adopt a methodological stance that social behavior can be viewed in a manner similar to the discipline of physics. A model of inquiry is adopted in which the individual is viewed as an essentially receptive, reflective organism whose qualities are shaped over time by the environment (see, for example, Blalock, 1982).

These assumptions about individuality however are not located solely in the scientific community. The underlying assumptions about method and theory in social science are linked to larger transformations of social relations, politics and economics that occur in the society as a whole. Behavioral inquiry historically emerges from the philosophies and psychologies of Hobbes, Locke and John Stuart Mill who sought to explain and justify the rise of the bourgeois class. As did Locke, the behavioral sciences consider human nature unalterable and seek to manipulate the environment in which that nature 'develops'. The public support and legitimacy given to the development of the behavioral sciences in universities at the beginning of the twentieth century were influenced by particular historical circumstances, including the need for data by the British government to ameliorate the condition of the poor (Abrams, 1968) and American philanthrophy to the university (see Chapter 5 in this volume).

A different intellectual tradition in social science, symbolic sciences, can be seen as responding to a different social vision of human affairs and the role of science in understanding and influencing conduct. (This view is discussed in more detail in Chapter 2). Drawing upon a blend of American and European philosophy and social theory, symbolic sciences view human behavior as fundamentally different from the natural biological world. The importance of communication processes among people and the development of meaning among actors in a situation are emphasized. Symbolic sciences, while also responding to the emergence of a middle class, are concerned with human responsiveness and adaptiveness. Faith is placed in a vision of a social world in which power and identity are negotiated among many interests and where meritocratic situations to foster opportunities and conditions for self-development are important.

At one level, we can say that the behavioral and symbolic sciences investigate different problems about our social conditions and pose different questions and 'find' different solutions to the riddles of our lives. The choice of science is seemingly one of perspective and approach which has no implication beyond science itself. But the conflict in root assumptions of these scientific perspectives is not the result of misplaced faith or erroneous methods that lead us away from Truth. The conflict involves a plurality of visions about society that exist in our social, political and philosophical thought and that we bring into the domain of research. While the nature of these pluralistic assumptions will be explored further in the following chapters, the conflict of ideas and resulting cross-fertilization that occurs in science are important to the development of imagination and the prevention of stagnation of ideas (Mulkay, 1972). The conflict can produce intense debate about which research questions and methods are appropriate and limit the crystallization of scientific concepts and theories.

The conflict and social character of science led Toulmin (1972) to argue that to understand science one must focus on the condition in which, and the manner in which, concepts change. The rationality of science is socially constructed and cannot be demonstrated by the ordering of concepts and beliefs into tiny structures. Rather, science exists in the preparedness of individuals to think up, explore, and criticize new concepts, techniques of representation, and arguments, as well as to tackle the outstanding problems of the field. To focus discussion only on predominant theories is to ignore the debate among scientists and the deeply rooted conflict that exists about the way the world is constituted and its possibilities.

Science As Responding to Social and Cultural Commitments

The control and conflict of scientific ideas must be considered in the larger context of social and cultural commitments. Disagreements in disciplines often involve an interplay of political, methodological, and epistemological issues.

In part, the relation of social and cultural commitments within science occurs because social researchers are members of their culture and inherit its history (Schultz, 1973). Their work contains assumptions developed and sustained in everyday conversations, behaviors and events. Social theory, for example, uses language drawn from everyday conversations. The form and content of language reflect beliefs, commitments, and values. Theories of totalitarianism, important in the 1960s, were built on people's daily experience. Totalitarian theories grew out of debates about a 'cold war'. People in the United States found themselves with allies who had been enemies just a few years before during a large-scale war. The new forces of evil were communism, not fascism. One response to the new situation and its alliances was to generate theories about totalitarianism. These theories not only reflected the changed situation, but lent credibility to our new political allies.

We can illuminate this relationship between research and social conditions more clearly by focusing upon a purpose of research. Inquiry can be viewed as a search for new metaphors for thinking about everyday affairs. The metaphors are 'lenses' which enable people to rethink and to give coherence to daily events that before seemed incomprehensible or troubling. The genius of Einstein and Keppler, for example, was their ability to put the physical world into sharp focus, different from what others accepted as common sense. The new lenses enabled scientists to consider different forms of questions and produce greater depths of understanding. The importance of the systems of thought provided by Freud, Marx, and Weber, as well, is to orient people toward their social and personal lives in new and different ways. The concepts of 'ego', 'ideology', or 'bureaucracy' have metaphoric value in enabling people to conceive of social reality from different layers of interpretation which were not readily apparent in everyday life.

The metaphoric quality of science is influenced by the issues, strains and struggles that confront the social theorist. Social theory is not so much a determination of 'facts' but an effort to make sense of unresolved experiences and to interpret the meaning of one's life (see, for example, Gouldner, 1970). Much of the classical work in sociology in the nineteenth and early twentieth century reflected the need to give definition and direction to the mass upheavals in values and relationships produced by industrialization. Tonnies' *Gemeinschaft und Gesellschaft* articulated his sense of a loss of community brought about by the new social and economic predicaments of his time. Weber's notion of bureaucracy reflected an attempt to rationalize the transformed social and economic affairs. Durkheim's theme of anomie represented a spirit of pessimism, moral uncertainty, and dislocation of norms produced in a period of material progress (Nisbet, 1976).

In more recent times, the Civil Rights movement, protests against the Vietnam war and changes in the social roles of women and men brought new themes for study. In part, the protest movements of the late 1960s and 1970s were perceived as a breakdown of moral and civil community. Political scientists and many educators became concerned about problems of political legitimacy and socialization. Curriculum designers responded to the conflicts in society by developing value clarification, public issues, and citizenship education programs. These efforts were to introduce instructional practices that could reassert the idea of community obligation and moral values into public and school discourse. More recently, changes in family and work structures have influenced the emergence of gender analysis in social and educational research, focusing upon ways to understand the contradictions produced. The economic crisis of the early 1980s, as well, has shifted the concerns among researchers. No longer is the basic concern how to produce greater economic mobility for the poor and the disenfranchised. The new mandate is elitist in a time of economic contradiction: to produce scientists, engineers and mathematicians who contribute to the productive outcomes of industry.

In focusing on a purpose of social science as metaphoric, I do not wish to play down the importance of giving detailed attention to the empirical world. Rather, I wish to suggest that all theory is language and this imposes an irony upon any study of our human conditions. The concepts that we use to look at reality can only be an approximate vision of that reality. Further, the particular dialects of science provide a structure to how we conceive of and interpret data: all data collection and analysis emerge from some theory about what the world is like and about how the phenomena of that world (the 'facts') are to be given coherence.

When we look historically to the significant contributions of social science, these contributions are located not in data *per se*, but rather in the ability of particular theorists to create new themes for considering the world, thus creating new questions and leading us to search for different data to provide insights into how our world is constructed and changed. Contrary to prevailing belief, the potency of social science is not in the utility of its knowledge but in its ability to expand and to liberate the consciousness of people into considering the possibilities of their human conditions. It is the visions that underlie our language and direct our observations that bring into play the metaphoric quality of science.

This discussion has, to this point, focused upon cultural dimensions of social research. First, the creativity of inquiry has sociological as well as psychological characteristics. Research exists within and is supported by a community of discourse. Second, the nature and character of scientific work are responsive to the larger social world. The social researcher participates in everyday conversations and these dialogues become part of the background for occupational endeavors. The cultural quality of research, however, is not complete until a third dimension is considered: a scientific community is an element in the general dynamics of the social world.

Science As an Occupational Community

Science does not stand by itself but is a cultural artifact. Social science is in demand and seems a necessary component of our everyday consciousness. Status is given to scientific knowledge in business, political, and social institutions. Political leaders use scientific techniques to 'poll' people about their actions and policies. Industrial psychologists and organizational researchers provide information about how to organize labor. Economic theorists guide people's interpretations about the relationship between work, capital, and consumption. Historians interpret a nation's past to help establish a collective identity. Curriculum researchers apply scientific thought for selecting, organizing, and evaluating schooling. In everyday choices, science is viewed as making life more manageable and social problems more solvable.

The cultural imperative of scientific thought can be illuminated by comparing Western science with the African Azande (Winch, 1977). The Azande maintain a system of magical thought which constitutes a coherent universe and discourse similar to science. It provides an intelligible conception of reality and a clear way of deciding which beliefs are and are not in agreement with that view of reality. Poison oracles or ghost rites to influence rainfall exist within a context of rules and conventions which gives these actions a sense of significance.

The Azande rationale is no less intelligent than the logic of science practiced by anthropologists who study these people. Its principles and rules arise out of the course of human conduct and are subordinate to existent cultural beliefs. The way of thinking found in

Western science would be incomprehensible to the Azande. In fact, science would seem to these people to have many of the same irrational 'magical' qualities that Western anthropologists see in Azande. The anthropologists' structure of thought becomes significant only within the context of the larger social forms and value structures that give it legitimacy.

The value placed on science represents one of the more profound changes in the nature and manner by which social authority is legitimated (see, for example, Gramsci, 1971; Gouldner, 1979; Edelman, 1974; Konrád and Szelényi, 1979). Whereas order patterns of authority have rested upon the social status of the speaker or on the word of God, the rules of logic and the reference to the empirical have become the new source of the validity of knowledge. The knowledge of the secular expert, the scientist, is believed to be transcendent, existing separately from social context, cultural location and biography. Scientific knowledge is treated as something that 'merely' describes or explains how things work, that orients us to the most effective practices and whose insights enable us to make more intelligent choices. The imagery of both physical and social science is that there is a technical expertise necessary for interpreting and finding solutions to our problems.

The rituals and ceremonies of technical expertise obscure the nature of social inquiry as a particular activity of an occupational community. The use of mathematics and an impersonal style of writing emphasizes a neutrality to the text. Yet, the knowledge of social science is the knowledge of a particular social group. To argue that rational styles of analysis and problem-solving are needed to deal with the complexity of industrial society is also to argue for the skills and sensibilities of the experts who maintain and develop those styles of analysis. While other possibilities exist — one could argue that folk knowledge or aesthetic forms, as well as scientific thought, can provide a vantage point for understanding and challenging the world — the reduction of knowledge to a particular style of discourse, the scientific, makes that single form of knowledge ideological. It legitimates a particular social group as the arbiter of human knowledge, responsibility and possibility. The technological claims of the expert sustain, bestow and create definitions of self, of society, and their interplay. These claims are not necessarily based upon the technological superiority of scientific knowledge but possibly upon the more effective control they permit the expert to exert over institutional sectors (Marglin, 1974).

The social location of social science discussed in this section can be summarized as: science is a community of discourse, a response to social and cultural commitments and an occupational community. Central to the argument is that the activities of research are human endeavors, reflecting the hopes, desires and tensions of our social conditions. The task now is to explore more concretely the implications of the argument for the problems of theory and the procedures of research.

Theory As Political Affirmation

At first glance, the suggestion that theory and research methods contain social and political values may seem misleading, if not in error. Our assumptions 'tell' us that theory is objective and neutral. Theories, it is believed, give coherence to data and expression to human regularities. The previous discussion, however, suggests that theories are products of human ingenuity and social context. Social theory exists within a social context that maintains purpose and commitment.

To consider social theory as part of its institutional setting, we must recognize that there is no meaning outside of practice. The language of research does not 'sit' as a logical artifact, outside social discourse and devoid of human interpretation and manipulation. Theory enters a world in which there are predefined institutional arrangements, linguistic conventions and established priorities. The language of theory contains assumptions and visions that are influenced by the strains and struggles of the larger world. Social sciences cannot be immune from such partisanship.

The social assumptions of theory can be understood by realizing there are different layers of meaning to social theory. A typical way of considering social science is through its explicit knowledge statements, that is, what is overtly said about society, government, schools, or students. For example, some school programs draw upon political theories to encourage participation. Underlying curriculum is a series of unpostulated and unlabeled assumptions about the world. The theory of participation, for example, may 'treat' the world as highly integrated and people as rational. These assumptions guide people in 'seeing' participation as a rational involvement in publicly sanctioned groups, such as a student council. The assumptions about participation also contain beliefs about how institutional structures should be challenged. Lack of participation, for example, may be viewed as lack of individual motivation rather than as an institutional defect. Often such political theories in schools ignore structural factors that preclude certain groups from decision-making processes. Political participation in the United States, for example, is highest among professional and business groups, groups whose work structures encourage and permit such participation. The assumptions, prescriptions and interests of a political theory remain tacit, and the values which favor and handicap certain groups are not scrutinized for possible latent implications or consequences.

The interests embedded in theory can be explored by studying the social values emphasized in its language. Social theory can function to

1   provide a rationale for changing social and economic conditions, making these changes seem reasonable;
2   provide a mechanism to legitimate institutional interests;
3   give direction to alternative social arrangements.

These interests of social theory are often obscured by the form of scientific discourse which emphasizes a formal and seemingly universal language.

Theory As Symbols of Reconciliation

One social function of theory is to provide symbolic coherence in periods of changing social, political and economic conditions. The political, social and economic upheavals of the American depression and revolutions in Europe during the 1930s, for example, produced a series of social theories that provided conservative responses to the crises of the times.[3] The dominant sociology of the period, structural-functionalism, maintained a posture that accepted dominant institutions in order to maintain traditional loyalties and to avoid discontinuities (Gouldner, 1970). New symbols of harmony and hope in those times of changing social order are found in political science as it responded to the changing political and economic world. New symbols of political inquiry provided a way to understand and give coherence to the expanded role of a central government and a sense of political importance among individuals in the United States (Merelman, 1976). The concepts of 'political culture', 'pluralism', and 'political socialization' could serve to re-establish values and beliefs about individual efficiency and community that were being challenged. The method of 'polling' public opinion could enable people to believe they were being consulted. The creation of these concepts and procedures produced by behavioral political science provided an organized response to the changing social conditions.

As with political theory and method, the larger context of strain and transformation provides an underpinning to theories of pedagogy. The introduction of 'new' theories of instruction or curriculum is one way in which people respond to perceived gaps between social belief and institutional conditions. For example, the late 1960s and 1970s produced a 'crisis of values'. An Asian war, urban riots, and government actions such as Watergate or FBI and CIA domestic spy activities threw basic values of American life into question. In this social context, educators used theories about 'moral development' and 'values clarification' to orient curriculum development. The concept of 'values clarification' helped monitor more closely the moral development of children. The pedagogical theories involved a therapeutic perspective in which remedial treatment is offered to resolve the questions of value conflict.

Theories of individualized instruction are also accounted for by locating pedagogy in larger contexts of belief and struggle (Popkewitz, 1983). The sanctity of the individual has received increasing ideological support since the early eighteenth century as a result of industrialization, shifts in power and the development of Western liberal democracies. The notion of individualism, however, has not been unidimensional: theories of pedagogy are rooted in social conflict about the location of social order and authority. The social efficiency curriculum movement of Bobbit, Charters and Snedden reflected an early twentieth century belief in the professional expert as providing mechanisms for social harmony and stability. Progressive educators, such as Dewey, responded to the need for social mobility produced by the new professional strata in society. Schooling was to stress the development of 'self' through social interaction. Knowledge was presumed flexible and negotiable, with legitimacy built by the consensus developed in interpersonal communication. Current debates about instructional management approaches and open education are also rooted in deeper conflict about principles of legitimacy and social interest. (For a discussion of how theories of individualization function in schools, see Popkewitz *et al.*, 1982).

Theories of pedagogy have political potency. They provide symbols which help people to express a variety of emotions associated with schooling and society. Theories enable people to resolve contradictions between the values they hold and the actual conditions of institutional life. Theories symbolically tie together seeming discontinuities and social strains, bringing reassurances of ethical commitment and institutional adaptiveness. The theories make it appear that professionals have a grasp of what should be done. Reassurances, however, do not necessarily alter or explain what actually occurs in schools.

Theory As Legitimation

Closely tied to the 'strain' function of theory is legitimation. Statements of research can enable certain social structures and interests to seem normal and reasonable. Legitimation occurs when the organizing categories of theory define what is to be taken-for-granted about institutional life.

Often social research is initiated in response to some administrative action and is guided by an administrator's definition of the problem. Many school research projects accept the objectives of pedagogical programs and are organized to 'explain' how the objective was reached. Research focuses upon whether the course material was learned, whether the teachers perceived the material to be clear and easy to use, and how well students understood and achieved project goals (see, for example, Angrist *et al.*, 1976). The results of the research do not question, but assume, the premises of the project, that is, that the problem of teaching was to have children master the content efficiently. The criteria of content selection or the ways in which the social conditions of schooling might unequally distribute knowledge are left unquestioned.[4] The consequence is an *ad hoc* pedagogical theory that justifies the agreed-upon design and content selection of project administrators.

'Basic' research, as well, often assumes the non-problematic character of administrative categories. Discussions of teacher instructional decisions, for example, often are concerned with how teachers make instructional choices based on information processing. In one such study (Shavelson *et al.*, 1977), the empirical problem was to present a group of graduate students in education with information about student aptitude, children's ages, family status (divorced, number of siblings, etc.), children's use of time in school, and intelligence. Sometimes the information was negative (the child did not do homework or the father was a machinist rather than an engineer). A second session for teachers was held to provide more information. The teachers were asked to revise instructional decisions based on the above information. The conclusion of the study was (a) 'subjects may use different kinds of information to make different kinds of decisions'; (b) '. . . decisions at time one and time two were influenced by other factors not measured in this study' (Shavelson *et al.*, 1977, p. 95).

With such common-sensical conclusions, one might ask what is the function of such research. The question can be answered in two different ways. Methodologically, researchers tend to believe that through the slow accumulation of data important generalizations about teaching will be made. Furthermore, there seems to be a technical elegance to the report itself, especially when data collection, literature review and findings are succinctly and carefully presented, and sophisticated techniques such as path analysis are used to increase data manipulation.

The social significance of the research, however, overshadows its methodological elegance. There are social and political ramifications which are as important as the tests of reliability. First, the research tacitly accepts institutional assumptions, some of which are defined by school professionals themselves. Achievement, intelligence, and 'use of time' are accepted as useful variables for stating problems about schools and these categories provide the basis for research and, often, the possibilities of our conditions. Inquiry enables researchers to see how school categories relate, but it does not test the assumptions or implications underlying the school categories. No question is asked about the nature of the tasks at which children spend their time. Research conclusions are conceived within parameters provided by school administrators and the rules and values by which organizational control are to be maintained. Second, to accept institutional categories as a basis of research is also to accept social myths as moral prescriptions. Social class, social occupation (engineer or machinist), or divorce are accepted as information which should be used in decision-making. These assumptions maintain a moral quality and criteria which may justify social inequality. Third, the acceptance of school categories often directs people to consider school failure as caused by those who happen to come to its classes. Problems of social location become problems of family life or individual motivation. Social and school organization are unscrutinized.

One could say at this moment that this is *only* research. People do use research in making decisions about schooling. I would argue, however, that research often has a way of entering into the domains of social interaction. This influence is indirect as well as direct. People adopt certain of the categories and definitions of research for understanding their own and others' actions. The research orientation defines as well as responds to our social situation. Educational administrators, curriculum developers, and teachers use the research to direct their practical activities, and the effect is to limit and predispose individuals in their actions and conceptions of educational possibilities.

Theory As Alternate Possibilities

Theory can also direct attention to the possibility of alternatives. The concern of theory is to identify ways in which existing institutional arrangements limit the fulfilment of certain cherished values and to offer metaphors that direct attention to new relationships. The use of theory for constructing different social possibilities involves at least two strands, one concerned with maintaining certain residual structures of society while transforming them to respond better to social and ethical imperatives, and another which focuses upon theory as leading to the emergence of new basic social structures.

'Open education' or the British infant school is a case in point. It emerges from the progressive theories of the 1920s and 1930s in which educators saw the school as an agency of reform and social change. It is also a response to the emergence of a 'new' middle class of professionals who demanded a socialization process that emphasized interpersonal communication skills. Open education is a contemporary response to demands of the professional and the limitations its advocates find in existing institutional beliefs and practices. Tabachnick (1976), for example, argues that there is a relationship between open education and the norms, beliefs and patterns of work that underlie social inquiry, the latter giving emphasis to an active search for knowledge and individual responsibility. Open education is believed to be a search for ways in which students could develop more autonomy in social relationships. Mutuality of roles, community, and reciprocity of relations are perceived to be central to the structure of school experience and are measures of its outcomes.[5] These dispositions of open education are related to the orientations and sensibilities of the professional strata.

Critical theory poses a different route for a search for alternative structures. Associated with the Frankfurt School (Institute for Social Research, Frankfurt, Germany), the task of theory is one of opposition, focusing upon the contradictions of advanced capitalist societies which produce domination and prevent emancipation (see, for example, Jay, 1973; Giroux, 1981, 1983a). The Frankfurt School has refashioned and rethought Marxism by focusing upon the formation of consciousness, culture and everyday life, and how these formations maintain the legitimacy of existing political and social interests. The language and intent of such theory is political — to consider the moments of domination, ideology, hegemony and emancipation in social life and social change. The purpose of social criticism is not solely one of opposition to social economic structure. Making problematic the nature of words, customs and tradition in our everyday life is to increase the possibility of human agency in providing for a social transformation that creates new social structures and emancipatory conditions (see also Giroux, 1983b).

In this section I have discussed three different social values embedded in theory — theory as symbols of reconciliation, as legitimation and as directing attention to alternative possibilities. These three different values require that we consider our scientific activity as continually involving elements of political affirmation. Social theory is potent because its language has prescriptive qualities. The selection and organization of research activities give emphasis to certain people, events, and things. These more abstract categories are not neutral; they define certain elements of institutional relationships as good, reasonable, legitimate, or 'bad' and in need of change. Visions of society, interests to be favored, and courses of action to be followed are sustained in theory. What values are served, however, are never straightforward, the different social functions of theory are always in tension and in need of critical scrutiny.

Research Practices and Visions of Social Order

A different element of social and educational research lies in the practices of study. As with theory, the suggestion that research practices embody values goes against conventional wisdom. Researchers often argue that methods are the only values in science. Kerlinger (1973), for example, defines methods of inquiry as procedures in which beliefs have no effect. The character of method, he argues, remains entirely independent of our beliefs, perceptions, biases, values, attitudes, and emotions.

The stance of neutrality is itself a value stance. It expresses a belief and a hope of researchers. As I will argue, the procedures of inquiry contain assumptions about social relationships which are interrelated with theory, human purpose and social affairs.

One approach to considering values in practice is to look at techniques. In many ways, the techniques of study are treated as skills which exist independently of the purpose or commitment of those who do research. The professional preparation of researchers, for example, consists of courses in statistics, field study, or survey research. It is assumed that these techniques of data collection and analysis can be learned as specialized skills apart from the actual process of inquiry. The techniques, to phrase the problem somewhat differently, are conceived of as neutral to the conduct of study.

A critical scrutiny of techniques yields a different perspective. Techniques emerge from a theoretical position and therefore reflect values, beliefs, and dispositions towards the social world. Factor analysis, for example, was created as a measurement procedure for faculty psychology. It was based on the assumption that the mind has different compartments which could be trained as independent units (Hamilton, 1980). While faculty psychology has been discredited, its techniques are still in use, thus maintaining the assumption that the mind is a cluster of parts. Embedded in field methods, as well, are assumptions about social relations, the power of individuals in effecting change and the appropriate way of considering individuality and human needs and wants. (These issues are discussed in Chapters 2 and 4.)

While we tend to place great faith in the mathematical expression of data as devoid of values, Fox and Hernandez-Nieto (1977) argue that mathematical models for research articulate value preference and underlying assumptions about social relations. Conventional statistical techniques, for example, are based on Euclidean geometry which has linear conceptions of time and space. In contrast, newer mathematical models contain principles of interaction. The development of the new models for research derives, in part, from a theoretical and value commitment to include dimensions of intention and historical setting.

The choice of technique is a moral responsibility. Moral questions are deeply intertwined with the general commitments of science. Social scientists are concerned with developing verifiable knowledge. This interest involves manipulating variables to test outcomes of a hypothesis and the predictive quality of theory. This commitment poses no dilemma to most physical or life scientists — they can change the heating temperature to combine elements or experiment with hybrid feed without any moral guilt. In high energy physics, molecular biology, or medical research, the manipulation of variables often does have direct implications for human beings. Various ethical and legal restrictions have evolved from this research.

Questions of morality and immorality are *always* involved in social research since the 'subjects' of social scientists are people. The problem of controlling variables is a moral one. It is immoral, Homans (1967) argues, to manipulate people. The alternative is to create statistical techniques which provide scientists with the necessary tools to manipulate data.

> It is certainly less easy in the social sciences than in some physical and biological sciences to manipulate variables experimentally and to control the other variables entering into a concrete phenomenon.... It is less easy to control the variables because it is less easy to control men than things. Indeed it is often immoral to try to control them: men are not to be submitted to the indignities to which we submit, as a matter of course, things and animals. Hence the relative prominence in some of the social sciences, even increasingly in history, of other methods of controlling variables, methods thought somehow less satisfactory, such as the use of statistical techniques (Homans, 1967, p. 22).

Ideology and Methods

The relation between technique and value in science implies that social research is based upon certain background assumptions about society and individuals. These assumptions, in the main, are drawn from the behavioral sciences and posit certain beliefs about how people should control and manipulate their world. While the original tenets of behavioralism in social and educational sciences were created to redress certain limitations in social inquiry, that original stance to inquiry has often been distorted in the professions where scientific forms have been incorporated into occupational settings concerned with rationalization and control. Techniques of managing variables have become a paramount consideration in determining scientific conduct, leading to a position that science is human engineering, a position which contains certain ideological qualities by establishing a style of discourse for determining the well-being and progress of individuals (see Giroux, 1983b; Therborn, 1980, Gouldner, 1976, for discussion about ideology and the debate about its meaning).

These implications of the background assumptions can be illuminated by looking at the particular commitments to science that underlie much educational research.[6] These commitments are as follows.

1 Social science is to be modelled after the physical sciences.
2 Social science aspires to be a deductive system of propositions which report the law-like qualities of human affairs. These laws are to explain and predict the actions of individuals in a manner similar to those developed in the physical sciences.
3 To identify these laws, it is important that the science be objective. Objectivity is the ability of the observer/recorder to develop techniques that place the data outside (away from) the particular meanings, interpretations, and values of social situations and researchers.
4 Mathematical expression of data is important to the development of techniques. Mathematics, it is believed, eliminates ambiguities (43 per cent *is* 43 per cent) and human values and permits stringent tests of validity and reliability of data.

These commitments form the basis of what is called the behavioral sciences and behaviorism in psychology and they dominate much of educational research in the United States. The commitments to behavioral sciences emerged to correct the legalistic and formal analysis of social institutions that existed prior to the 1930s. As such the behavioral sciences do provide an important corrective to previous intellectual traditions. (This tradition of 'empirical-analytic' science is explored in the discussion of paradigms in Chapter 2).

For many researchers in the 'helping' professions, however, the historical and intellectual roots of the behavioral sciences have become lost as there is a consuming emphasis on the rules of data collection and analysis. The commitment to a notion of objectivity leads many to assume that the sole criterion of science is the detail given to the development and use of rigorous procedures. Graduate research programs, for example, entail a proliferation of technical courses in statistics, computer programming and research design. These courses give focus to the problem of data collection/analysis as separate from the problems, exemplars and curiosities that guide a field of inquiry. Science is taught as procedures of data collection/ analysis; objectivity is determined by following the rules which reduce data to statistics and sampling theory. Anything not following the preset procedures becomes 'soft', that is, intuitive, descriptive or anecdotal; labels that suggest the work is anything *but* scientific. The outcome of this position, I believe, is a trivialization of science itself (and of behavioral science) and the establishment of a particular ideological definition of practice as the sole legitimate path to truth.

We can trace the movement from science to ideology in the following way: first, there is the commitment to rigorous techniques as overshadowing theoretical interests by focusing on those aspects of research which can be numerically expressed. In a typical study of teacher effectiveness (Cooley *et al.*, 1977), the authors discussed student outcomes as involving dimensions such as citizenship, attitude towards learning, conceptions of 'self', creativity, and achievement. However, since achievement is the only dimension which has reliable testing, achievement was treated as the sole empirical interest.

This superimposing of technique over theory needs to be considered as contrary to good science. In a classic statement about behavioral theory, Easton (1971) argues that an important dimension of social theory is its relevance to social problems and variables that focus upon the complexity of the situation. However, as illustrated above, the commitment to rigorous techniques removes that theoretical dimension and, in fact, simplifies the situation in a manner that hinders the search for understanding. The rigorous techniques of the study enable us to learn less and less about the social affairs researched.

Second, objectivity is narrowly defined. Researchers maintain the belief that there are regularities or laws of human nature which lie outside personal intentions and motives. To discover these laws, it is argued, data must be obtained that can be devoid of human values and bias. The method to achieve this lies in mathematics and statistical computation which, it is believed, eliminates or reduces human values and ambiguity from science. This commitment to objectivity reinforces the need for the rigorous application of techniques and attention to procedural questions.[7] The view of objectivity, however, is itself procedurally rather than philosophically grounded. Scriven (1972) argues, for example, that the merit of judgments provided by instruments may, at any one time, not be as adequate as the judgments of a human observer. He continues that we must not confuse subjectivity and objectivity with a comparison of individual, personal experiences and the number of experiences in the public domain.

Third, the stress on procedures of science leads many to consider only those questions and problems that conform to its procedures rather than to having methods and procedures respond to and develop from theoretical interests.[8] This has certain consequences. Since reflection, criticism and development become tied to the improvement of techniques, the root assumptions about the world embedded in scientific practices are not examined but are crystallized.

One of these assumptions is that science is to identify and to make the laws of nature work more efficiently through the manipulation of variables. The science of social institutions becomes management of people. The quote by Homans cited earlier about the moral hesitancy of social scientists to manipulate people, thus turning to statistics as a means of accomplishing this goal, is turned around. What was originally a methodological device for collecting data becomes a view of the world which includes definitions of how people should act, believe, and feel.

The pedagogical sciences provide a case-in-hand. A central strategy in educational research is to define the purpose of education as one of a management strategy, such as 'changing children to some desired end'. Educational theories are the technical apparatus that guide the manipulation of children. Experimental techniques are implemented as the means of instruction. Behavior modification is thought of as a teaching strategy. The moral hesitancy of social scientists to intervene in human life is non-existent, from this perspective, as it assumes a professional prerogative.

The belief that teachers are human engineers is exemplified in a popular book on curriculum development entitled *Instructional Product Development* (Baker and Schultz, 1971). The authors define curriculum design as a technological problem which involves stating educational results in terms of precise, observable performances of children. For example, an acceptable objective of a history lesson is to teach a student to 'order four wars of the 19th century chronologically' (p. 10). The goal of educational research is to find more efficient ways of obtaining correct performances from children. To test these performances, criterion-referenced measures are constructed. These measures provide clear, precise test items that refer to objectives (that is, a child chronologically lists wars). The authors define professionals as 'personnel' whose function is 'management of human resources which will lead to more efficient administration of instruction and the greater likelihood that prescribed outcomes will be attained.' A professional's task is to measure teaching efficiency and a researcher's task is to identify levels of mastery.

In much curriculum thought and educational reform, the science of education is translated into a technology. Choices exist only when they make the existing system more rational, efficient, and controllable. Science is administration of people; research is a team effort, user-oriented, and devoid of the imagination described earlier. The skepticism and self-criticism which characterize science are made irrelevant. Curriculum is no longer an ethical task. In fact, the technical nature of professional work makes the image of the Renaissance man, as Baker and Schultz (1971) suggest, an image 'for his time, not ours'.

The image of science exudes a belief that 'the laws' of nature or the knowledge of human existence have been discovered. Educators are to manipulate and control children as physical scientists manipulate objects of the physical world. Although the belief that the laws of social life are known is a chimera, human engineers act upon educational affairs as though there were no difficulties or uncertainties. The ceremonies and rituals of research give the practice legitimacy and sanctity. The moral implications of control, dominance, and power are eliminated from discussion as the only problem of schooling is implementing technologies.

The concept that social science is similar to the physical sciences is an ideological one. Gouldner (1970) argues, for example, that behind methodologies and techniques is a belief that (a) people might unite in order to subdue a 'nature' that is regarded as external to man, and (b) technologies might be developed which would transform the universe into a 'usable' resource of mankind as a whole. These assumptions led to a belief that people could control the rest of the universe and have the right to use the universe for their own benefit. When the assumptions of the physical sciences were applied to studies of people, specific problems arose.

> The humanistic parochialism of science with its premised unity of mankind, created problems, when the effort was made to apply science to the study of mankind itself. It did so partly because national or class differences then became acutely visible, but also, perhaps more important, because men now expected to use social science to 'control' men themselves, as they were already using physical science to control 'nature.' Such a view of social science premised that a man might be known, used, and controlled like any other thing: it 'thingafied' man. The use of the physical sciences as a model fostered just such a conception of the social sciences, all the more so as they were developing in the context of an increasingly utilitarian culture (Gouldner, 1970, p. 492).

The role of the researcher in direct planning and reproduction involves a more fundamental shift in the role of the intellectual. The intellectual is more appropriately and precisely called professional. The task is not to create new knowledge and to seek a humane social construction. The intellectual as human engineer formulates an ideological program in which that intellectual knowledge is to be the dominant legitimating principle in the exercise of power. This new role of the intellectual will be returned to as we consider the problems of educational change and reform.

Conclusions

Social research involves values which emerge from an interplay of various communities. Research is influenced by a community of scholars who follow accepted lines of reasoning, standards of discourse, and definitions of problems. The character of research is also responsive to the issues and dilemmas confronted by the larger society. Research is often initiated to resolve possible institutional contradictions. Studies of poverty, deviance, moral dvelopment, or gender are examples of such responses to conflict.

The values affirmed in research *are political*. Theories and methods imply what the customary ways of behaving in society are. Certain ways of participating in social affairs are given emphasis and, hence, preference through research activities. Rather than being aloof and detached, engagement in research affirms social values, beliefs, and hopes.

The values of social inquiry also can have ideological implications. As argued earlier, the perspectives of social science not only describe but also give direction to how social events are to be challenged. The perspectives of research are increasingly incorporated into common-sense reasoning and professional definitions. The theories of social and professional research help to define political, social, and educational problems. These practices tend to favor certain interests and handicap others through the underlying social visions and definitions of power contained in research.

The normative quality of the work of research makes it especially potent when applied in schools because schools are designed to impose ideas and work patterns upon children. Much of what occurs in schools is justified and made credible by the activities of the educational research community. Scientific evidence provides the rationale for curriculum development, instructional approaches, and evaluation strategies. Theories about social affairs, childhood, and learning guide educators in their choice of content and in the procedures they use to conduct everyday activities at school. It is to this role of the researcher and the particular values, patterns and implications of that research that we now turn our attention.

The discussion of ideology raised a concern about a transformation in the role of the intellectual. For some the intellectual is more precisely a professional, assuming a direct role in planning and processes of reproduction. This role as a technical intelligentsia, however, needs to be juxtaposed with the more general task of the intellectual to establish moral will and direction. As the discussion indicated, this function is not unidimensional and the theories of science respond to different interests in schooling and society.

Notes

1 I will use the label 'social science' as a general term which includes the traditional social sciences (political science, sociology, psychology, and history). Educational research is a special type of social science, having an institutional focus on schooling. The generic label, social science, gives emphasis to the social nature of all the disciplines.

2 I have explored the social and cultural quality of inquiry in 'Myths of social science in curriculum' (Popkewitz, 1976b) and 'Craft and community as metaphors for social inquiry curriculum' (Popkewitz, 1977).

3 Many of the theoretical perspectives and research techniques developed at this historical time have become important to educational analysis. Among these are the theory of functionalism in sociology and the survey methodology of behavioral science.

4 These assumptions are challengeable. The discipline-centered curriculum tends to provide a crystallized notion of 'science' which distorts its creativity and maintains values which are conservative (Keddie, 1971; Popkewitz, 1976a).

5 While the vision of open education does have the potential to guide people in a search for social alternatives, the practice of open education has tended to be non-political. Puppetry, 'creative' writing, or stitchery often replace sustained disciplined thought. Mutual satisfaction among class participants becomes the purpose of schooling rather than a search for community in relation to some general intellectual problem or social issue.

6 There are other commitments in educational sciences which are discussed in a later chapter. The focus upon the following set of commitments at this point occurs for two reasons. One, they form an essential part of the dominant approach to educational research. Two, the commitments are often narrowly conceived and acted upon in such ways that produce ideological consequences.

7 The idea of objectivity in research can be treated in a different manner. Berger and Luckmann (1967) define reality as being socially constructed and maintained through a dialectic process; thus arguing against research perspectives and rules that crystallize social structures.

8 An insightful discussion of the relation of theory, method and technique is found in the work of Vygotsky (1978).

References

ABRAMS, P. (1968) *The Origins of British Sociology, 1834–1914*, Chicago, University of Chicago Press.

ANGRIST, S. *et al.* (1976) 'Development and evaluation of family life courses', *Theory and Research in Social Education*, 4, 2, pp. 57–79.

BAKER, R. and SCHULTZ, R. (Eds) (1971) *Instructional Product Development*, New York, Van Nostrand Reinhold.

BERGER, P. and LUCKMANN, T. (1967) *The Social Construction of Reality: A Treatise in the Sociology of Knowledge*, Garden City, N.Y., Anchor Books.

BLALOCK, H. (1982) *Conceptualization and Measurement in the Social Sciences*, Beverly Hills, Ca., Sage Publications.

COOLEY, W. *et al.* (1977) 'How to identify effective teaching', *Anthropology and Education*, 8, 2, pp. 119–26.

CRANE, D. (1976) *Invisible Colleges, Diffusion of Knowledge in Scientific Communities*, Chicago, Ill., University of Chicago Press.

EASTON, D. (1971) *The Political System: An Inquiry into the State of the Political Science*, New York, Alfred A. Knopf.

EDELMAN, M. (1974) 'The political language of the helping professions', *Politics and Society*, 4, 3, pp. 295–310.

FOX, T. and HERNANDEZ-NIETO, R. (1977) *Why Not Quantitative Methodologies to Illuminate Dialectic or Phenomenological Perspectives?* Paper presented at the meeting of the American Educational Research Association, New York.

GIROUX, H. (1981) 'Culture and rationality in Frankfurt School thought: Ideological foundations for a theory of social education', *Theory and Research in Social Education*, 9, 4, pp. 17–56.

GIROUX, H. (1983a) *Critical Theory and Educational Practice*, Geelong, Australia, Deakin University.

GIROUX, H. (1983b) *Theory and Resistance in Education: A Pedagogy for the Opposition*, Hadley, Mass., Bergin and Garvey.

GOULDNER, A. (1970) *The Coming Crisis of Western Sociology*, New York, Basic Books.

GOULDNER, A. (1976) *The Dialectics of Ideology and Technology*, New York, Seabury Press.

GOULDNER, A. (1979) *The Future of the Intellectual and the Rise of the New Class*, New York, Seabury Press.

GRAMSCI, A. (1971) *Selections from the Prison Notebooks*, Q. HOARE and G. SMITH (Eds and trans). New York, International Publishers.

HAGSTROM, W. (1965) *The Scientific Community*, New York, Basic Books.

HAMILTON, D. (1980) 'Educational research and the shadows of Francis W. Dockrell, Galton and Ronald Fisher', in HAMILTON, D. (Ed.), *Rethinking Educational Research*, London, Hodder and Stoughton.

HOMANS, G.C. (1967) *The Nature of Social Science*, New York, Harcourt, Brace and World.

JAY, M. (1973) *The Dialectical Imagination: A History of the Frankfurt School and the Institute of Social Research, 1923–1950*, Boston, Mass., Little Brown.

KEDDIE, N. (1971) 'Classroom knowledge', in YOUNG, M. (Ed.), *Knowledge and Control: New Directions for the Sociology of Education*, London, Collier and Macmillan.

KERLINGER, F. (1973) *Foundations of Behavioral Research*, 2nd ed., New York, Holt, Rinehart and Winston.

KONRÁD, G. and SZELÉNYI, I. (1979) *The Intellectuals on the Road to Class Power: A Sociological Study of the Intelligentsia in Socialism*, R. ARATO and R. ALLEN (Trans), New York, Harcourt, Brace, Jovanovich.

KUHN, T. (1970) *The Structure of Scientific Revolutions*, Chicago, Ill., University of Chicago Press.

MARGLIN, S. (1974) 'What do bosses do? The origins and functions of hierarchy in capitalist production', *Review of Radical Political Economics*, 48, pp. 32–64.

MERELMAN, R. (1976) 'On interventionist behaviorism: An essay in the sociology of knowledge', *Politics and Society*, 6, 1, pp. 57–78.

MULKAY, M.J. (1972) *The Social Process of Innovation*, New York, Macmillan.

NISBET, R. (1976) *Sociology As an Art Form*, New York, Oxford University Press.

POPKEWITZ, T. (1977) 'Craft and community as metaphors for social inquiry curriculum', *Educational Theory*, 5, 1, pp. 41–60.

POPKEWITZ, T. (1976a) 'Latent values of the discipline-centered curriculum', *Theory and Research in Social Education*, 4, 1, pp. 57–79.

POPKEWITZ, T. (1976b) 'Myths of social science in curriculum', *Educational Forum*, 60, pp. 317–28.

POPKEWITZ, T. (1983) 'The sociological bases for individual differences: The relation of solitude to the crowd', in FENSTERMACHER, G. and GOODLAD, J. (Eds), *Individual Differences and the Common Curriculum*. 82nd Yearbook, Chicago, Ill., National Society for the Study of Education.

POPKEWITZ, T. et al. (1982) *The Myth of Educational Reform: A Study of School Responses to Planned Change*, Madison, Wisc., University of Wisconsin Press.

SCHULTZ, A. (1973) *The Problem of Social Reality. Collected Papers 1*, M. NATHANSON (Ed.), The Hague, Martinus Nijhoff.

SCRIVEN, M. (1972) 'Objectivity and subjectivity in educational research', in THOMAS, L. (Ed.), *Philosophical Redirections of Educational Research*, 71st Yearbook, Chicago, Ill., National Society for the Study of Education.

SHAVELSON, R. et al. (1977) 'Teachers' sensitivity to the reliability of information in making pedagogical decisions', *American Educational Research Journal*, 14, 2, pp. 83–98.

STORER, W. (1966) *The Social System of Science*, New York, Holt, Rinehart and Winston.

SUPPES, P. (1974) 'The place of theory in educational research', *Educational Researcher*, 3, 6, pp. 3–10.

TABACHNICK, B. (1976) 'Open education: Ideology and alternative visions of schooling', Paper given at the National Council of Social Studies Convention, Washington, D.C., April 1976.

THERBORN, G. (1980) *The Ideology of Power and the Power of Ideology*, London, Verso.

TOULMIN, S. (1972) *Human Understanding: The Collective Use and Evolution of Concepts*, Princeton, N.J., Princeton University Press.

VYGOTSKY, L. (1978) *Mind in Society, the Development of Higher Psychological Processes*, M. COLE *et al.* (Eds), Cambridge, Mass., Harvard University Press.

WINCH, P. (1977) 'Understanding primitive society', in DALLMAYR, F. and McCARTHY, T. (Eds), *Understanding and Social Inquiry*, Notre Dame, Ind., University of Notre Dame Press.

1
Science As Discourse and Interest

Chapter 2

Paradigms in Educational Science: Different Meanings and Purpose to Theory

The last half century has seen the emergence of a particular way of thinking and reasoning about social science which has come to dominate the cultural outlook of the United States, Australia and, to some extent, Britain. The view is commonly associated with the behavioral sciences. Its argument assumes a detachment of science from moral and ethical questions, a view of the social world as systems of distinct empirical variables (such as the classroom, economic or welfare systems), and the movement towards formal and mathematical languages for expressing social relationships and progress. For many social scientists, these assumptions present the most advanced form of rationality available to Western culture and the only legitimate heir to social science.[1] The assumptions have become so much a part of our everyday definitions that the more general meaning of empirical as giving detailed attention to actual events is ignored; instead a narrower definition is assigned to suggest that empirical means only that which is quantifiable. The dominance of this particular form of scientific reasoning is often accompanied by the reduction of methodological issues to those techniques. Problems of procedural and statistical rigor seem paramount; generalizations become determined by tests of sampling rather than criteria of substantive theory.

Lost in this hegemony is the socially constructed and sustained quality of reason and logic. Behavioral sciences are recent social inventions and only one of the possible ways to be rational and systemmatic. Developed in the United States during the 1930s, these sciences did not receive prominence in the universities until the 1950s (Easton, 1971). The development of behavioral sciences, however, did not occur in isolation from other American and European thought and the social strains and transformations that underlay the formation of social science itself. To understand social science is to understand the relation of its dominant and counter-traditions and their differing definitions of purpose, value, practice and social interest.

This and the following two chapters will focus upon the differing logic and values that are embedded in discourse of social science. The idea of science as paradigms or constellations of commitments, values, methods and procedures that shape and fashion research guides the analysis. In the second part of the book, the discussion will shift to the social and historical conditions that influence the development of educational paradigms. The social values that underlie inquiry and the historical position of the academic intellectual are interrelated and must be considered in any discussion of science.

The social values and interests in scientific discourse can be illuminated by focusing upon three different intellectual traditions that compete in American social and educational sciences. These traditions are: empirical-analytic sciences, of which the behavioral sciences form the largest and most powerful segment; symbolic or linguistic inquiry; and critical sciences. Each of these traditions will be viewed as paradigms which contain different assumptions about the social world, questions about the social predicament of institutions and solutions to the problems of social and school life. In responding to the social world in different ways, these paradigms pose particular purposes for a theory of institutions and individuals. One is a search for law-like regularities; another focuses upon how human interaction produces rule-making and rule-governing actions; and the third is concerned with how social relations have developed historically and the way that history obscures human agency and interest. Also to be considered are the different purpose and meaning imposed upon the techniques of research, such as the manner in which 'qualitative' methods are used.

In considering the different paradigmatic assumptions, this chapter will focus first upon the social and political nature of social scientific communities, then upon social assumptions that influence the three paradigms. Different meanings of theory will emerge, related to the visions of social affairs, assumptions about the purpose of science and the location of the intellectual within a more general context of social contradictions.

Paradigms and Scientific Communities

We can pursue the idea of the social construction of rationality by considering further Kuhn's (1970) idea of scientific paradigms. Scientific communities have particular constellations of questions, methods and procedures that form disciplinary matrixes or paradigms. As people are trained through participation in a research community, the dispositions implicit in that work are often internalized: they become the scientists' imputed world.

The idea of paradigm directs attention to science as having constellations of commitments, questions, methods and procedures that underlie and give direction to scientific work. The importance of paradigmatic elements in science is that they do not appear as such but form the 'rules of the game' or dispositions that guide everyday practices. Kuhn (1970) focuses upon the paradigmatic elements of research when he suggests that science has emotional and political as well as cognitive elements. As people are trained in a research community, they learn ways in which to think, 'see', 'feel' and act toward the world. These dispositions towards the world are implicit in the exemplars of a field that the researcher learns as s/he defines the scope and boundary of inquiry.

We can distinguish the underlying assumptions of a paradigm by viewing its discourse as having different layers of abstraction. These layers exist simultaneously and are superimposed upon one another. The 'ordinary' language of science focuses upon the questions, content and procedures of research, such as logical consistency, concept validity or instrument and technique reliability. At a deeper layer, we can view inquiry as metalanguage in which the narrative creates a style or a form for thought. The metalanguage maintains assumptions which are unconscious in the formal debates of science but by which the content and procedures of inquiry are made sensible and plausible.

To engage in the discourse of science is to build images about the social world through the words and rules of the language. The concept of culture, for example, is a convenient abstraction anthropologists use to invent questions and to direct observation and interpretation of human affairs (Kluckhorn, 1949). To conceptualize the world as 'culture' is to perform a transitive operation on reality; it neither mirrors nor copies experience but allows people to suppose that things are happening after a fashion. The concept of culture allows us only a partial vision of what exists. The concept emphasizes certain objects, processes, and qualities; it says to an investigator, 'notice this' or 'these things belong together'. The structure of this language is never neutral. It is replete with unconscious assumptions about what the world is like and about the nature of things.

One way of illuminating the assumptions of social inquiry is through the historian's notion of world view: a pattern of *weltans-chauung* imposes upon people in an age a particular use of intelligence or special type of logic for looking at human activity. Each age has suppositions that provide people with certain unpostulated and unlabeled assumptions about what the world is like. These assumptions may be that society is highly integrated and cohesive or that people are rational or irrational. The assumptions are so deeply rooted in the personal reality of a researcher that they become 'facts' that structure the perceptions of the theorist and shape his/her subsequent theorizing. A medieval assumption exemplified in the writings of St Augustine, for example, was that existence was a cosmic drama written by God according to a central theme and rational plan. A function of intelligence was to reconcile experience with a pattern determined by God rather than to inquire into the origin of existence.

In modern social science, there are conflicting assumptions that underlie our social science language and guide our reasoning about social affairs. Contemporary approaches for clarifying problems of poverty, for example, involve different sets of preconceptions (Lowry, 1974). One assumption is a notion of deviance which projects a disease analogy — events are to be identified which interfer with the normal functions of society. A second orientation contains an assumption of social and cultural disorganization, focusing upon disorganization in society in which the victimized and helpless are forced to live. A third assumption is a 'functionalism' which defines social affairs as bound to other institutions in a self-sustaining and interrelated fashion. In each case, causes are assigned to social problems and certain preconceptions of social order and social myth maintained. These themes act metaphorically to create analogies by which we structure and organize events, defining causes of poverty and the possibilities for correcting this social problem.

We can also locate unpostulated and unlabeled assumptions about the world in the conventions and customs of modern science. Tools of modern social science, such as regression analysis, analysis of variance or random sampling involve 'seeing' our social situations as having a number of separate and individual elements that can be combined in aggregates. These assumptions emerge, however, not from science itself, but from political and social movements. The philosophical beliefs of John Stuart Mill that have their origin in the realignment of interests that resulted from the industrial and political revolutions in the late eighteenth and early nineteenth centuries have become embedded in much of our empirical research tradition

(Hamilton, 1979). An examination of recent use of field methods or ethnography in educational research, as well, reveals that certain underlying political and social themes guide the direction and interpretations of investigations (see Chapter 4). These themes are of community, pluralism and a negotiated social order. The themes respond to perceived discontinuities between cultural traditions and the technological structures in our society.

The different themes underlying our theories and techniques point clearly to how general yet divergent social assumptions are rooted in the activities of social science. The discourse of science contains different and sometimes conflicting assumptions about what constitute social facts *par excellence* and how people are to make sense out of the disparate events of their social world. The power of the underlying assumptions in science is that they do not appear as such but are contained in the different customs, conventions and findings of research.

The different and sometimes competing definitions and assumptions about social inquiry are 'normal' responses of an occupational community which is struggling to make sense of a morally complex and profound human condition. The work of social theory is to give coherence to what previously seemed contradictory or without purpose (Gouldner, 1970). The social scientist lives in a world of different social visions, human possibilities and contradictions. As people respond to the contradictions of their world with different purposes and visions, this pluralism becomes an inherent characteristic of the intellectual community of that society.

The concept of paradigm provides a way to consider this divergence in vision, custom and tradition. It enables us to consider science as having different sets of assumptions, commitments, procedures and theories of social affairs. In the disagreements are fundamental issues about values and visions of social order. The conflict revolves not only around technical issues but around the essence of social institutions. The disagreements and conflict enable us to consider more adequately the meaning of a science of society and schooling and the issues that underlie that endeavor.

Three Paradigms: Empirical-Analytic, Symbolic and Critical

In educational sciences, three paradigms have emerged to give definition and structure to the practice of research.[2] These research traditions are discussed as having distinct sets of assumptions, values and interest. While general tendencies will be explored here, the actual patterns are in flux and contain debate about the conduct of research. Further, the different traditions are part of a dynamic context. The conflict occurs as part of the discourse of science itself as proponents seek journal and convention space to argue their views. The conflict is also rooted in problems of social reproduction and transformation, as each paradigm offers a response and challenge to the basic contradictions and strains found in the contemporary world. This latter aspect of the social location will be discussed at the end of this chapter and in later chapters.

Empirical-Analytic Sciences: Lawlike Theories of Social Behavior

One approach to educational research is subsumed under certain commitments and assumptions related to an empirical-analytical approach to social inquiry. Dominant in the Western social science community, the purpose of study is seen as similar to that of the physical and biological sciences.[3] It is believed that the natural sciences progressed once they freed themselves from pre-Enlightenment religious and social premises, in which inquiry was to understand the word of God. Knowledge was to be developed only upon that which could be observed or made observable (the empiric); that knowledge was to be analytical rather than synthetic, that is, observations were to separate human behaviors into its constituent elements. It is from these commitments that many called the science 'Behavioral'.

While recognizing that social conditions have certain characteristics that make them distinct from physical objects, the norms and procedures of 'the older' physical sciences were to be operating guides for a social science. As with these older physical sciences, social affairs are believed to contain law-like regularities which can be identified and manipulated as can objects in the physical world.

At least five interrelated assumptions give form to empirical-analytic research. First, theory is to be universal, not bound to a specific context or to actual circumstances in which generalizations are formulated. The most highly developed theory, for example, is believed to be one which is axiomatic — that is, there is a set of original principles, rules of inference that can be deductively arrived at to describe and predict social occurrences (see, for example, Snow, 1973). The basic principles or axioms are abstract and free from specific social or historical context (for example, principles sought between concept acquisition and engaged academic time in school, increases in stages of moral reasoning through instruction, or of influence of birth order and family size on intellectual growth). Each relationship has qualities that seem to transcend any particular time or context. The axioms of science are to conditionally predict behavior, in a manner similar to Newton's law for universal gravitation. While these axiomatic models have not yet been developed, the lack of such models is thought to be due to the youth of social science itself.

Second, and related to the universal quality of theory, is a commitment to a disinterested science. The purpose of science is analytic. The statements of science are believed to be independent of the goals and values which people may express within a situation. By eliminating contextual aspects, theory is only to describe the relationship of the 'facts'. Suppes (1974), for example, argues that educational sciences are technical activities whose interest is to understand how particular aspects of educational systems work. Educators, he argues, 'do not need wisdom and broad understanding of issues that confront us. What we need are deeply structured theories of education that drastically reduce, if not eliminate the need for wisdom.' The notion of disinterest involves a distinction between scientific theory and moral theory (for discussion, see Bernstein, 1976, Part I). Empirical theory is an explanation of how things work, that is, about what is. It is separate from the differing social interests of people who operate in social and human context. The latter are expressed in moral or normative theory about what ought to be.

Third, there is a belief that the social world exists as a system of variables. These variables are distinct and analytically separable parts of an interacting system. Variables are studied independently of one another (see, for example, Easton, 1971; Rosenshine and Furst, 1973). Teaching is thus reduced to specific variables that can be measured independently of other elements in the system. Teacher praise, for example, is separated out from a myriad of other factors in classroom or teaching practices and compared to achievement in order to understand whether praise influences this school outcome. It is believed that by identifying and interrelating variables, the specific cause of behavior within the system can be known.

The notion of a system of variables provides a specific meaning of causation within the empirical-analytical sciences. A cause is a relationship among empirical variables that can be explained or manipulated to produce conditionally predictable outcomes. This causality is typically defined as: 'If X occurs, then Y will be the effect.'

Fourth, there is a belief in formalized knowledge. This involves making clear and precise the variables of inquiry prior to research. Concepts should be operationalized, defined in such a way that there is an invariant definition which can be used to test and compare data. A concept (such as intelligence, academic achievement) means only and always what results from performing certain operations. The idea is borrowed from physics. For example, concepts about teaching are ordered into specific variables that have invariant meaning and can be measured concretely, such as types of questions asked in a lesson, a teacher's use of praise or the number of student-initiated responses.

By making units of analysis invariant, the researcher can create 'independent' and 'dependent' variables to identify how one unit influences others, and how manipulation of one variable can produce 'effects' upon other variables. Teacher's praise, for example, is related to achievement in order to understand whether praise influences a school outcome. The comparison and manipulation of variables is to confirm or falsify hypotheses as they relate to the development of theory. Operational variables and reliability of measures assume importance in defining and limiting the scope of empirical-analytical theory. Concepts and generalizations are to be rooted only in what is operational.

Fifth, the search for formal and disinterested knowledge creates a reliance upon mathematics in theory construction. Quantification of variables enables researchers to reduce or eliminate ambiguities and contradictions. It is also to elaborate the logical-deductive structure of knowledge by which hypotheses can be tested and improvements in theory made. 'Mathematical models are extremely powerful tools, not only for systematizing research on individual theoretical formulations but also for controlling comparisons between competing formulations' (Snow, 1973, p. 96).

The use of mathematics as a tool should be seen in relation to the other commitments of universal theory, disinterested science, systems of variables and operational definitions. While other paradigms use mathematical models and formal logic, they have a premier position in the empirical-analytic sciences. The goal of formal, mathematical modelling, however, is sometimes misinterpreted to mean that all data are to be quantified and that the only reliable data are those which can be reduced to numbers.

An illustration of the commitment to an empirical-analytic theory can be found in much of the research on teaching. One central approach is to study the relation of teacher questioning to student achievement (see Winne, 1979). The concern is to manipulate teacher questioning during lessons to study its impact on student ability or achievement. Typically, two groups of students are compared: one of which is taught by a teacher who uses mostly factual questions (convergent or lower cognition questions) and a second group taught by a teacher who uses relatively higher cognitive or divergent questions. The independent variable is either training programs in questioning techniques or the experimentor prescribing the manner of questions used during a time-sequenced lesson. The intent of the research is a theory of teaching which can provide a set of specific propositions that would describe and prescribe teaching practice in a given domain. The identified causal relationships are to be described formally and to apply deductively to all teaching situations.

Many empirical-analytic researchers recognize that at certain stages of research, the premature quantification of variables may restrict the inventiveness of the researcher to refine and test hypotheses. It is at this point that non-quantifiable methods are deemed important. Observations and interviews are considered the first steps in initially identifying the essential elements and working hypotheses that can be tested to develop formal theory. The purpose of field work within the empirical-analytic paradigm is to lead to the development of behaviorally oriented concepts and propositions that are testable and predictable.[4] The goal remains quantitative theory with observational techniques a step in that direction. Bellack (1978), in an analysis of paradigms of research, views the results of the study of teaching from the empirical-analytic paradigm as dismal. This occurs, in part, because researchers have not given enough attention to observing and analyzing the phenomena needed in the development of fruitful conceptual structures for significant correlational, predictive or causal studies.

The meaning of theory produced in this paradigm imposes a distinction between theory and practice. Researchers create, discover, or invent theories about social behavior. These symbol systems are separate from practice, as value is separate from fact. Empirical-analytic theory is believed descriptive of what exists. It also has predictive qualities. At one level, this relation between predictors and the descriptive poses no dilemma. How people use the theory to guide practice is a question not of science but of politics. Many social scientists make a distinction between basic science (one which develops broad, context-free generalizations) and applied science, arguing that basic theory is a more enduring and fruitful endeavor.[5]

The choice of use lies not with the scientist, but with the society. At a different level, most empirical-analytic researchers in fields like education are interested in problems of 'knowledge utilization' and school reform. They believe that the outcomes of research can make a difference in teaching and learning. This reformist stand, however, is defined as providing technical expert-neutral knowledge.[6]

The emphasis on developing systematic, lawlike generalizations defines a specific type of cognitive interest for science: it is concerned with the appropriate application of technique to realize defined goals under given conditions. Theories of teaching, learning, or school organization are to define appropriate or inappropriate means to achieve some pre-established criteria. Teaching theories, for example, are concerned with identifying the most efficient ways to produce acquisition of predetermined outcomes (typically achievement). Change theories of school organizations give attention to the most efficient administrative technique for organizing means to achieve 'desired' goals, with the goals assumed as an *a priori* aspect of the social context. Goals are seen as distinct from practice and examined separately: a theory of instruction 'is to settle the question of how the instructional sequences of concepts, skills, and facts should be organized to optimize the rate of learning for a given student' (Suppes, 1974). Theory is not concerned with the total social framework by which social goals and interests are chosen, technologies applied, and systems established. Its sole concern is with technical, cognitive, rational procedures for testing, validating or rejecting hypotheses about observable social events.

Symbolic Sciences: Social Life As Rule-Making and Rule-Governing

A second paradigm in social and educational sciences defines social life as created and sustained through symbolic interactions and patterns of conduct.[7] Through the interactions of people, it is argued, rules are made and sustained to govern social life. The ideas of 'rule-making' and 'rule-governed' can be contrasted to the law-like generalization of the empirical-analytic sciences. In the latter, it is methodologically assumed that there is an invariant nature to human behavior which can be discovered. The idea of 'rules' shifts attention from the invariant nature of behavior to the field of human action, intent and communication.

The rule-making/rule-governed approach distinguishes social life from the physical world. It is argued that the unique quality of being human is found in the symbols people invent to communicate meaning or an interpretation for the events of daily life. To an atom, the language of culture means nothing. To people immersed in Azanda or American life, the ideas, concepts and languages of interactions create ways of expressing and defining the possibilities and limitations of human existence. A cultural science gives focus to the unique human capacity to invent and use symbols.

This second approach to science can be viewed as 'symbolic' (others have used the notion of interpretative, hermeneutic or micro-ethnographic to give expression to this approach to a cultural science). Rather than making the behavior of peoples the 'facts' of science, attention is given to the interaction and negotiations in social situations through which people reciprocally define expectations about appropriate behaviors. One can talk about the role of a teacher, for example, in some abstract and objectified form. But the meanings and rules governing teacher behavior are developed and sustained as people engage in teaching activities. One might compare the roles of a teacher in an urban high school and a suburban elementary school to understand the importance of social meanings and social context in defining roles. In each situation, the behaviors, expectations, and demands made upon teachers are different. Further, the basis of the authority of the role is negotiated differently.[8]

At one layer, the purpose of a symbolic and an empirical-analytic science is the same: to develop theories about social affairs. The notion of theory, however, shifts from a search for lawlike regularities about the nature of social *behavior* to the identification of the social *rules* that underlie and govern the use of social 'facts'. Mehan (1978) argues that 'objective social facts' of schooling, such as students' intelligence, scholastic achievement, career patterns, or routine patterns of behavior, such as classroom organizations, are accomplished and defined through interaction among teachers, students and principals. As people interact, they mutually define what characteristics 'make' for intelligence or achievement and assign categories to describe those elements. Analyses of social situations are to understand what social rules govern and direct the use of these social categories. The sequence and hierarchical organization of a lesson contain rules that govern the acts of initiation and response as a lesson progresses (Mehan, 1978). The research to understand classroom communication involves fieldwork to identify how participants reason about a situation, and the language that enables individuals to participate in a world of collective symbols and shared meanings.

Central to the theoretical work of symbolic social sciences are the concepts of intersubjectivity, motive, and reason. In every situation, people interact and develop consensual norms that bind them in patterned ways of acting. Social categories and definitions (deviance, competence, achievement) are achieved through social interactions and generation of social rules. The rules contain implicit epistemological models that provide guides to actions, practices, and institutional structures. The models enable people to meet and understand the expectations and requirements of the situations they confront.

The consensual norms in a situation involve intersubjectivity. What is 'real' and valid is so because of mutual agreement by those who participate. Objectivity, then, is not a law that guides individuals, but the result of an intersubjective consensus that occurs through social interaction. The 'objective' nature of IQ scores or achievement testing is not in the innate qualities of the people being tested or of the tests themselves, but in the social agreement that enables people to interpret the test results in a particular way and agree upon the validity of the tests.

The notion of intersubjectivity has implications for the scientific community itself. The knowledge of a science is considered valid and 'truthful' only insofar as it reflects the consensus of the scholarly community. The scientific community presupposes conventions and agreement about appropriate knowledge.

Motive and reason are also important elements in social theory. Symbolic researchers argue that there are two types of causation in social affairs. One type of cause is the 'because of'; that is, an event occurs because of a previous one. Empirical-analytic sciences tend to focus on this type of causation. A second type is the 'in order to' cause. An individual does a particular act in order to bring about something in the future. The 'in order to' cause of social affairs involves human motive and reason. A social theory, it is argued, needs to account for both types of causation in explaining social affairs.[9]

Winch (1971) explores the use of reason and motive in social affairs through the following example. One may cite the fact that a person votes in an election and this fact may be understood behaviorally. The behavioral act, in itself, is not adequate to understand that behavior. Voting is voting for a candidate, which involves reasoning about what it means to vote in a society, understanding that the act of voting relates to relevant social rules that operate in a society, and that voting is seen as a rational act because of the existing cultural rules within which the action takes place. Unless motive and reason are explored, the theory of human affairs is inadequate.

We can look at a study of patterns of communication to illustrate the implications of a symbolic science (Barnes, 1975). The study considers the personal and conversational interaction that exists within classrooms as the way in which curriculum is realized and learning occurs. Talk in the class is viewed as based upon tacit agreements between teacher and pupils 'about who writes where, in what way and about what subject-matter and for whose eyes', and about who talks to whom and when and how. These patterns of communication provide children with expectations about how to interpret teacher's remarks and experiences provided in the class-room. The language processes of the classroom have another impor-tant function for learning: they make knowledge and thought proces-ses available for introspection and revision. Thus, the communicative life of classrooms has both a passive and an active tense; with the meanings open to interpretation and change.

Using transcribed conversations from classrooms, Barnes analy-zes the functions of discourse to provide broad and contextually defined definitions for learning and for curriculum. Small group interactions, for example, are examined to illustrate how children work out interpretations through talk and how language strategies develop that to enable children to take responsibility for formulating explanatory hypotheses and evaluating them.

The language of discourse is considered in two complementary ways: that which distinguishes the different forms of knowledge control from that which distinguishes aspects of discourse which control the social order of the classroom. In a study of secondary teachers' attitudes to written work for pupils, two different know-ledge categories were identified: teachers who viewed teaching as transmission, the recording and acquisition of information, and those who saw teaching as interpretation, emphasizing cognitive and personal development. Barnes suggests that there is a relationship between a teacher's view of his/her own role and the evaluation given by pupils' participation (p. 144). This becomes embedded in the communicative life of the institution and is part of the school curriculum.

Symbolic science maintains certain fundamental similarities to an empirical-analytic science. One, its purpose is a descriptive 'neutral' theory about social affairs. By descriptive and neutral, I mean that the interpretive theories of a symbolic science are not thought of as a necessary catalyst within which the social complex of life is con-fronted. Rather, the theories of communication are contemplative of and detached from social situations. As with the empirical-analytic sciences, questions about actions to change social conditions, while informed by theories of communication patterns, are guided by other than scientific questions, such as political, social or philosophical considerations. This neutrality does not mean, however, that the underlying conceptions of symbolic sciences do not have political and practical implications. The idea of negotiation, for example, is derived from liberal democratic theory and contains implicit principles of power and authority.[10] Nor does neutrality mean that the investigators cannot take explicit value stances about what they ought to be; in fact they do (see, for example, Cusick, 1973). The value stance, however, is distinguished from the theoretical. Interpretation is to objectify reality through reflection and the reflective act is fundamentally different from acting on the practical matters of changing that reality.

Two, symbolic scientists do not necessarily reject the formal requirements of empirical-analytical sciences. Mehan (1978) argues that a social-cultural science is concerned with the retrievability of data, exhaustive data treatment, and verification of knowledge. In contrast to the empirical-analytic science, however, the purpose of a theory is not technical. It is to clarify the conditions for communication and intersubjectivity. Three, while its cognitive interest is different (social norms vs. technical rules), there is a separation of theory from practical matters. Theory helps to illuminate, to clarify and sometimes to give social-technical recommendations to social affairs but does not necessarily serve a practical purpose in giving moral direction to social affairs; that is, theory is essentially contemplative. Four, formal logic is important in illuminating inconsistencies and fallacies, although the reliance on mathematics to develop knowledge is not essential. Five, inquiry is ahistorical, focusing upon the rules of what is now occurring. Like the empirical-analytic, it is concerned with aspects of 'what is' not 'why it is' or 'what might be'.

Symbolic theory shifts the focus of theory to the nature of discourse rather than behavior. The parts of the whole are to be understood in relation to the totality of the situation; thus it is not reductive of phenomena. The situation, however, is typically defined by the interactions of the participants. While there are attempts to consider how institutional and social structures influence negotiations, the responses remain partial and unclear (Hall and Hall, in press).

Critical Science: Social Relations As Historical Expression

A critical perspective to social science is an approach for understanding the rapid social changes in the Western world as well as responding to certain social problems that these changes have brought about.[11] In part, critical social scientists see the rapid technologicalization of work, the growing importance of mass communication, and the growth and fusion of institutionalized sectors of life as having social and political consequences. The social alternatives available have been limited, and the domination of public and private life by particular groups in society has increased. Knowledge, for some, has become 'professionalized'. Certain occupations have license to provide the rationality of determining how children are to grow, how families are to live, how social deviance is to be defined, and how work and leisure are to be practiced. A consequence of the professionalization of knowledge is to make individuals more dependent upon certain experts in society. In identifying such trends that limit human possibilities, the goal of critical science is to demystify the patterns of knowledge and social conditions that restrict our practical activities.

We can distinguish between two major movements or tendencies within a critical science. To borrow from Williams (1977), one strand can be called 'residual', the other 'emergent'. The residual tendency refers to that aspect of a critical science which, while maintaining some distance from the effective dominant culture, incorporates major residues of the past culture into its critique for considering alternatives to the dominant culture. Berger and Neuhaus (1975), for example, give focus to mediating structures in society. They suggest that the modern state is here to stay, indeed that it ought to expand the benefits it provides — but that alternative mechanisms are possible to provide welfare-state service (p. 1). The purpose of their research, according to Berger and Neuhaus, is to make the political order less alienating and more meaningful. An emergent tendency, a second strand of critical science, offers arguments that are in opposition to the dominant culture and institutions.[12]

A critical social science is, at root, normative and substantive as well as formal. The way in which we think, argue, and reason about social affairs has implications for the scope and boundaries placed upon social affairs. The function of critical theory is to understand the relations among value, interest, and action and, to paraphrase Marx, to change the world, not to describe it.

The relation between theory and practice, fact and value, is not direct. Theory is not prescriptive as in the empirical-analytic sciences. Were it so, theory would play a role of legitimating and justifying what is done. Practice involves strategic choices in political negotiation. To have theory prescribe action would make that theory technical and mechanical.

> Therefore, theory cannot have the same functions for the organization of action, of the political struggle, as it has for the organization of enlightenment. The practical consequences of self-reflection are changes in attitude which result from insight into causalities *in the past* and indeed result of themselves. In contrast, strategic action oriented towards the future, which is prepared for in the internal discussion of groups who (as the avant garde) presuppose for themselves already successfully completed processes of enlightenment, cannot be justified in the same manner by reflective knowledge (Habermas, 1973, p. 39).

The purpose of theory from Habermas' perspective is to enable individuals to know themselves and their situation through retrospection, and thus bring to consciousness the process of social formation which, in turn, provides conditions in which practical discourse can be conducted. Practical discourse is prudent action: questions of ethics, morality and politics are interrelated with science to orient individuals to what is right and just in a given situation. Theory, in this context, provides an orientation for practice rather than providing calculated administrative rules, regulations or norms for making life possible.

While critical theorists do give explicit attention to the relation of science in society, the issue is plagued with ambiguities and unresolved issues about the social role of the intellectual (Bernstein, 1976; Ball, 1977). It is an issue that has been continuously debated from the time of the ancient Greeks to the present. The significance of the current dialogue within the critical sciences lies in the struggle with this issue — that is, that the consideration of the language and occupation of a social science as an instrumental part of people's world-creating and sustaining activity. Descriptions of science are at the same time prescriptions and advocacy in the political struggles of that world.

Because of the interests in practical discourse, critical science is akin to historical analyses of social processes. The daily routines of our social life obscure many strains, struggles, and interests which have coalesced to define the conduct of schooling, of nationhood, gender, and work in our society. The historical development of tradition and institutions contains reifications and mystifications which make social affairs and social interests opaque. The interaction between subject and object in society is lost. A critical science investigates the dynamics of social change, of past and present, to unmask the structural constraints and contradictions that exist in a determinant society. The task of inquiry is to illuminate the assumptions and premises of social life that are subject to transformations and those propositions which are not (see, for example, Giroux, 1981).

The notion of causation in critical science concerns the intersection of history, social structure, and biography. Causation involves historical determination (that is, the regularities of social action that result from historical processes), structural conditions, and the actions of particular individuals who influence and modify their social situation.

The assumption that science illuminates the historical processes of social relations involves considering social affairs as having a dialectical quality. Dialectics, according to Ilyenkov (1977), concern the way in which the structure of society performs its specific functions in a manner that not only conforms to its own structure 'but according to the scheme and location of all other things' (p. 51). Each chain of events has, as its consequence, a new formation that not only interferes within the events but rejoins the events each time there are new conditions and circumstances in action. Gunn (1977), from an emergent perspective, suggests that the dialectical quality of inquiry involves 'seeing' the world in a continuous flux in which there is negation and contradiction. Every substantive change manifests itself as a change in relation to the whole and itself, and thus changes the form of objectivity.

Berger and Luckmann (1967) offer a residual approach to a critical science. They define the dialectical quality of social life as involving three moments: society is a human product; society is an objective reality; man is a social product. 'At any moment, it is important to emphasize that the relationship between man, the producer, and the social world, his product, is and remains a dialectical one. That is, man (not, of course, in isolation but in his collectivities) and his social world interact with each other' (p. 61). A theory of social reality, they argue, must consider these three moments and their interaction.[13]

By considering social reality as 'moments', the notion of generalization is transformed from that found in the two previous paradigms. Hamilton (1981) argues that much of twentieth century Western positivistic philosophy involves the separation of logic (explanation) and cognition (understanding) which has weakened the power of systematic inquiry.[14] The emphasis on 'logic' focuses upon the verification of knowledge and the world as an assemblage of discrete facts. The reaction to positivistic philosophy which emphasizes cognition is limited as well. Knowledge is thought available only through the craftlike qualities of the researcher. Emphasis is given to the importance of history, culture, and the subjective. The problem of inquiry is to abandon the cognitive-logical polarity and produce an educational theory that

> has four elements which, collectively, go beyond the assumptions of the 'received' and 'craft' standpoints. First, it acknowledges the dynamic (i.e., non-steady-state) quality of human history; second, it accepts the open-ended nature of research and action; third, it aims to reduce (or codify) the apparent complexity of human experience and finally, it operates through the translation of private accounts of the past, present or future in a form that can be 'tested' through further action and inquiry (Hamilton, 1981, p. 235).

The stance of a critical science toward social reality redefines the notion of systems and their relationships. Whereas the empirical-analytic paradigm defines 'systems' as independent sets of variables, critical scientists seek to understand the totality of systems and how they interrelate. But, in comparison to symbolic sciences, a particular system is considered not in isolation but in relation to other aspects of society that influence its own form as well as that of others. A view of the dynamics of the whole, with its contradictions and issues, is necessary to enable people to develop a more adequate sense of how to penetrate institutional structures and to inform practical actions.

> As a mode of reasoning, the category of totality in the dialectic allows educators not only to become more critically interpretative, it also suggests new ways of acting in the world; it helps teachers and students alike to link knowledge with specific normative interests, with specific frames of reference (Giroux, 1979, p. 10).

The relationship of institutional forms and structures is documented in Noble's (1977) study of the professionalization of engineering. He illuminates how university training was a response to industrial and business demands for more efficient production. The university's incorporation of programs that certified engineers had, in turn, an effect upon the business community. The certification procedures influenced who occupied the positions of authority in business and what the business community began to accept as an appropriate rationality for production processes and social relations at work. The latter, the definition of social relations as problems of human engineering, had consequences for social affairs that went beyond the production process itself as it was incorporated in other social institutions, such as schooling.

If we return again to the use of technique, we find, as in the other paradigms, multiple approaches are used to develop theory. Wright (1978), for example, uses survey data and statistical techniques to test the appropriateness of existing definitions of class structure. Field methodologies assume particular importance in pursuing questions about cultural reproduction and transformation (see, for example, Connell *et al.*, 1982).

The influence of the assumptions of a critical science on the practice of study can be illuminated by focusing upon an investigation of the transition from school to work of twelve non-academic English working-class boys (Willis, 1977). The research involved case study work, interviewing, group discussions and participant observations as the boys proceeded through their last two years at school and into the early months of work. The questions that guided the field study were related to understanding the underlying meanings, rationality and dynamics of the cultural processes in which the working class is located and how these cultural processes maintain and reproduce the social order. The use of field method, Willis argues, is dictated by his interest in culture: 'These techniques are suited to record this level and have a sensitivity to meaning and values as well as an ability to represent and interpret symbolic articulations, practices and forms of cultural production' (Willis, 1977, p. 3). Also the method was viewed as allowing a degree of activity, creativity and human agency to come through in the analysis.

The central argument of the study is that working-class youth learn to take on a subordinate role in Western capitalism through their interactions with school and with the culture of the workplace. The working-class 'lads' were a counter-school culture. They maintained a general and personalized opposition to authority in school and a rejection of those students who conform. This opposition occurred through dress, mannerism and sexual aggressiveness. The 'lads' also became adept at managing the formal system of schooling and limiting its demands. The opposition to school culture, however, is viewed in relation to larger patterns of working-class culture. There is social pressure for the boys to take their place on the shop floor and to gain acceptance in that culture. The racism, sexism and masculine chauvinism which characterize the counter-school culture are the locating themes of the shopfloor culture.

The rejection and resistance of the 'lads' to the school culture becomes a contradiction in which the subordinate roles are experienced as 'true learning, affirmation, appropriation and as a form of resistance' (p. 3). There is some illumination of the social myths and ideology of schooling by which the lads understand some of the determining conditions of the working class. The lads 'see', for example, the false logic of school career counseling that all jobs are satisfying to a range of human aspirations. The penetration, however, is only partial. The myths are turned back upon themselves through general ideological and school processes in ways that the working-class assumptions of sexism, racism, and anti-intellectualism serve to legitimate social and economic devisions within society.

In the Willis study we can begin to identify some of the assumptions which underlie a critical science. The research was concerned with how forms of domination and power are maintained and renewed in society. The intent of the research is not just to describe and interpret the dynamics of a society, but to consider the ways in which the processes of social formation can be modified. Finally, it posited the social world as one of flux, with complexity, contradiction and human agency.

Paradigms As Artifacts of Social/Cultural Conditions

The commitments to generate scientific knowledge about schooling are fraught with different assumptions, commitment, and interests that underlie the ongoing work. These assumptions do not necessarily have their source in the discourse of science itself. Visions of social reality found in social theory are not testable by science but, rather, reflect root values about the ways in which larger issues of social strain and contradiction are to be explained and resolved.

The location in larger social issues enables us to ask the question, why do these three paradigms exist *now* as competing forms of discourse? The question, I believe, can be answered in a variety of ways. One is to locate the paradigms within the 'science as conflict' view. Earlier it was argued that Western sociology and history of science identify conflict as essential to scientific imagination and creativity. This answer, I believe, can now be extended to consider a second response. That response seeks to understand the general social and cultural conditions in which the idea of conflict is seen as plausible and reasonable. Here we must begin examining the general conditions of capitalism and political liberalism in the United States. Science exists within a general system which stresses the rules of the market. While these rules do vary in time and circumstance, the intellectual has been located within that system which enabled the intellectual to seek different sponsors and to respond to different interests. In contrast to the East where the intellectual has been historically part of the state apparatus, Western science has relied upon patronage of different interests, as well as, in later stages, the state apparatus. These Western structural conditions tended to produce divergent interests and the legitimation of pluralism. In what is an irony to some, the view of intellectual life as being a 'marketplace of ideas' has enabled a certain degree of dissent and development of residual and emergent perspectives.

The importance of capitalism in legitimating intellectual conflict, however, does not explain a different order of question: Why these three paradigms? As will be discussed in the following chapter, these are not the only possibilities, as a different set of assumptions and procedures have been adopted by Soviet researchers. It is important that an understanding of the plausibility and appropriateness of the three paradigms be considered not only by the ideas generated but by considering the larger historical and political setting in which the paradigms exist. Each paradigm offers a response to the social predicament of the contemporary situation of the United States. It is on the particular historical setting that we need to focus, for each paradigm responds to a different moment in the social conditions being confronted.

Empirical-analytic science responds to a host of social, economic and historical factors. As a historically young country, the United States had none of the strong humanistic traditions that are found in Western Europe, and its science and literature developed a strong pragmatic ideology. Biddle (1981) argues, for example, that individualism, pragmaticism and technology took on specific meanings within the frontier society of the United States. These root values and circumstances provide the underpinning for contemporary research on teaching. One also needs to consider the dominance of empirical-analytic sciences in relation to the changing economic and social conditions in which major interests called for social engineering approaches in both physical and cultural production. The administrative focus of the empirical-analytic sciences provided one response to control the transformations that were occurring as a result of industrialization, immigration and, more recently, the development of high-technology industry and finance capitalism.

The symbolic and critical sciences can be viewed as a different response to those same social and cultural circumstances. In a later chapter, symbolic sciences will be considered as responding to certain contradictions in United States capitalism — its ability to provide, for most, material progress but not spiritual satisfaction. This period was also one of great economic and university expansion, creating many new academic positions. The critical science offers a different moment in our contemporary conditions. Critical sciences have long been a part of American intellectual heritage but were reasserted as an important part of academic debate during the 1960s when the Vietnam War and urban riots highlighted certain inequities and structural limitations. Many graduate students during that period sought to incorporate European Marxist and critical perspectives into American scholarship to deal with the contradictions and inequities of social conditions. These graduate students of the 1960s now have major professorial positions and their critiques have refocused upon the state fiscal crisis and the institutional contradictions that emerge more clearly in times of social strain.

As with society as a whole, science contains multiple visions and methods for coming to grips with social reality. These visions and methods are deeply rooted in the contradictions and transformations that occur in society. The different paradigms provide one institutional response to unresolved aspects of everyday life and the attempt of individuals to locate themselves in society. If we look at other institutional structures, we would find similar root conflict as people engage in defining themselves, society and their intersections. While a particular dynamic in society, science is also a part of history and an expression of its struggles and conflict.

Competing Paradigms and Change

The unpostulated and unlabeled assumptions about the social world embedded in educational research have implications not only for knowledge of the world, but also for the ways in which that world is challenged. In organizing, categorizing, and defining objects in social life, inquiry gives direction to what possibilities are seen as plausible and reasonable in our daily encounters. To adopt a language for structuring existence is to give organization to the ways in which the existence is to be changed. The stances taken in the different paradigms, then, should not be considered as only providing rules about what is valid in scientific discourse. The rules for generating knowledge about reality also provide guidelines for determining appropriate operations for transforming that reality. The languages of science contain thought, ideas, and values, as well as 'mere' descriptions.

The problem of change implicit in research is clear when we transpose the characteristics of the paradigmatic stances into questions about altering existing institutional structures. The empirical-analytic sciences enable us to consider how formal knowledge of schooling is distributed among groups, such as pointing to disparities through intergroup comparisons on achievement tests or attendance in universities. The symbolic sciences focus upon how knowledge is negotiated in schools. The critical sciences enable educators to understand the social and economic roots of the knowledge maximized in schooling. The problem of change becomes tied to the manner in which the problem of schooling is articulated: each paradigm locates the issue of schooling in different patterns of social life.

Some Concluding Thoughts

In identifying three paradigms in educational research, the argument illustrated how competing commitments, purposes and values work themselves into definitions of knowledge and method. The definitions of what is appropriate knowledge predispose one's way of thinking and challenging social conditions and institutions. Each of the paradigms provides a different view about the 'nature' and 'causes' of our social situation and seeks to give coherence in different ways to the social predicaments that seem unresolved.

Science as a social occupation suggests that categorical distinctions often made in the philosophy of science cannot be sustained. Distinctions between normative and empirical theory, fact and value, theory and practice, descriptions and evaluation can mislead and possibly distort the scientific enterprise. Discussions of science need more subtle ways of describing the interactions between norms and rules of science, scientific knowledge, and larger communal aspects that influence inquiry. Otherwise, researchers are faced with comforting mystifications about their own occupational work.

The question of paradigm raises a further consideration. Often discussions have posed the problem of conflict in research as between doing 'qualitative' and 'quantitative' methods. This distinction makes science technical, and the process of research mechanical. Field techniques, surveys, and mathematical interpretation of findings are deemed useful in each of the paradigms discussed. What is important in considering these various techniques of science is how they relate to paradigmatic commitments and how the techniques are placed within a context of problem, scientific intent and interest.

We must again consider the emergence of these three paradigms in contemporary educational and social science as an artifact of our time. The empirical-analytical sciences developed in relation to the growth of a corporate society and the needs of a science of management, especially after the 1930s. The symbolic sciences developed as a science of education, in part from anomalies that could not be resolved by the empirical behavioral sciences. It also responded to a general social malaise in which some felt that the technological successes of society have not been able to accommodate the spiritual and community needs of people. These needs demanded that new scientific approaches focus upon communicative competency and social cohesion. The critical sciences, vital during the 1930s, received a renewed credibility from the turmoil and conflict of the 1960s and early 1970s, when institutional structures were placed in question and conflict became a visible element in society, and legitimacy in the 1980s as those critics assumed central positions in universities.

What I cannot argue for is the superiority of any single paradigm for considering the complexities of schooling. Each intellectual tradition provides a particular vantage point for considering social conduct. The different paradigms can enable us to gain greater insight into the whole and into the relationship of the elements to that whole. It can also enable us to consider the possibilities and limitations of that enterprise of science. In this sense I am willing to adopt a liberal-democratic perspective to the problem of social science. While it is clear to the reader that my own sense of the problem lies in the critical sciences, the symbolic and empirical-analytic sciences do provide particular insights into our human conditions. We must guard against, as we did in the previous chapter, the reduction of science to technique in which attention is given to problems of rigor that are separate from the questions, purposes and assumptions that guide inquiry.

Notes

1 This faith does break down periodically in our society. Events such as the study of how to pacify rural populations in Latin America (Project

Camelot) or the scientific reporting of the nuclear mishap at Three Mile Island point to the vulnerability of these *occupations*. However, once the furore dies down it is the expert, and his or her scientific knowledge, that is called for to right the wrongs that have brought about by previous actions.

2 My attempt in this and the following sections is to point to central tendencies and dimensions of each paradigm. At points this may cause omission of certain distinctions within a paradigm and of the internal disagreement about perspective and procedures.

3 Discussions of empirical-analytic sciences are in Easton (1971) and Homans (1967). While these arguments differ as to what are the basic 'data' of human experience, I believe the authors do maintain certain general commitments that allow their arguments to cohere.

4 Louis Smith (1981) reflects upon this assumption in his early research efforts and how they have evolved.

5 For arguments about this distinction, cf. Easton (1971) and Shaver (1979).

6 The problem of reform through social science is discussed in more detail in Chapters 5–8.

7 Symbolic sciences are discussed in Winch (1971), Schutz (1973), Luckmann (1977), and Cicourel (1969).

8 To see how different paradigmatic assumptions lead to different emphases, questions and solutions to school problems, compare Cusick's (1973) symbolic interactionist perspective and Willis's (1977) Marxist perspective to the study of high schools.

9 In an insightful analysis of competing research paradigms, Bellack (1978) argues for a synthesis. An adequate research perspective, he suggests, requires both an observer's and a participant's view for interpretation and description of classroom events. Each view of research provides a different but essential dimension to the study of human events; no one view is adequate. Further, explanation of classroom events involves interrelating reason and intentions with causes found in the contextual factors of schooling. (For discussions of generalizations, see Popkewitz and Tabachnick, 1981.)

10 See Chapter 4 for a discussion of the political conceptions that underlie symbolic field study approaches.

11 Critical stances are discussed in Bernstein (1976) and Lukacs (1971).

12 Some current writers who might be considered as having a residual orientation are Oliver (1976) and Bruce-Briggs (1979). Because of both residual and emergent tendencies, we have labeled this paradigm 'critical science'. Critical theorists are a particular 'school' that has been called the Frankfurt School. Their arguments are along emergent lines. There is a rejection of earlier social formations and values in a search for new meanings, practices and relationships. Current Marxist analyses of contemporary society can be viewed as emergent (see, for example, Wright, 1978; Apple, 1982). Both residual and emergent tendencies, however, contain political visions to guide social inquiry.

13 To consider the political qualities of Berger's argument, see Berger and Neuhaus (1977).

14 In this chapter the cognitive (understanding) perspective is discussed as symbolic social science, logic (explanation) as empirical-analytic sciences.

References

APPLE, M. (1982) *Education and Power*, Boston, Mass., Routledge and Kegan Pual.

BALL, T. (Ed.) (1977) *Political Theory and Praxis, New Perspectives*, Minneapolis, Minn., University of Minnesota Press.

BARNES, D. (1975) *From Communication to Curriculum*, Harmondsworth, Middlesex, Penguin.

BELLACK, A. (1978) *Competing Ideologies in Research on Teaching*, University Reports on Education, 1, Uppsala, Department of Education, University of Uppsala, September.

BERGER, P. and LUCKMANN, T. (1967) *The Social Construction of Reality: A Treatise in the Sociology of Knowledge*, Garden City, N.Y., Anchor Books.

BERGER, P. and NEUHAUS, R. (1977) *To Empower People; The Role of Mediating Structures in Public Policy*, Washington, D.C., American Institute for Public Policy Research.

BERNSTEIN, R. (1976) *The Restructuring of Social and Political Theory*, New York, Harcourt Brace Jovanovich.

BIDDLE, B. (1981) 'Ideology, social planning and research on teaching in the United States', in TABACHNICK, B. *et al.* (Eds) *Studying Teaching and Learning; Trends in Soviet and American Research*, New York, Praeger.

BRUCE-BRIGGS, B. (1979) *The New Class?* New Brunswick, N.J., Transaction Books.

CICOUREL, A. (1969) *Method and Measurement in Sociology*, New York, The Free Press.

CONNELL, R. *et al.* (1982) *Making the Difference, Schools, Families and Social Division*, Sydney, George Allen and Unwin.

CUSICK, P. (1973) *Inside a High School Student's World*, New York, Holt, Rinehart and Winston.

EASTON, D. (1971) *The Political System: An Inquiry into the State of Political Science*, New York, Knopf.

GIROUX, H. (1979) 'Dialectics and the development of curriculum theory', Unpublished paper, Boston University, August.

GIROUX, H. (1981) *Ideology, Culture and the Process of Schooling*, Lewes, Falmer Press.

GOULDNER, A. (1970) *The Coming Crisis of Western Sociology*, New York, Basic Books.

GUNN, R. (1977) 'Is nature dialectical?' *Marxism Today*, February, pp. 45–52.

HABERMAS, J. (1973) *Theory and Practice*, Boston, Mass., Beacon Press.

HALL, P. and HALL, D. (in press) 'The social conditions of the negotiated order', *Urban Life*.

HAMILTON, D. (1979) 'Educational research and the shadow of John Stuart Mill', in SMITH, J. and HAMILTON, D. (Eds), *The Meritocratic Intellect: Studies in the History of Educational Research*, Aberdeen University Press.

HAMILTON, D. (1981) 'On generalization in the educational sciences: Problems and purposes', in POPKEWITZ, T. and TABACHNICK, B. (Eds), *The Study of Schooling; Field-Based Methodologies in Educational Research and Evaluation*, New York, Praeger.

HOMANS, G. (1967) *The Nature of Social Science*, New York, Harcourt, Brace and World.

ILYENKOV, E. (1977) *Dialectic Logic; Essays on Its History and Theory*, Moscow, Progress Publishers.

KLUCKHOLN, C. (1949) *Mirror for Man: Anthropology and Modern Life*, New York, McGraw-and Hill Book Company.

KUHN, T. (1970) *The Structure of Scientific Revolutions*, 2nd ed., Chicago, Ill., University of Chicago Press.

LOWRY, R. (1974) *Social Problems: A Critical Analysis of Theories and Public Policy*, Lexington, Mass., D.C. Heath.

LUCKMANN, T. (Ed.) (1977) *Phenomenology and Sociology*, Harmondsworth, Middlesex, Penguin Books.

LUKACS, G. (1971) *History and Class Consciousness; Studies in Marxist Dialectics*, R. Livingstone (Trans), Cambridge, Mass., MIT Press.

MEHAN, H. (1978) 'Structuring school structure', *Harvard Educational Review*, 48, pp. 32–64.

NOBLE, D. (1977) *America by Design: Science, Technology, and the Rise of Corporate Capitalism*, New York, Knopf.

OLIVER, D. (1976) *Education and Community: A Radical Critique of Innovative Schooling*, Berkeley, Ca., McCutchan Publishers.

ROSENSHINE, B. and FRUST, N. (1973) 'The use of direct observation to study teaching', in R. TRAVERS (Ed.) *Second Handbook of Research on Teaching*, Chicago, Ill., Rand McNally.

SCHUTZ, A. (1973) *Collected Papers*, Vol. 1, M. NATANSON (Ed.), The Hague, Martinus Nijhoff.

SHAVER, J. (1979) 'The productivity of educational research and the applied-basic research distinction', *Educational Researcher*, 8, 1, pp. 3–9.

SMITH, L. (1981) 'Accidents, serendipity and making the commonplace problematic: The origin and evolution of the field study "problem"', in POPKEWITZ, T. and TABACHNICK, B. (Eds), *The Study of Schooling, Field-Based Methodologies in Educational Research and Evaluation*, New York, Praeger.

SNOW, R. (1973) 'Theory construction for research on teaching', *Second Handbook of Research on Teaching*, Chicago, Ill., Rand McNally.

SUPPES, P. (1974) 'The place of theory in educational research', *Educational Researcher*, 3, 6, pp. 3–10.

WILLIAMS, R. (1977) *Marxism and Literature*, Oxford, Oxford University Press.

WILLIS, P. (1977) *Learning to Labour*, Farnborough, Saxon House.

WINCH, P. (1971) *The Idea of a Social Science and Its Relation to Philosophy*,

New York, Humanities Press.

WINNE, P. (1979) 'Use of higher cognitive questions and student achievement', *Review of Educational Research*, 49, 1, pp. 13–50.

WRIGHT, E.O. (1978) *Class, Crisis and the State*, London, New Left Books.

Chapter 3

Soviet Pedagogical Sciences: Visions and Contradictions

The organization of science in the Soviet Union provides a set of historical constraints, social assumptions and interests different from those in the United States. State policy is that Marxist-Leninist thought provides the framework for the formation of science. Further, science is to serve directly the policy goals of the state. On the surface, these commitments might lead one to consider Soviet educational science as utilitarian in purpose, similar to the managerial focus of the empirical-analytic sciences in the United States. This similarity in general purpose, however, is transformed by the fundamental differences in the social, philosophical and methodological assumptions of Soviet pedagogical research. There is an emphasis upon interrelations of social elements, the role of social environment upon learning and a recognition of the moral/political imperatives of science.

The different posture of Soviet pedagogical research is explained, in part, by its relation to the state. Historically, the intellectual in the East has developed as part of the state bureaucracy (Konrad and Szelenyi, 1979). In the current political setting, the Soviet intellectual has direct responsibility for rationally distributing goods, services and values. This direct role in social reproduction and distribution of surplus values has implications for the conduct of science. There is little official room for shifting values and subcultures. The intellectual is not able to choose the content of his/her work by appealing to pluralist interests.

Pedagogical research is premised upon the Soviet interpretation of Marx. Marx's analysis of Western economic and political history was one of critique and opposition. He sought to understand the historical contradictions in the development of labor processes and how those contradictions provide elements that could foster a more progressive society. But Marx did not prescribe the forms of institutions in that new society and how day-to-day life is to be interpreted, explained and changed. As Marxism became an ideology of power rather than opposition, the problem of science became programatic. Marxist sciences had to be modified and adapted to orient practice towards social goals.

A single paradigm emerges that is drawn from Marx but given definition by Russian experience and thought.[1] The philosophical root of science is called dialectical materialism and this establishes ground rules that guide Soviet research practice. Debate and methodology evolve around interpretations of the nature, character and implications of dialectical materialism. While one could argue that the tying of Soviet research to the state and an official philosophy has limited social inquiry, the assumptions of dialectical materialism have been constructive in certain areas of pedagogical research.

This chapter will consider the paradigmatic assumptions and practices of Soviet pedagogical research. First, the idea of dialectical materialism will be discussed. Second, research approaches to pedagogical problems will be considered. The intent is to provide a critical appraisal of how these philosophical assumptions are incorporated into problems of research. A distinction is made between the research approaches in psychology and didactics and that of curriculum research. The former focuses upon human development and the logic of teaching as a dynamic, historical process; the latter focuses upon the establishment of predefined laws that regulate the physical and social world. This difference, which poses a contradiction in the research community, also establishes a functional relationship that ties the research community to state goals.

Some caveats need to be entertained in this discussion.[2] To discuss scholarship is to enter into a world that assumes tacit understandings, rules and a horizon in which language and practices are made reasonable. As an American, I see only faint glimmers of the rules of Soviet scholarship as I cannot have full access to the nexus of social, intellectual, material and political conditions that comprise intellectual life in the Soviet Union. Language is a case in point. While I had read about Soviet history, intellectual thought and pedagogy, I was unprepared for their talk about 'knowing activity', 'upbringing activity', 'individualization', or 'problem-solving'. The conversations seemed to have no concrete reference, a jumble with no relation to empirical facts or syntactical structure. I soon found, however, that the words are part of a dialogue that began after the Soviet revolution as people began to search for sciences that reflected the new image of socialist man. To understand the words is to understand that history of politics, struggle and visions that captured many intellectuals in the Soviet Union.

Further, I had entrance into only parts of Russian society and Russian intellectual life. The psychoanalytic work in the Republic of Georgia or the intellectual perspectives of the non-Russian Republics rarely enter Western literature about the Soviet Union or its official publications. Yet the non-Russian population is about half the population of the Soviet Union. Finally, I realize that many of the research efforts discussed here may have little bearing upon the actual workings of schooling. Understanding what occurs in schools involves a more complex consideration than the sociology of its research community.

Dialectical Materialism: Social and Philosophical Commitments to Guide the Conduct of Research

Turmoil, idealism and social experimentation followed the 1917 Russian Revolution. While the Bolsheviks consolidated physical power by re-establishing a state apparatus, there was a practical quest to establish a socialist consciousness and institutional forms (Bauer, 1952; Joravsky, 1961). The writings of Marx provided a critique of a society to which Russian experience only partially conformed. Just as important, Marx was not prescriptive about the organization of the new socialist system. He believed that critique would produce direction and possibility. The task of the collectives, government ministries and individuals who believed in the revolutionary ideals was to create the necessary infrastructure (Fitzpatrick, 1978).

Intellectual excitement and experimentation in the 1920s occurred not only among Russians but throughout many intellectual circles in the Western world where the Soviet experiment was seen as a noble one. A problem of the new Soviet government was to create sciences, social services and education that conveyed the world view underlying a socialist commitment. In the writings of Luria (1979) and Vygotsky (1978), founders of Soviet psychology, there is a compelling search to place the ideals and premises of socialism into method for scientific studies. These psychologists admitted to being only partially aware of Marx prior to the revolution. They became partisans in transforming its ideals into concrete research programs. The same zeal can be found in the work of Makarenko (1973), a Soviet educator who sought to transform youth orphaned by the Civil War into productive social members. His schools were based upon the development of collective norms and sanctions to achieve social goals.

From these and subsequent activities grew a social philosophical view of society, of the relation of people to production and of the formation of consciousness. This view was drawn from Marx but labeled by early Russian revolutionaries as 'dialectical materialism'. It is the official interpretive scheme of the state and Soviet scientific communities. As a social philosophy, dialectical materialism poses fundamental questions about the nature of people and the transformation of the social and physical world. The social philosophical assumptions are interrelated with state mandates to guide the formation of schooling and pedagogical research.

Man As a Social Animal

Central to dialectical materialism is the belief that man is a social, historical animal. Drawing upon the writings of Hegel, Marx and Lenin, the individual is seen as emerging from social, historical and cultural processes in which people act upon their external environment to modify and or improve their world. Thus the ideas, categories and thoughts in a society are not produced by the independent will or consciousness of separate individuals but rather from people's interactions with their material world. The emergence of consciousness and personality is considered an aspect of a people's involvement in creating and responding to events of their world. The relation of psychology to the social world is basic to the Soviet attempt to eliminate a dichotomy between thought and practice or subject and object that underlies much Western philosophy and social theory.

The unity of objective and subjective world is achieved by considering the subjective (thought, reason, ideas) as socio-historical phenonema. Thought appears in the course of actually shaping the world and the making of things. The mind is a special form of activity, '. . . the product and derivative of the development of material life . . . which is transformed in the course of social-historical development into internal activity, the activity of consciousness' (Leont'ev in Davydov, 1981, p. 6). For Soviet social and psychological scientists, an individual does not embrace reality through theoretical ability (contemplation), preconception or knowledge alone, but through a practical ability in which production and action take precedence over knowledge.

The mediating link between the objective and subjective world is labor and production. It is the productive process that transforms the objects of nature into objects of contemplation. Vygotsky (1978) viewed social interaction as analytically prior to individual consciousness and categorical behavior. Emphasizing the *material* basis of psychology, Vygotsky argued that development does not proceed towards socialization, but towards the conversion of social relations into mental functions. Maintaining the Marxist assumption that labor is a mediating link between the objective material world and human consciousness, Vygotsky focused upon language as a tool in social activities. Language brings transformation of the objects into ideas, concepts, and thoughts of our consciousness. The process is not linear (material to subjective consciousness) but dialectical, one in which thought and practice become interrelated, involving tensions and contradictions which produce change and progress.

Contradiction As Principle of Social Life

Contradictions give reference to the principle that life involves a unity of mutually exclusive opposites. Actual experience always contains contradictions that cannot be resolved through formal logical operations. Relative to any one thing or object in the universe are two mutually exclusive points of view. In looking for invariant determinants, there is also the discovery of differences; with necessity and stability comes change; change is a part of stability; new knowledge infringes upon the old by refuting and revising it; diversity co-exists with homogeneity; what is negative to the debitor is positive to the creditor. Contradictions, it is argued, are essential to human conditions and to the problem of change because human experience is always unfinished. To eliminate contradictions is to eliminate half of human experience.

The problem of contradiction merges into that of dialectics. Dialectics direct attention to the world in motion, to evolution and development as central to thought and nature. The emphasis on movement and connections focuses upon the social-historical process of individual development. Human understanding is to understand how structures of thought and culture perform their specific functions in a manner that not only conforms to its own inner logic 'but according to the scheme and location of all other things' (Ilyenkov, 1977). Each chain of events has as its consequence a new formation that not only interferes with the events but also rejoins the events in such a way that each time there are new conditions and circumstances in action. Every substantive change manifests itself as a change in relation to the whole and itself, thus changing the form of objectivity. This notion of change has implications not only for the study of individuals but for understanding social transformation. Attention is directed to the multiplicity of 'cause', the historical quality of change and the relatedness of human events in history.

The Relation of Thought and Activity

The primacy of social/cultural conditions foreshadows a theory of activity as the central problem of pedagogical research. Thought is seen in relation to human activity in which things and events are created. Thought is the ideal component of the objective activity of social man. It emerges as an individual acts to transform both external nature and 'self' by labor. Psychological reality becomes a part of a total life activity of a human being. Thus, the problematic of Soviet psychology departs from American educational practice of separating thought from practice. Soviet psychology does not seek to identify the inner structure of an individual's thought but the relationship and formation of thought in social-historical development (Wertsch, in press). A task of research is to identify the processes of practical activity that mediate the relations of the subject with the world.

As a heuristic and prescriptive concept, 'activity' considers the complexity found in human situations and social relations. In addition to behavioral aspects, one is to consider social institutions as providing background assumptions and expectations in the forming of social activity and consciousness (see Wertsch, in press). Activity also addresses attention to the relation of quantitative and qualitative change. It is argued that quantitative changes produce qualitative changes and that one cannot sum an aggregate, as in much behavioral research, to understand the significance and meaning of change. For example, a child that learns to do more arithmetic examples undergoes qualitative changes in the conceptual and analytical abilities associated with those examples. Further, this development may not be linear. Growth is viewed as moving in spurts, with a child doing some tasks at one level of development while performing other tasks at a different level.

As the meaning of dialectical materialism is continually debated in the Soviet Union, so too is the meaning of 'activity' debated. For some, the notion of activity gives reference to the ways in which symbolic forms are internalized. Symbolic modeling for students is important to this research orientation. Others give attention to the idea of activity as contained in the patterns of social and linguistic interactions among children. The ideal of activity is also used in reference to the identification of cultural systems and cultural technical agents (curriculum designers) whose task is to impose these systems in classrooms. These different meanings and interpretations of 'activity' are a vital part of Soviet pedagogical conferences and discussions.[3]

A science of pedagogy is related to the ethical and political system it is to explain. The relation of philosophy to science suggests that the former dominates the formation of theoretical thought, that science is thought morphological rather than deterministic. The laws of science are to explain the unity and interconnectiveness of the whole. Dialectical assumptions are to prevent compartmentalization of complex phenomena in which objects and processes are considered in isolation from their connection with the whole. The relation of quantity and quality directs attention away from a reductionism in which phenomena are thought of in terms of combinations of simple or elementary attributes. Finally, the unity of theory and practice is to tie research to the social purposes defined by the state, although the links are sometimes indirect.

As Graham (1974) points out, there are both official and unofficial views about the predominance or tentativeness of the statements underlying dialectical materialism. Many Soviet scholars accept the general assumptions of Marxism as a working set to propositions, but see the propositions as ones which are to be examined and modified (but not refuted in their essential qualities) by the findings of science. For others, the assumptions are the dogma of immutable laws. This tension between the tentativeness and immutability of laws is found in the interpretations of Lenin's views of the formation of consciousness (see Lenin, 1927; Hoffman, 1975). The debate has concrete implications for pedagogical research. The practices of psychology and didactics focus, to some extent, upon the historical quality of our human conditions; in contrast, curriculum research assumes that knowledge is fixed and unyielding. Before considering these different research practices, however, a Soviet distinction between methodology and method needs exploration.

Pedagogical Research: Methodology and Method

The Soviet research community is self-conscious about the relation of philosophy and science. Discussions of methodology and methods entail reflection about the presuppositions and assumptions that guide inquiry. *Methodology* gives focus to the underlying assumptions of science as a human activity, focusing upon presuppositions about the world that guide the creation of concepts and procedures. Discussion of *method* of inquiry is more directly related to inquiry. The general philosophical commitments are to guide the formation of concepts and procedures of research. The interrelation of social vision and philosophy in discussions about method is contrasted to the Western logical-positivist tradition in philosophy and empirical-analytic sciences. The latter is concerned with the internal logic of knowledge, efficiency and organization of research procedures. While the Soviets are concerned with logic and efficiency, they place these concerns in an explicit normative, epistemological and conceptual context.

Methodology

For Soviet social scientists and philosophers, methodology is the study of science as a cognitive activity that involves production (practice) and thought (logical structures of knowledge). An essential element of this activity is its antinomies, paradoxes or contradictions. Contradictions are resolved at two different levels of discourse (Shchedrovitsky, 1960, 1977). One is within a discipline to solve concrete problems with specific methods, such as defining the velocity of two moving bodies. A second level is methodological — the existing contradictions that involve general issues of how science transforms objects of the real world into cognitive *things*. These cognitive *'things'* are to be analyzed and interpreted by symbolic representation — concepts, models and theories.

This distinction between object and thing is important to the conduct of science: the thing is a product of human cognition and, as such, obeys laws which are not identical to the laws of the object. The 'things' of science are not mirrors of those social affairs. The processes of science objectify 'things' by fixing the content of science into symbols. The things to be analyzed (for example, ideology, socialization, learning) seem to stand apart from the object from which they have been abstracted.

Objectification of scientific symbols requires a methodological analysis of the manner in which 'things' become substituted for objects, thus 'ensuring' that science properly connects the two. Shchedrovitsky (1960), a prominent Soviet pedagogical methodologist, argues that the concepts of 'structures' and 'systems' require such an examination because the two concepts are central to all sciences. Systems and structures have been only partially understood as functionally united. It is argued, for example, that the structural connections within a system produce change in the position of all elements when the position of an element is changed. This occurs because of the indirect as well as direct relationship of elements. The study of a system's structure involves investigating the history of the system and interrelating its development (genesis) and functions. Through logical analysis, Shchedrovitsky challenges the assumption of consistency of elements found in American experimental research and a limitation of relying upon mathematical models to assess the relation of symbol systems to the original object.

Shchedrovitsky's methodological work has been part of a continuing seminar in Moscow for the last twenty years. The seminar involves students and faculty in such diverse fields as engineering, psychology, special education and mathematics. It is assumed that the application of dialectics to presuppositions of science can identify laws of discourse that pertain to diverse disciplines. Little empirical work, however, has been carried on through these methodological studies.

Development of Method

The Soviet approach to methods of inquiry is best exemplified in the writing of Vygotsky. After the Soviet Revolution, Vygotsky came to find Marxist thought important for a foundation to a psychological science. In the 1920s, he argued that Soviet psychologists had to create a science in response to the new conception of 'man' posited by the Revolution. He recognized the need to interrelate the new approach to social philosophy, suggesting that to apply the assumptions of dialectical materialism 'inevitably leads to new methods of investigation and analysis, requiring far more than the simple modification of previously accepted method' (Vygotsky, 1978, p. 58).

Vygotsky's experimental method draws from Engel's discussion of a dialectical approach to understanding human history (see Scribner, 1981). Vygotsky suggested that psychological development has qualities similar to historical development. Quoting from Marx, 'It is only in movement that a body shows what it is,' Vygotsky argued that development occurs in relation to complex social-cultural processes of change (Vygotsky, 1978, p. 65). Further, the relation between man and nature has qualities in which man can affect nature and create 'through his changes in nature new material conditions for his existence' (Vygotsky, 1978, p. 60).

Vygotsky rejected both naturalism (the assumption that natural conditions determine historical development) and stimulus-response methods, in which there is a unidimensional reactive relation between human behavior and nature. In their place, an experimental method is proposed to identify 'a dynamic display of the main points making up the processes of history.' The experimental method is to make 'visible processes that are ordinarily hidden beneath the surface of habitual behavior.' The investigation telescopes 'the actual course of development of a given function' (p. 12). This purpose led Vygotsky to focus upon methods that illuminate how *performance* is achieved.

The purpose of the experiment is different from those characteristic of the West to control conditions of behavior to produce a certain performance under those conditions. The emphasis on process involves a rejection of psychological analysis which has treated processes as stable, to be broken down into their components (such as attribute-interaction-analysis). The Soviet experiment gives attention to explanation of the origin of behavior, 'its causal dynamic basis', rather than description of its outer behavior appearance.

Procedures of Inquiry

It is within this context of historical development that procedures are defined. *Research is observing systematically the processes in which behavior occurs to understand its origin and logical formation.* Little attention is given to problems of statistical sampling and problems of reliability.

The 'process' approach is illustrated in Soviet problem-solving research. A task becomes a problem when it is relative to the individual. A problem is defined by the way a child tackles the given task rather than as defined by the curriculum organizer. A task may be a problem for one student; it may be an exercise for another; and it may just involve frustration for a third. Landa, for example, studied the processes of proof to determine thought operations involved in carrying out a geometric proof and also evaluated the effects of these operations on pupils who had demonstrated various degrees of ability to carry out a geometric proof (in Rachlin, 1979). Through observations and interviews with children, the qualitative evidence of students' analytic-synthetic operation is emphasized.

The study of pedagogical processes has been called ascertaining and teaching experiments (Kieran, 1981). Ascertaining experiments collect data in schools but do not have a teaching component. They may involve interviews and observations of students to assess the knowledge acquired or the acquisition processes used in a long-term situation. The study of learning occurs under given instructional conditions without any systematic intervention. In an ascertaining experiment, for example, students may be asked about the procedures they followed. Periodic interviews provide another approach to investigate long-term learning. Students in different grades, for example, may be given the same tasks and interviewed to assess their stages of learning.

A teaching experiment involves the development of a teaching strategy to stimulate children's learning. It proceeds according to some predefined goal and is to assess the effectiveness of the strategy and its psycho-pedagogical basis. Depending upon the research question, the investigation may be with individual children, small or large groups. The 'experiencing' method involves understanding how methods of teaching influence instruction. It is usually done first with an individual to understand the specific processes, and later with larger groups. A 'testing' method, usually done at the beginning of research, is used to identify how a method of instruction influences mastery of information.

How the methods of inquiry are translated into concrete re-search practices is examined in the next two sections. Educational psychology and didactics, the studying of teaching and learning, it will be argued, maintain a commitment to process and development. But the content of that development is assumed predefined. The school curriculum is not considered as a problem of historical development but one of mastery of predefined rules and prescriptions. The result is a reification of culture and society, denying human agency. This treatment of curriculum contains a surface layer of social values different from those found in the United States. At a deeper layer, the epistemological assumptions are similar as philosophy passes into the realm of practice. It is to this contradiction of unity without unity that attention is now turned.

Processes without Content: Educational Psychology and Didactics

While the relation between theory and practice remains a public principle, the meaning of this relationship assumes a particular definition in the organization of Soviet school research. A distinction is made between the developmental processes of consciousness and the knowledge provided in the content of curriculum. The former emphasizes two aspects of classroom research. One is educational psychology. It focuses upon the processes by which children reason about and internalize content in school tasks. A second process concern is didactics, how teaching and instruction can be organized.[4] Educational psychology and didactics are to identify developmental processes for implementing the predefined structures of subject-matter knowledge and values. Whereas Marx defined knowledge as historically located and socially developed, the actual practice of school research dichotomizes practice from knowledge and treats each separately.

The current emphasis of Soviet pedagogical research can be viewed against a backdrop of changes in the more general cultural and economic demands of the Soviet system. Following World War II, a reorganization of the economic base in Soviet society occurred, placing greater emphasis upon science and technology. The changing economic demands and cultural requirements required different socialization patterns of schooling. This involved greater emphasis on analytic and synthetic ways of thinking, prerequisites of an industrial, scientifically-based society. The psychological and didactic studies need to be considered in relation to this large social and economic transformation. It is historically interesting to note that Vygotsky's work did not receive legitimacy until the post-war period. One can only speculate that the renewed interest in the psychology of Vygotsky is related to the larger changes in the economic and cultural system of the Soviet Union. Vygotsky's ideas are theoretically appealing when demands of schooling emphasize scientific and technological thought.

Educational Psychology

Educational psychology is to identify the most efficient and effective means for improving children's cognition and upbringing or social/moral behavior. Efficiency, however, is defined by a different set of assumptions from those found in the empirical-analytic sciences. Schools are artificial creations of culture and the most important task of the sciences of schooling is to foster the transmission of culture. Studies in schooling are phenomenological explorations of how thinking and practice are related, designed to identify the mechanisms for internalizing the material and ideological goals of schooling. The purpose of pedagogical psychology is to integrate the logical stages of thought, classroom conditions and principles of activities into a comprehensive view of the formation of consciousness.

Certain aspects of educational psychological research serve to illustrate how philosophical and methodological assumptions work in practice. One aspect involves the integration of research programs with the development of a comprehensive theory of activity. Another is the role of social relations and sign systems in forming consciousness. In both instances, research problems in psychology are drawn from larger theoretical issues.

An emphasis of Soviet pedagogical research is on making a more coherent and integrative theory of activity. Istomina's study of remembering and recall, for example, defines acts of memory in a functional relation to contextual factors (in Wertsch, in press). In an experimental setting, pre-school children were asked to memorize a list of items. In a second play setting, Istomina had the children learn the list in relation to purchases made at a store. The interrelation of thought processes rather than its distinctive constituent elements is the focus of classroom studies. The findings of the study were cast in a more general theory of activity. Memory was related to problems of motivation, cognition and social setting.

The role of social relations and sign systems in the formation of consciousness is another important aspect of research. Tikhomirov, for example, considered the role of computers in cognition (in Wertsch, in press). He suggests that computers should be considered as a sign system other than speech. Drawing upon Vygotsky's theory of signs and mental development, he sees the computer as a tool of mental activity which transforms activity. He rejects the idea that there is a 'mere' substitution of elements between human cognition and computer information processing operations; the problem is how computers provide new possibilities for mediation of cognitive activity. The study of computers involves the quantitative and qualitative change of existing capacities.

The importance of social interaction gives focus to the idea of the collective. V.V. Rubstov (1981), director of a new psychological laboratory, is concerned with how cooperative (collective) activities foster the development of individual mental activities. The idea of collective is ideologically formed and distinguishable from the neutral meaning associated with the term 'group'. The emphasis is on mutual responsibility, the setting of a civic aim, self-management and practical activity among people. Rubstov's research examines which types of cooperative activity provide specific models for the development of the intellect. In one experiment, children work with objects of different shapes to construct a circle. In the organization of the joint planning solutions emerge which determine the methods to transform the materials. Children learn to 'see' the relationship of discrete parts to a whole rather than as a self-sufficient and closed unit unrelated to other parts. Rubstov concluded that these findings challenge Piaget's work.

> This indicates that the genesis of intellectual structures of thought in the child is linked to the appearance of new forms of organization of joint activity. The relations determining the logic of an intellectual structure consist of compact condensed forms of mutual relationships among the participants in cooperation (p. 59).

The emphasis on signs that mediate cognition and personality is illustrated in the work of V.V. Davydov, former director of the Institute of General and Educational Psychology. Davydov's work is developed in relation to Vygotsky and the previous institute director, Leont'ev, who sought to understand consciousness as a sensate, practical activity that emerges as people enter into contact with objects and act upon them (Davydov, 1981; Davydov and Zinchenko, 1981). Internalization involves transferring of external activity to reflection, perception, representation and conception. Davydov's pedagogical work reverses the assumption found in the United States that students learn from the concrete to the abstract. In contrast, he argues that students progress from abstract to concrete and from general concepts to specific examples. For example, a child might learn the concept of measure by manipulating objects. Then the related learning symbols (less than, equal to) follow, prior to the introduction of concrete number systems (see, for example, discussion in Gibson, 1980). Davydov's research provides the theoretical basis for a number of experimental pedagogical programs in science, mathematics and language.

The emphasis on development is not always concerned with the transmission of knowledge. Although most problem-solving and 'creativity' research involve learning answers to questions that are already known, there are discussions of ways to produce a skepticism and playfulness. At one Soviet pedagogical research conference, for example, the topic was play. The discussion had different foci. One was the development of play to learn efficient strategies for problem-solving, such as in simulation games or children's play as a means for internalizing social norms. At another level, play was thought of as a social point in which individuals begin to make problematic social forms and institutional arrangements, thus making possible the rethinking of social relationships. While this notion of cultural production is covered in scholarly discussion, it has not received much attention in scholarly writing.

The Study of Didactics

The study of didactics maintains a similar emphasis on processes of development. The focus of didactics is upon the tasks in which teaching develops. Observations of classroom interactions are to identify a logical order in the development of a lesson. This logical order is presented to teachers as the procedures for ordering classroom lessons. Didactics, however, does not consider the social dynamics of classroom life.

The problem of teaching research is to identify the correct logical sequence in coursework or lessons. A study of teacher education conducted by the Institute of General and Adult Education, for example, defined the problem of 'the perfection of teaching' as identifying the relationship between existing teacher education courses and how teachers perceive their work. The research was to find more efficient ways of providing new teachers with experiences that regular teachers found lacking (such as more pedagogical and psychological preparation) and a reordering of courses to give more emphasis to practice than theory (a dichotomy that officially does not exist).

The idea of development assumes a limited meaning in didactics. By this I mean that the organization of teaching, the sequence of lessons or the approaches by which children are to master some curriculum goal are seen as a problem of logically ordering the tasks of instruction. A pedagogical syllabus defines a teacher's lesson as a teacher posing the problem, subdividing it into separate problems that can organize instruction. The teacher's task is to direct children to identify and plan the solving of the problem. Research on self-development, a recent emphasis in Soviet education, involves an historical analysis of how the concept changed from prior to the revolution, through the years inaugurating the Soviet regime, to the present. Pedagogical researchers argue that the social conditions made self-education inappropriate during the 1920s and 1930s, but progress in social development has made it possible now. The outcome of the analysis is a set of stages for self-development: the lowest stage involving no aim to the organization; a second stage where an aim appears; and a final stage involving the realization of abilities and aims (such as planning without wasting time). In each instance, teaching is characterized as having a logical organization in which the social/interactional quality of school life is ignored.

The logical character of didactics can be illustrated in the problem of 'overloading' of work.[5] According to Ippolitov (1981), approximately one-third to one-fourth of middle and upper grade children are 'victims of overloads' — expending much time and effort on school work but unable to keep up with classroom processes. Ippolitov argues that this occurs due to pressures from above (increased demands for curriculum materials) and from below (demanding teachers who give pupils assignments in excess of textbook and curriculum requirements). While stating the problem in this manner, the discussion ignores the roots of the problem. The focus is upon a reformulation of rational study skills lessons to help students cope with the problem of overload. The recommendations include: to help overloaded students distinguish between basic, derivative, supplemental and illustrative aspects of their study material; to improve the quality of assignments through independent work with textbooks; to include regular correcting and surveying of pupil assignments; to provide logically and linguistically appropriate assignments for pupils to learn the terminology and symbols of a given discipline; and to give library research assignments.

The approach to didactics is often drawn from psychological research. Studies in self-education, for example, begin with the study of development (Markova, 1981). The psychological research is designed to link self-education to a general theory of activity. Various characteristics of the children's self-study are identified and specified according to the problems to be solved. A first psychological level of self-education involves identifying an indeterminate problem to be solved; at a next level specific goals (passing an examination) become important; then there occurs a selective assimilation of information and inclusion of material from the curriculum; and, finally, long-range objectives associated with choice of an occupation and self-directedness. The different levels of self-education are seen as a function of age, for example, students between the ages of 15 and 17 are to be involved in study of vocational activities related to the pupil's chosen occupation.

The outcome of research is a set of procedures to guide the teacher in instilling the new attitude associated with, in this case, self-education. This is done by setting up the logical tasks to be followed in the classroom (pedagogical supervision), such as identifying and conveying the components of self-education so children may perform them independently. The study techniques may be to learn how to consolidate study materials or how to identify general ideas, principles and rules.

Pedagogical Research and Innovation

The study of self-education is illustrative of a Soviet approach to pedagogical change. The research is normative and phenomenological. The problem is to find procedures that can introduce a predefined policy effectively. This occurs through observation of how children react to innovations in classes, studying both psychological and didactical elements. The identification of psychological aspects of self-learning leads, for example, to a set of logical techniques and procedures for organizing instruction.

Perhaps the most extensive study of development and pedagogy to influence actual school practice was conducted by Zankov (1977). The experiments responded to a more general demand made upon schools by what the Soviets call 'the scientific-technological revolution', the demand for greater emphasis upon science and technology. Zankov's experiments were based upon four principles of pedagogy which reflected the cultural as well as knowledge requirements of a technological society. These principles of socialization in school were:

1   Instruction should be at the highest level of difficulty;
2   Children should learn at as rapid a pace as possible;
3   Theoretical knowledge should have a leading role in pedagogy;
4   Children should be consciously involved in learning by making them aware of the learning process.

Underlying the experiments was Vygotsky's notion that a child's mental functioning is social in nature, that cooperation and teaching are the source of development and that the educational process should be constructed so as to draw upon contradiction. In this case, contradiction involved the relation of children's expected mental functions to the present stage of a child's development. Zankov did not look at teaching/learning as a simple sum of lessons but he looked for the lines of general relations by which children are linked to the external world.

The experiments, begun in a single school in Moscow, expanded to involve over 1000 classrooms in eight of the fifteen constituent Republics of the USSR. The results provided a general reorientation of primary school teaching.

The experiments illustrated ways in which the methods and principles of development could be implemented. These experiments proved that children could learn the proposed material in three rather than the regular four years of primary school. One result of the research was the reduction of Soviet primary schooling to three years. Textbooks were developed that reflected the developmental and pedagogical principles of the research.

Zankov's experiments are illustrative of Soviet faith in science. The work represents a belief that for every teaching problem there is a solution; that the laws (principles) of Marxism can provide the guidelines for improving and implementing social goals.

Psychological and didactic research are directed by an optimism that is drawn from both Soviet philosophy and politics. Philosophically, it is believed that the material world determines consciousness; therefore planning correct environments will produce the necessary results in the development of children. Politically, the optimism is related to the public belief that the Soviet Revolution introduced a transformation of society that to no small extent provides for the progress of human civilization. Underlying the progress is a Marxist science which has identified the general laws and methods to bring about this new condition. Scientific planning is the cornerstone of the rational distribution system and guides the conduct of social relations, social welfare and schooling.

Content with Process: Unity without Unity

A fundamental principle of dialectical materialism is the unity of theory and practice. That unity is based upon a number of epistemological, social and political elements. Marx opposed speculative philosophy and hoped to transcend philosophy by 'actualizing' it. He sought to unite the subject and object that had dichotomized philosophy by focusing upon the material basis of society. Part of that discussion rejected theory as being contemplative, an ideal element in the social world; theory was a part of human relations and social history.

The unity of theory and practice serves to direct attention to the al relationship of 'affective' and 'cognitive' dimensions, upbringing or moral formation and intellectual development, and the dispositional elements embedded in work patterns. There is also a recognition of the social/communal aspect of knowledge. This is developed philosophically in dialectical materialism and historically through Marxist analyses of bourgeois traditions, customs and theories. Yet, the unity of theory and practice collapses in curriculum research. There is a dichotomy between the content of schooling and ways of acquiring knowledge. The dichotomy is subtle and can be illustrated by contrasting two approaches to explaining science.

One approach is to look at knowledge as containing community and craft qualities (Popkewitz, 1977a). The community qualities direct attention to the pattern of interactions, norms of discourse and standards of truth that evolve in any one discipline. From this perspective, the 'nature' of sociology or physics is determined by the conditions in and manner of discourse among participants in a field (Toulmin, 1972). Thus, to understand sociology or educational research is to consider their central concepts and how those concepts evolve, are challenged, and are extended through the debates and circumstances of a discipline. The bodies of knowledge in a discipline are viewed as tentative and changing in relation to changes in a community's discourse. This view can help us locate the importance of Vygotsky to current Soviet psychology. It involves considering not only the internal coherence of Vygotsy's work but relating Vygotsky's work to the ongoing debates and social-cultural circumstances of psychology in the Soviet Union.

The craft-quality of knowledge points to what would seem a contradiction to that of community. It directs attention to the role of personal autonomy and responsibility of individuals within a community. While the community provides certain standards, norms and commitments to the conduct of science, the vitality and imagination of research is dependent upon human agency (see Chapter 1). An individual's craft-quality guides the use of techniques: particular events and data are 'seen' in relation to a conception of the whole, the use of intuition and the aesthetics of the situation. Some American sociologists of science have argued that science is organized to provide for the development of the craft-skill and autonomy necessary for imagination.

The craft and community qualities of science are essential to a consideration of scientific practice. They draw attention to the ways in which structural aspects of science interrelate with subjective elements. What seems at first contradictory about the craft and community qualities of science becomes mutually related as the problems of imagination, creativity and change are considered.

The curriculum implications of the community/craft quality of science are several. It makes knowledge problematic and tentative rather than fixed. The concepts and findings of science are seen as emerging from both community discourse and the productive activities of individuals. Methods of inquiry are related to concepts and problems rather than determining them. Knowledge and methods are understood to be in a state of flux and containing limitations that are related to their human quality. Finally, the problem of creating a community pattern to support scientific norms and interactions becomes a problem of pedagogical design and research.

An opposite view of science focuses upon the fixed quality of scientific knowledge. The US 'discipline-centered' curriculum movement of the 1960s, for example, focused upon how to make the structure of disciplined knowledge accessible for curriculum development. The problem of instruction was

1 to identify the concepts, principles and generalizations that seemed to give structure to knowledge in a field,
2 to develop strategies of instruction for learning the knowledge, and
3 to explore the psychological mechanism by which concepts can be efficently internalized.

Much of this notion of 'structure' was sketched in Jerome Bruner's *The Process of Education* (1962). In fundamental ways, the structure of the discipline approach denies the community and craft quality. Knowledge is defined as a logical entity which psychology and didactics are to reproduce effectively among children.

It is this second approach that Soviet educational research has adopted for curriculum design. This reified view responds to issues of legitimacy in contemporary industrial nation-states. One of the first languages into which Bruner's book was translated was Russian. A consequence of the Soviet approach is to separate knowledge from its methods; to isolate craft and community elements from the products of science.

The 'clear issue' in curriculum becomes teaching knowledge or attitude acquisition. The consensual knowledge of a field is accepted, posing no sense of the debates, ambiguities or tentativeness of inquiry. The study of history is to establish the sacredness of the laws of social development of the state (Koloskov and Liebengrub,

1977). Curriculum improvement is to improve students' comprehension and involvement in learning 'the leading role played by the Party in the Communist construction and strengthening of its unity with the entire Soviet people' or 'the indisputable advantages of socialism over capitalism'. The curriculum research question is how teachers can direct children to use the proper reasoning to reach these conclusions; 'to approach generalizations and theoretical conclusions with awareness'. In part, the research problem is to identify an appropriate logical sequence. This might involve the inclusion of material about the problem of social order in seventh grade textbooks or teacher procedures that will enable children to recall definitions and use the definitions 'to analyze factual materials and determine *independently* what kind of social order developed in ancient Russia' (Koloskov and Liebengrub, 1977, my emphasis).

The reification of knowledge and social order underlies the study of labor. Polytechnical education has its philosophical roots in dialectical materialism in which labor is seen as a mediating link between consciousness and the objective world. The study of labor is directed not only 'towards learning about the world but toward transforming one's surroundings . . .' (Atutov, 1981). The theoretical concern is to create a 'harmonious development' of the individual through a curriculum that balances ideas, attitudes and actions. Actual educational research, however, is tied to practical concerns of economic stability and change. Research is not to understand how children learn about the relation between social consciousness and modes of production, in a manner that emphasizes the labor process as a way to understand society and human activity. Research is to identify approaches to improve production, to improve students' attitude towards existing work patterns and to increase work skills. The pedagogical research and curriculum practices legitimate officially defined modes of production.

The teaching of physics also maintains a dichotomy between knowledge and process. The problem is to identify the structure of knowledge in physics as a logical structure to be taught. A curriculum problem may be to learn how resistance to electricity is formed through understanding symbolic models and doing practical experiments. Pedagogical experiments may seek to identify the way in which cooperative activities interrelate with the structures of physics and thus improve the quality of learning.

Teaching physics illustrates a particular role of educational psychology. The problems of pedagogy and psychology are treated as different from the problem of the content. The origin of development is in the development of individuals as observed in school. What is not considered is that the origin of development can also be understood by focusing upon distinct cognitive styles of a disciplined field. From this perspective, a study of cognition is located within the activity structures of scientific communities. This 'psychology' of the discipline has a different point of reference from the developmental processes found in the institutional contexts of schooling.

To assume that psychological investigations in school can be superimposed upon 'structures' of a discipline in ways that maintain the integrity of the latter is problematic. The insights of Vygotsky or Piaget, while valuable, were not formed as a way of talking about the cognitive styles of historians, physicists or sociologists. In effect, a psychology of children's reasoning about science or mathematics in school is concerned with identifying how predefined logical structures of knowledge can be efficiently internalized. A consequence is to lose the community/craft quality of science and the dynamic nature of knowledge.

While a reader might concentrate on the imposition of Soviet values in the curriculum approach and consider solely this aspect of the curriculum, I believe that would miss the more important meaning. All knowledge contains bias, establishes certain dispositions towards social affairs and favors certain interests. This is clearly the case in the Soviet Union. It is as true in the United States or Britain, but the manner in which it occurs is more subtle. Textbooks and curriculum materials do maintain a hegemonic orientation (see, for example, Anyon, 1978; Popkewitz, 1977b). Political liberal theory and economic assumptions of capitalism underlie the stories and legends of American school studies. To understand how hegemony becomes represented in the United States, one would have to look at factors different from those in the Soviet Union. This would include looking at the ways textbooks are produced, how local school boards are organized and communication patterns maintained and legitimated. The argument, though, is not that visions of social order appear in school content. Rather, it is directed to the relationship of knowledge to curriculum methods and its implications for principles of authority and social order.

Conclusions

A particular form of reasoning and logic emerges in the pedagogical community of the Soviet Union. Research is based upon the idea of dialectical materialism in which human and social development is defined as a historical process and in which change is bound to the contradictions found in individuals' relationships to society. As a philosophical position, dialectical materialism articulates a hope and vision of remaking society and the individual's relation to that society.[6] The assumptions of pedagogical research have provided the Soviet pedagogical research community with an integration and coherence to its theory. But this integration occurs with contradictions.

To understand these contradictions, one needs to consider Soviet pedagogical sciences within Russian history and politics. The label of dialectical materialism is one that emerges from Russian history and receives the full sanction of the state and Communist Party. The definitions and interpretations have been dictated by Party politics and scientists discredited when attacked for practicing science defined as having 'bourgeois assumptions', especially during Stalin's reign (see Bauer's, 1952, discussion of the changing emphasis in Soviet psychology). State intellectual mandates, however, have not gone unchallenged. Members of the scientific communities continually give attention to the problem of dialectical materialism so as not to leave its articulation solely within the state apparatus. This jockeying for position and definition does not mean that the assumptions of dialectical materialism are not taken seriously. Intellectuals in the Soviet Union do maintain a general commitment to Marxism as a method of analysis and dialectical materialism as a philosophical cornerstone to that analysis.

The relation of pedagogical sciences to state history and politics is general phenomenon of our epoch. In both the West and East, pedagogical sciences are rooted in the mandate of the school to socialize the youth of a society to the interests of those in power. The empirical-analytic sciences of the West and the pedagogical sciences of the Soviet Union are concerned with increasing the efficiency of schools as they relate to larger social goals. The differences in these sciences, however, are not adequately expressed by focusing upon their utilitarian purposes. The differences are in the historical and social circumstances in which goals are decided. These include different presuppositions, philosophical traditions and institutions that mediate and give direction to the dynamics of schooling and its research community.

The importance of psychology in pedagogical research needs further scrutiny. In the West and East, psychology is the root discipline of pedagogical sciences. This is so well entrenched that people take this condition for granted. Yet when one looks at schooling, the psychological focus seems odd. The overriding problems of schooling are those of groups of children and the social organization of people. Teachers are rarely able to deal with particular psychological dimensions of children or learning. The problems of curriculum are those of philosophy (the nature of knowledge), ethics (what should be taught) and politics (in whose interest). Curriculum problems cannot be reduced to psychology.

One might respond to the question of psychological dominance with the observation that it is the oldest and most respected social discipline in the Soviet Union. This response, however, needs to be enlarged to consider historical and social elements. If it is correct that pedagogical sciences are occupations that traditionally serve the state, the development of psychology can be seen within that perspective. The focus upon 'learning' assumes rather than questions social and system goals. This is true of the psychology embedded in the empirical-analytic sciences. It is also applicable to Soviet psychology. Where research gives attention to social conditions, such as collective learning, the focus is upon how individuals develop strategies that contribute to the goals of the social system. How the individual can transcend a problem and redefine the situation is rarely considered. Also ignored in conventional school psychologies are the biases of institutions which maintain inequities and limit opportunities.

Making schooling a psychological problem obscures the social tensions and contradictions in adult society, drawing attention away from differential conditions of schooling and the biases of those conditions. Psychology tends not to focus upon the historical and social development of the school. Its horizon is the individual and possibility of the individual within a group. The cultural-social content of transmission is not problematic.

This position of pedagogical sciences also helps to explain a particular contradiction between psychological-didactic and content research. The former assumes an historical world; the later reifies the world. The reification of knowledge makes the social and physical worlds seem stable, uncompromising and 'natural'. This point of view underlies most curriculum development in the United States and the Soviet Union. Where challenges to this view do emerge (such as in progressive education or the British infant schools), they receive support among the intellectual or professional strata of the society and do not become important moments in the general development of schooling.

What originally seemed a contradiction between curriculum

research and research in didactics and psychology also provides a coherence. The definitions of psychology and didactics as historical processes take for granted the cultural and social content of schooling. There is an assumption that the laws of physics or society are well-known and stable. The problem of research is to find the most effective social arrangements (activity structures) to bring about children's learning. The idea of development as an historical process assumes a one-dimensionality. It is functionally related to curriculum definitions of a stable world.

This leads to a conclusion that is often submerged in current debates about school research. The definitions and forms of rationality associated with schooling are typically responsive to the priorities of the state and its major interests. An overriding pressure of institutional life is the creation of legitimating canopies that make reasonable the everyday priorities of the state. This is a major task of pedagogical research communities. In the West, the degree of leeway from that dominant position is wider but the pressure is still present. Researchers do appropriate the categories of existing relations as the categories of research. The arguments about the Soviet pedagogical research community enable us to understand the function of the intellectual in establishing and legitimating moral direction and will in society. While the research programs can be viewed in this light, the analysis does not consider the social and cultural messages actually transmitted in the patterns of school conduct.

Notes

1 I use the word 'Russian' rather than 'Soviet' to recognize the hegemony of Russian experience in giving official definitions to Soviet life.
2 This discussion is based, in part, upon work done as part of a US Fulbright-Hays award under which I spent the spring 1981 with the USSR Ministry of Education and the USSR Academy of Pedagogical Sciences' Institute for General and Pedagogical Sciences.
3 For social and political reasons, many of the vital discussions about theory do not become part of the published literature. While institutes have publishing quotas as part of their overall plan, each published article must go through several layers of political as well as scholarly review.
4 Didactics are discussed in Tabachnick *et al.* (1981).
5 In the United States the problem of overloading is generally defined as one of remediation or discipline. The overall tone is very different from that found in the article cited.
6 A related statement could be made about the dominant position of American pedagogical science in which corporate individualism is made sacred.

References

ANYON, J. (1978) 'Elementary social studies textbooks and legitimating knowledge', *Theory and Research in Social Studies*, 6, 3, September, pp. 40–55.

ATUTOV, P. (1981) 'The polytechnical principle in teaching basic science', in TABACHNICK, B. *et al.* (Eds) *Studying Teaching and Learning, Trends in Soviet and American Research*, New York, Praeger.

BAUER, R. (1952) *The New Man in Soviet Psychology*, Cambridge, Mass., Harvard University Press.

BRUNER, J. (1962) *The Process of Education*, Cambridge, Mass., Harvard University Press.

DAVYDOV, V. (1981) 'The category of activity and mental reflection in the theory of A.N. Leont'ev', *Soviet Psychology*, 19, 4, Summer, pp. 3–29.

DAVYDOV, V. and ZINCHENKO, V. (1981) 'The principle of development in psychology', *Soviet Psychology*, 22, 1, Fall, pp. 22–46.

FITZPATRICK, S. (Ed.) (1978) *Cultural Revolution in Russia, 1928–1931*, Bloomington, Ind., Indiana University Press.

GIBSON, J. (1980) 'Soviet pedagogical research: Classroom studies: Cognitive theories of development and instruction', *Contemporary Educational Psychology*, 5, pp. 184–91.

GRAHAM, L. (1974) *Science and Philosophy in the Soviet Union*, New York, Vintage Books.

HOFFMAN, J. (1975) *Marxism and the Theory of Praxis, a Critique of Some New Versions of Old Fallacies*, London, Lawrence and Wishart.

ILYENKOV, E. (1977) *Dialectical Logic: Essays on Its History and Theory*, Moscow, Progress Publishers.

IPPOLITOV, F. (1981) 'On the problem of the overloading of school pupils with work', *Soviet Education*, 23, 8, June, pp. 20–34.

JORAVSKY, D. (1961) *Soviet Marxism and Natural Science, 1917–1932*, New York, Columbia University Press.

KIERAN, C. (1981) 'The Soviet teaching experiment', Paper prepared for NCTM research presentation on 'Alternative research methods in mathematics education', St Louis, Mo.

KOLOSKOV, A. and LEIBENGRUB, P. (1977) 'Increase the effectiveness of history teaching', *Soviet Education*, 19, 7, May, pp. 70–90.

KONRÁD, G. and SZELÉNYI, I. (1979) *The Intellectuals on the Roads to Class Power, a Sociological Study of the Role of the Intelligentsia in Socialism*, New York, Harcourt, Brace, Jovanovich.

LAURIA, A. (1979) *The Making of Mind, a Personal Account of Soviet Psychology*, M. Cole and S. Cole (Eds), Cambridge, Mass., Harvard University Press.

LENIN, V. (1927) *Materialism and Empirico-Criticism, Critical Notes Concerning a Reactionary Philosophy*, Vol. 13, D. Kvitko (Ed.), Moscow, International Publishers.

MAKARENKO, A. (1973) *The Road to Life*, I. and T. LITVINOV (Trans), Moscow, Progress Publishers.

MARKOVA, A. (1981) 'The self-education of school pupils', *Soviet Education*, 23, 8, pp. 5–19.

POPKEWITZ, T. (1977a) 'Craft and community as metaphors for social inquiry curriculum', *Educational Theory*, 27, pp. 310–21.

POPKEWITZ, T. (1977b) 'The latent values of the discipline-centered curriculum', *Theory and Research in Social Education*, 5, 2, pp. 41–60.

RACHLIN, S. (1979) 'Soviet approaches to the study of problem-solving processes in mathematics', in DAVIS, R. *et al.* (Eds), *An Analysis of Mathematics Education in the Union of Soviet Socialist Republics*, Columbus, Ohio, ERIC Clearinghouse for Science, Mathematics and Environmental Education.

RUBSTOV, V. (1981) 'The role of cooperation in the development of intelligence', *Soviet Psychology*, 19, 4, Summer, pp. 41–62.

SCHRIBNER, S. (1981) *Vygotsky's Use of History, Culture, Cognition and Communication*, J. Wertsch (Ed.), New York, Cambridge University Press.

SHCHEDROVITSKY, G. (1960) 'Methodological problems of systems research', *General Systems*, 5, pp. 27–52.

SHCHEDROVITSKY, G. (1977) 'Problems in the development of planning activity', *General Systems*, 22, pp. 3–16.

TABACHNICK, B. *et al.* (Eds) (1981) *Studying Teaching and Learning Trends in Soviet and American Research*, New York, Praeger.

TOULMIN, S. (1972) *Human Understanding: The Collective Use and Evolution of Concepts*, Princeton, N.J., Princeton University Press.

VYGOTSKY, L. (1978) *Mind in Society, the Development of Higher Psychological Processes*, Cambridge, Mass., Harvard University Press.

WERTSCH, J. (in press) 'A state of art review of Soviet research in cognitive psychology', *Storia e Critica Della Psicologis*.

ZANKOV, L. *et al.* (1977) *Teaching and Development, a Soviet Investigation*, B. Szekely (Ed.), White Plains, N.Y., M.E. Sharpe.

Chapter 4

'Qualitative' Research: Some Thoughts about the Relation of Methods and History

---

One of the more provocative dimensions of social and educational inquiry is the discussion of a 'paradigm crisis', a renewed debate about the multiple patterns, emphases and concerns of the social disciplines. This debate has focused upon the failure of positivism and its social science offshoot, empirical-analytic research, to provide adequate knowledge. Approaches previously refuted or judged irrelevant and moribund have taken on a new vitality within the discourse of social and educational research. In this debate, the notion of paradigm gives legitimacy to the establishment of alternative intellectual and conceptual traditions in research. It is suggested that truth is, to some extent, historical and situational, and that conflict among different intellectual perspectives is important to the imagination and development of science itself.

With the critiques of empirical-analytic sciences has emerged a community of researchers who give attention to the symbolic sciences, emphasizing the communicative patterns found within social interactions. Once reserved for the anthropologist living in a remote field setting, ethnographic, ethnomethodological, and other 'qualitative' modes of analysis have become more accepted in what had been previously considered the 'hard' social sciences. This type of research is legitimated by the attention it has been given in the American Educational Research Association's publications and in the types of sessions organized at its annual convention, and through large-scale federal grants which include case studies as an important dimension of social policy research and evaluation. The research is publicly considered 'qualitative' to emphasize the observer's participation in the ongoing events and the construction of narrative descriptions and interpretations. While the notion of qualitative is a technical definition, obscuring conflicting conceptual and paradigmatic comments, many believe that a paradigm crisis is at hand and the symbolic sciences provide an alternative for the development of scholarly knowledge about schooling.

The current American debate about paradigms can be viewed as emerging from a variety of historical, social and intellectual sources. The social unrest of the 1960s, the feeling of loss of moral will and direction in the 1970s, and the economic uncertainties of the early 1980s gave increasing attention to the values, conduct and purposes of everyday life in America. Themes worked out in the history and philosophy of science also contribute to the reconsideration and search for alternative directions in our social sciences. Conceptual inquiries in linguistic philosophy challenge the epistemological foundations of the empirical-analytic sciences. Developments in the history of science offer new interpretations to the development and significance of scientific knowledge. Phenomenology and hermeneutics have been reinserted into American scholarly discourse.

The controversy over the symbolic and empirical-science is not new to the academic disciplines, to society or to our culture. Such thinkers as Husserl, Cassirer, Ortega y Gasset, and Marx have pointed to the many serious flaws in Western culture that have become the current focus for methodological alternatives. Fundamental questions about the logic of positivism were discussed by Popper in the 1940s, Dewey at the turn of the century, Kierkegaard and Nietzsche in the not too distant past and Vico in the 1700s.

At first glance, it is puzzling to note that the methods of new possibilities are only now beginning to receive an adequate hearing when oppositional and alternative scholarly traditions have existed. With long scholarly traditions challenging the epistemological and social basis of positivistic thought, why is it that the arguments of discreditation and its antithesis are only now beginning to receive an adequate hearing? To answer this question, critics point to the failure of empirical-analytic science to provide powerful generalizations or to offer practical help in our social affairs. These critics call for a shift in metaphor and forms of analysis.

In part, these arguments have some merit, but another form of accounting can be used to understand why qualitative research now appeals to a scientific community. This second type of argument focuses upon the social sciences as special types of social organizations whose activities are maintained, renewed, and sustained in relation to other institutions in society. The debate about paradigm crisis provides a way to locate underlying social values and issues that shape and fashion our research endeavors. The legitimation of symbolic sciences within the educational research community can be considered as a response to larger issues of social strain and trans-formation. To understand changes in our standards of reasoning, the larger historical trends and issues which impinge upon the work of social inquiry must be considered.[1]

The purpose of this chapter is to locate the emergence of symbolic science in issues of social strain and transformation. The focus will be upon two particular styles of research that are central to the symbolic sciences in the United States — symbolic interaction and ethnomethodology. The discussion will consider these approaches to inquiry within a context that involves a breakdown in a liberal hope for social solidarity and political democracy. It is argued that 'qualitative' research provides legitimating symbols for those liberal ideas that are being challenged by contemporary conditions.

Locating symbolic sciences in a context of social strain and contradiction raises questions about the substantive difference be-tween the empirical-analytic and symbolic sciences. At one layer, differences are apparent in epistemology. However, the argument of this chapter is that both intellectual traditions are responses to a liberal democratic society, offering complementary perspectives to issues of authority, tradition and social change. By suggesting that the two research paradigms are complementary, labels of qualitative and quantitative can be misleading as to the social implications and consequences of a research paradigm. Further, the portrayal of symbolic sciences as one that develops and is sustained in relation to social conditions outside the discourse of science compels us to recognize a role of the intellectual in our social affairs. It is a role of re-establishing cohesion, will and direction in periods of cultural crisis.

Social Science and Its Evolution: An Internal Perspective

The challenge posed by symbolic sciences to the dominant empirical approach to school research can be understood by focusing upon certain dimensions of change within scientific communities. The argument for interactional studies is often one of the need for new conceptual perspectives for considering the conditions, relations, and meaning of institutional life. Ethnomethodologists and symbolic interactionists argue that conventional approaches to schooling either ignore or obscure significant questions about the implications of the social relations and communication patterns produced in institutions.

Much of the argument for a paradigmatic shift draws upon

Kuhn's (1970) analysis of scientific revolutions. He views scientific advancement as a series of 'non-cumulative-developments', and maintains that such developments result neither from purely rational choice nor from the accumulation of knowledge. His analysis of the history of change in the physical sciences suggests that science evolves when the 'normal' methods of a discipline can no longer resolve the discrepancies and abnormalities that have arisen. Kuhn suggests that a new constellation of methods appears to solve riddles that the conventional paradigm could not.

While Kuhn's analysis focused primarily upon the natural sciences, social scientists reacted on heuristic grounds, rather than to the structure of Kuhn's ideas (Heyl, 1975). Kuhn's historical and philosophical analyses of change in the natural sciences have an important legitimizing function in contemporary social and educational research. Social scientists were provided with a language, a method, and a focus for reappraising the history and present conditions of the social disciplines. Kuhn's ideas are used to argue that disciplines such as linguistic analysis or hermeneutics are normal and acceptable divisions within academia and there is a methodological and theoretical autonomy to their studies (see, for example, Drietzel, 1972; Friedrick, 1972). The 'post-Kuhn' period has made a plurality of perspectives acceptable and even a valued dimension of social scientific work.

From Kuhn's perspective, the symbolic sciences can be interpreted either as a response to abnormalities or as a response to changing relevances. The old paradigm, many would suggest, does not adequately deal with certain questions and discrepancies. California, for example, initiated a study of the beginning teacher to identify teacher competencies to be used in a mandated teacher certification procedure. The identification of competencies, it was soon found, could not be handled by conventional survey techniques. Prior observational and ethnographic studies were required. While no behavioral competencies were ever identified, the use of field methods provided a way of responding to the new questions about schooling.

Social Science and Its Evolution: Social Dimensions

When we consider the debate within the social and education disciplines as a historical phenomenon, arguments about the poverty of positivism and the richness of field study are found to have their origin in the works of such people as Max Weber, Ortega y Gasset,

Carl Becker, and Alfred Schutz. These men argued about the dehumanizing effect of a positivistic social science and by the early 1900s decisively portrayed what are now seen as the 'new' requirements for a social science. Yet many of these critiques and alternatives were contemporaneous with the Chicago School of behavioral analysis and Talcott Parsons' work at Harvard. The graduate students from these institutions dominated social study into the 1960s, and it was not until the last decade that the social disciplines began to revive works of phenomenology, Marxism, and social philosophy, reintroducing them into mainstream American discussions about social inquiry.

To understand this historical phenomenon of 'acceptability', we need to relate scientific inquiry to larger social and cultural trends. Scientific communities, as products of their social world, are responsive to the issues and dilemmas that people confront in that world. Each paradigm organizes social and psychological processes, renders culture and politics interpretable, and provides competing ways for individuals to mediate more complex meanings than would seem available in ordinary discourse. The debate about field methodologies, while it poses important questions about the foundations of human studies, also reflects historical debates about social institutions and social ideas.

The coherence provided by a paradigm is understood not only as a descriptive, analytic task. A significant aspect of a paradigm is its response to perceived social incongruities and institutional contradictions. Gouldner (1970) considers social theories as expressions of personal struggles in order to make sense of those experiences that seem unresolved and to interpret the meaning of the life one has lived.

> It is my suggestion that a significant part of social theorizing is a symbolic effort to overcome social worlds that have become unpermitted and to readjust the flawed relationship between goodness and potency, restoring them to their "normal" equilibrium condition, and/or to defend permitted worlds from a threatened disequilibrium between goodness and potency (Gouldner, 1970, p. 486).

The classical sociological works of the late nineteenth century are attempts to redefine flawed relations and assert goodness and potency. The social science revolution of the 1930s, too, can be considered the creation of a symbolic universe to resolve problems of institutional legitimacy.[2] One sociological theory to emerge in that period, structural-functionalism, provided a particular disposition towards how people should conceive and act towards social affairs. This 'theory' accepted certain master institutions and thus created a disposition to social affairs that maintained traditional loyalties and avoided institutional discontinuities. The underlying sentiments of this intellectual position are understood when placed in the context of the 1930s. Social institutions were threatened by depression in the United States and by revolution in Europe. (See also Merelman's (1976) discussion of the emergence of behavioral political science which points to a similar symbolic function of social science.) The theories of social science made the social situation comprehensible; they made it possible for people to believe that they could act purposely.

It is within another period of social upheaval and disorientation that we have become involved in the re-examination of social science and in a discussion of paradigm crisis. The themes of the symbolic sciences enable us to grasp, formulate and communicate about social strains and tensions that dominate our social conditions.

Symbolic Sciences: New Symbols of Reconciliation?

In the previous section, it was argued that the potency of social inquiry is not only in its facts *per se*, but in the way its theories and methods create a form and style to thought that expresses hopes and beliefs about a changing social and moral order. From this perspective, the possible social significance of symbolic sciences can be considered. The emergence of symbolic sciences can be related to certain cultural contradictions between liberal ideals and institutional processes; its methods of organizing social 'facts' provide underlying themes that reaffirm the possibility of community, individualism and personal efficiency. These themes, important to our cultural and political mythologies, are threatened as the older symbols of reconciliation seem no longer viable.

The style of thought associated with symbolic sciences articulates a vision of social world that

1 re-establishes the idea of community at a time when people feel threatened, alienated and estranged;
2 makes plausible pluralistic beliefs through an emphasis on group diversity and individualism; and

3 reasserts a belief in the efficacy of individuals through the conception of negotiating roles

The concepts and methods of study are, in part, a reaction to the patterns of specialization and fragmentation in social affairs and the dissolution of moral life. The concepts and methods of the symbolic sciences establish underlying themes and visions by which we consider the permitted and the potency of our human condition. It is to this latter, dispositional quality, that this essay is directed.

In the following discussion, two variations of this research paradigm will be analyzed. One is symbolic interactionism as exemplified in the work of Phillip Cusick (1973). The second is the ethnomethodology of Hugh Mehan (1978). These two researchers provide styles of analysis that represent, I believe, the dominate characteristics of the symbolic sciences in America. The range of assumptions is similar to that found in most research labeled 'case studies', ethnographic or qualitative research. (See, for example, Willis, 1978; Cicourel, 1974). The argument here is not about the 'scientific value' of these traditions but the sentiments and dispositions carried in the analysis and interpretation of data.

'The Belief in Community and Its Loss'

The idea of community and its loss is a recurrent theme in modern society. Nineteenth century sociologists wrote of the leveling, atomization, alienation of society that left large numbers of people without neighborhood, religion, kinship and community. Marx, for example, perceived an absence of legitimate community and a sense of estrangement and isolation from both community and its moral value. The sociologist, Tonnies, provided a distinction between the traditions of community and of the large-scale, secular, individualistic industrial society that had grown in the latter part of the nineteenth century. The consequence of *Gesellschaft*, it was believed, was to increase anonymity, displacement, deviation and isolation.

In recent years the notion of community has again become a powerful symbol. Some believe that the increasing bureaucratization of American life and the professionalization of private and public affairs have made personal life seem isolated, insecure and without purpose. Institutions have come to be seen as abstract and antagonistic to the meanings and values people hold for them.

One of the more popular discussions of the demise of community is Daniel Bell's *The Cultural Contradictions of Capitalism* (1976).

Bell argues that there is a disjunction between culture and the social, techno-economic structures of capitalism. Nineteenth century capitalists valued self-discipline, delayed gratification and personal restraint. The work ethic was based upon rationality, solutions to organizational problems, efficiency, and the right balance between cost and benefit. The material bounty produced by the techno-economic structure created a different culture. The emergent bourgeois culture made sacred the principle of change and novelty, and emphasized values such as personal 'feeling', gratification, and the total fulfilment of self. Personal experience was no longer shaped by tradition or expressed in ritual. The singularity of experience became the criterion of what is desirable.

The disjuncture of culture and social structure, Bell continued, produces a break-up of institutions, the erosion of tradition, the loss of authority and the disintegration of normative rules by which to define the common good. Aesthetic justification is replaced by the instinctual; new conventions and forms are to create a world in which individuals live for self-realization. Psychoanalysis, formerly inseparable from helping people to act in a moral way in society and not instrumental and psychologistic, is now directed toward 'freeing' the person from inhibitions and restraints so s/he can easily express impulse and feeling.

Bell believes that the problems of culture in modern capitalism point to the need to find a new 'social cement' for society. He reaffirms his commitment to a liberal faith and advances two central questions for our society: 'how to find common purposes, yet retain individual means of fulfilling them; and how to define individual (and group) needs and find common means of meeting them' (p. 279).

The psychologization of culture has implications for the very conception of politics that permeates society. No longer is there a focus upon historical forces which influence roles. Cultural matters and social issues have been reduced to matters of personality, politics is reduced to the believable public person rather than believable actions. This tying of personality to social action denies political community and makes self-criticism and change difficult.

The theme of lost community is found in educational discourse. Cagan (1978), for example, suggests that the American preoccupation with the individual has escalated dramatically in recent years, reaching a point of narcissism. The moral and political primacy of the individual over the group is presented by many as a *sine qua non* of American democratic society. The remaining fragments of social bonds such as responsibility, loyalty and caring are stifled in the

American context. Collective education is suggested as a contrasting source to develop a sense of community which promotes higher forms of moral reasoning and a set of principles which considers the relationship of individual to community. Oliver (1976) takes the theme of fraternity and community as a focus for educational revitalization. He suggests that most educational activity has been technically concerned with coordinating activities. The division of labor in schooling maintains criteria related solely to usefulness. The problem of education, Oliver continues, is to reinstitute a sense of community in society.

The lost community theme, to summarize, is one which reappears in contemporary social and educational criticism. An atomization of human affairs, an alienation and depersonalization produces a renewed search for forms of corporate living, political participation and moral order. While faith in the individual and liberal society does not wane, there is a search for new symbols of reconciliation which can give expression to these ideals. The symbolic sciences are one source for re-establishing a belief in community, the sanctity of the individual, and the power of people to determine their destiny.

The Theme of Community and The Method Of Study

The search for community is an underlying orientation in symbolic research. The basic orientation of such study is to gain a systematic understanding of the whole, its parts, and how the parts relate to one another. The method of study gives attention to how social order is maintained and to alternative structures for institutional life. Relationships among participant feelings, emotions, language and patterns of conduct are examined in order to understand how symbolic ties are established and social cohesion produced. The metaphor is one that gives reference to people involved in a binding community, changing it and being changed by it. Smith (1978), for example suggests that 'case studies are "totalities"'. That is, they have a 'holistic' or 'systematic' quality. By their very nature they can contain or tend to all the elements.

The methodological approach of understanding social cohesion assumes a particular set of meanings. The school, for example, is defined as groups which exist within its formal setting. The problem of study is to give attention to how definitions of the situation and social cohesion occur. While it can be argued that the study of groups provides a limited conception of community because of its sole attention to the common interests of participants, the focus is not without implication.

Drawing upon the perspective of symbolic interaction, Cusick (1973) defines schools as groups of individuals who develop reasonable ways of behaving in their environment. He posits that individuals 'must have developed some ordered understanding of their relationship to the school' (p. 2). The pattern of interaction is that which can produce personal involvement and pleasure. To find involvement, the investigation focuses upon student groups where independence and power over activities can be exercised and students have 'the immediate pleasure of participation in human interaction' (p. 214).

The search to understand how community develops gives direction to the possibilities of schooling. Cusick believes that schooling fails in its responsibility to have students actively participate in their learning. Recent innovations which provide students with opportunities 'to express themselves' include more varied scheduling patterns, the elimination of dress codes and the removal of other restrictions on student freedom and interaction. The Cusick study begins with the idea that a notion of community is valued and developed through norms of interactions: the conclusions reassert this assumption, stressing the importance of interactions in formal and informal groups.[3]

Mehan's (1978) methodological approach, often called ethnomethodology, emphasizes social interaction as well. Rather than look at groups, as does Cusick, Mehan assumes that social cohesion exists in school settings and seeks to identify how rules and social order are created through interaction between role-types, such as teacher and student. In a study of a classroom, for example, minute details of the interactions are gathered to illuminate the rhythmic, cooperative activities and interactions, the sequence and hierarchical organization of school events and the boundaries of interactional sequences and events. The 'methodology', Mehan tells us, 'reminds us that the classroom can be viewed as a small society or community' (p. 48).

Cusick's and Mehan's research builds certain images and rules about the social world. The emphasis upon the whole, the system or totality, is a way of emphasizing the ability of people to work against the bureaucracies that inundate them, the dislocations that confront them and the lack of relatedness that might be felt in their daily lives. A particular notion of community emerges from this orientation, one in which the group is central to the building of consensus. People create rules and norms in the limited affairs of the groups to which they affiliate, but it is the group which articulates interests and provides psychological support for individuals.

A contrasting set of assumptions about community can be seen in Sharp and Green's (1976) study of a British primary school. The authors explicitly reject the ethnomethodological and symbolic interactionist stances because of the assumption that social consciousness is the major determinant in social action and development of meaning.[4] While Sharp and Green do view systems of meanings as important to the study of social settings, they argue that researchers must also consider how material structures limit and fashion the world view of the acting subject. From their perspective, the purpose of school study is 'to socially situate the classroom and intra-classroom processes within the wider structure of social relationships' (p. 13) and 'to develop some conceptualizations of the situations that individuals find themselves in, in terms of the structure of opportunities the situation makes available to them and the kinds of constraints they impose' (Sharp and Green, p. 22).

The notion of community is redefined by Sharp and Green; the researchers consider the conflict within, rather than the consensus of the social world of schooling, and are concerned with relating school relations to macrostructures in social life. The emphasis is upon how social structure and its implicit hierarchy, status, and power create forms of domination and thereby prevent a more just world. The concept of power is central to this examination.

In contrasting the work of Cusick and Mehan to that of Sharp and Green, we can consider two different visions of community. Cusick and Mehan adopt a liberal philosophical and political stance.[5] They emphasize the autonomy of the individual, in that one's actions and thoughts are not determined by agencies or causes outside one's personal control. They believe in the ability of individuals to expand upon their nature through active involvement in daily discourse. Morality and ethics are derived from individuals, with disparate groups giving substance and form to the social contract. Sharp and Green focus upon the communal in cultivating the self and seek to locate structural restraints that limit the individual in society.

The liberal dispositions of the symbolic interactionists' and ethnomethodologists' stance tend to make them more acceptable in the American context, and, in fact, they dominate the current work in what we might generally label field-study or qualitative research. The importance of these studies, however, may not be in what is found but rather in the illusion created: that community does exist, that it is a viable concept and belief that can be maintained unscathed, at least in our linguistic forms.

The Individual and Pluralism

The emphasis on the group to define community involves two other beliefs of liberalism: individualism and pluralism.[6] The practices of symbolic sciences offer particular ways of giving vitality to these ideals. The emphasis is upon the particular situation. There is an in-depth focus to the interactions, beliefs and patterns of behavior produced in a particular setting. Uniqueness or individuality become important to examining concrete interactions of people in groups. The fact that there are many different and distinct settings in which people can express themselves is significant. Legitimacy is given to the idea that diverse groups permit or deny individual involvement and growth.

The importance of the group as giving expression to individual, social, and political needs is a basic premise of pluralistic theories of democracy (see Bachrach, 1966). The diversity, size and complexity of a modern society make the idea of organized interest groups a mainstay of a democracy. The group is the agent for allocation of values in society.

The group also provides a mechanism for psychological development. Group participation enables the individual to strive for goals, to articulate personal decisions and to engage in purposeful action. Conflict is now interpersonal rather than political or social. Because there are many different and diverse interests in society, pluralistic settings are available to foster personal idiosyncracies. The focus on groups is a variation of the theme of individualism. It is through groups that individuals articulate their values; it is through individual interaction in groups that social cohesion and commitment are produced.

In *Inside High School* (Cusick, 1973), the group is the mechanism for meeting psychological and political ideals. Viewed as the central unit for communication and the development of meaning within the school, the group enables individuals to express their uniqueness, provides the psychological climate for the fulfilment of personal needs, and maintains the organizational arrangement by which students can act in a purposeful manner. It is in the small student groups of the school that Cusick believes individual characteristics are expressed:

> ... the premise of this chapter is that consideration of the group as a whole will capture something usually missed in observations of individuals. The group was, after all, a real

unity. It had its own meeting places, roles, patterns of communication, topics of discussion, and was definitely purposeful. That is, as the boys associated with one another in school they worked out a pattern of collective behavior which enabled them to fulfil some of their personal needs (Cusick, p. 83).

The group also has a political function. Groups compete for the center of attention and provide the mechanism by which students can influence the larger organization. 'Those small group associations', Cusick argues, 'can and do strongly effect other aspects of the school organization such as the teachers' classroom behavior, the extra-curricular activities, the vice-principal's actions, and the behavior of other students' (p. 205).

Although Cusick laments the fragmented and hierarchical nature of schooling itself, he does not suggest that the small groups are to be defined solely as a result of the pathology of schooling. To the question: Should students be in a position to seek and discover activity and involvement from one another in groups? Cusick comments:

Is that bad? I do not think so. While some of it may appear inconsistent with our stated goals, it seems to me that the best and worst of any society can be seen most clearly in those formal processes by which it transmits itself to succeeding generations (p. 235).

The ethnomethodologist takes a somewhat different stance toward understanding groups but maintains a similar commitment to locating the 'nature' of individuality within groups. The cohesiveness of social groups is assumed; the method is to unpack how specific groups interact and structure the events of their particular situations. Mehan (1978) is concerned with the creation of social facts and member competence in social situations such as classrooms, counsel-ing, or testing interactions. This involves monitoring the interactions between those who have roles of power (teacher, counselor, or tester) and the clients, students.

While Mehan argues the need to combine various discrete studies into a constitutive study of school events, the focus is upon the specific and concrete patterns of discourse in singular events. This focus is important because it directs the reader away from the linkage of the school to other institutional settings. It also suggests

1   that the social-psychological determinate of 'self' arises from the specific interaction, and

2   that there may be some cumulative (additive) quality in the structuring activities in various interactional settings.

The particularistic perspective found in these studies gives emphasis to the possibility that important social commitments in American life can be fulfilled. The legitimacy of many different systems of social meaning establishes a sentiment that, while there may be efforts towards conformity within the larger society, there is an opportunity for individuals to create their own, unique environments and to engage in an active public life. Pluralism reinforces a belief in individual self-actualization by its attention to the role of small interest groups in achieving the good life. There is also a relativism, in that it considers no one way of life or view better than others and thus relies upon the market-place of competing interests to produce consensus.

The method by which the symbolic sciences gives organization and meaning to social life is not neutral to that life or the cherished beliefs that seem threatened by institutional contradictions. Underlying the 'facts' are certain visions of society and its individuals. The vision is that while more complex institutional patterns may be beyond the control of individuals, participation and self-development in public life are still possible in specific and limited contexts.

Negotiation and Political Potency

The idea of negotiation is an integral part of symbolic research.[7] This idea suggests that before a meaningful action can take place, participants must act purposefully. Individuals must evaluate a situation in terms of their own orientation and the orientation of others. People then have to enter into a series of interactions in which they can communicate their definitions and arrive at a satisfactory way of working cooperatively. The idea of negotiation is a potent political symbol; it establishes the belief that people have the power to alter situations by the redefining and reordering of social events.

Inside High School emphasizes the active role of individuals in establishing the scope and boundaries of social reality. 'It [the symbolic interactionist perspective] assumes that a human being is an active agent, constantly engaged in the process of constructing his social self, and that what he does depends on how he perceives himself in relation to various features of his environment' (Cusick, p. 31). The negotiation process is seen as important for establishing the social dynamics of schooling and how the various interests interrelate.

> If one walked in the class and saw the teacher talking and gesticulating he might assume that the teacher is clearly in charge. But the social dynamics of that room are such that the teacher is in charge only in a very narrow sense. Should he fail to conduct himself with great care, he will no longer be in charge, and other forces will take over (Cusick, p. 200).

Negotiation is a powerful symbol for counteracting belief about institutional coerciveness and bureaucratic control. Typically, individuals derive personal meaning and identity from involvement with family, friends, and with a variety of voluntary associates. This private life is typically segregated, both physically and socially, from the vast institutions of modern life. To assert that negotiation is a part of public and institutional life is to reassert efficacy and the primacy of the individual in social life.

The power of the individual to shape the meanings and values in institutions is located in the negotiated action of various people as they act out roles. Social reality is a 'joint production' and the result of 'collaborative interactional work'. Through interactions between teacher and students or tester and tested, the 'objective social facts' of schooling are established. The study of the social structuring of classroom events, for example, is to understand how interaction 'reflects a strategic relationship between the teachers' and students' agendas and the practical classroom situations on a particular situation' (Cusick, p. 49). Analysis of the testing situation, as well, focuses upon how individuals exert influence and power. The testers 'puppeteering, cueing, and cutting off practices are not the result of sloppy test administration, but are inevitable aspects of social interaction that comprise testing encounters' (Mehan, p. 55).

By focusing upon the negotiated actions and the specific discourse of interaction, research offers a methodology that 'describes' reality. Mehan, for example, argues that data collection techniques provide researchers not only with an analytic device but with the actual mechanisms that guide participants. The researcher is able to identify the 'real' rules and patterns which give substance and definition to the social setting. For Mehan, ethnomethodology has resolved the social scientific problem of detachment and objectivity which has so plagued positivistic science. It appears, however, that

Mehan has succumbed to the metaphor; once invented and adopted, the metaphor is mistaken for the things interpreted.

The idea of negotiation affirms the American beliefs in individualism and political life as organized through social contracts. It suggests that institutions can be changed through processes of negotiation and that reality is that which is defined solely through the intersubjective processes that occur in particular situations. The idea of negotiation *denies* any overriding objectivity in society by focusing upon what individuals do in interaction with other.

Conclusions: The Contradictions of Study

Many in our society believe that scientific discourse provides the only 'reasonable' way of documenting and interpreting the course of cultural events. The expressions of social science are considered authoritatively different from other knowledge in thinking about and challenging the presumed relationships found in society.

The sacred quality of 'science' makes one lose sight of the 'as if' quality of organized knowledge. It is easy for people to react to their conception of affairs rather than to the actual state of affairs.

The discourse of social science is analogous to mythic structure. In a modern secular society, social science replaces religion as a major legitimating (and debunking) structure of social arrangements. The content or storyline of findings provides a way for people to reconcile contradictions and ambivalences encountered in everyday life. The language of inquiry, though, gives expression and cognitive definitions to the prevailing myths of society. That myth structure is not testable but a part of the assumptions and presuppositions of thought itself. The behavioral revolution of the 1930s provided new collective symbols capable of welding together a consensus about the relationship of people and government. The so-called paradigm crisis of our epoch may be viewed as a new attempt by people to confront the strains and contradictions of their existence.

Each age has to invent overarching symbols to legitimate social institutions. Theories and metatheories are necessary to make social order seem plausible and individual life seem satisfying. The metaphors of community, pluralism and negotiation in symbolic sciences provide one way of reaffirming ideals. In a society where people feel isolated, alienated and cut-off from community, the metaphors are persuasive. While underlying themes of the field method are, in many ways, impoverished notions of the relation of community and individual, the importance of the style of thought is its ability to create a new form of credibility for beliefs felt threatened by institutional contradictions. As the outcomes of our ideas are often different from what was hoped for and planned, we must be concerned about the creation of new forms of mystification through the languages of our sciences.

The themes of symbolic sciences raise an issue of the social location of science. That issue concerns the role of the intellectual. The assumptions and storylines of the symbolic research provide sets of symbols for establishing moral and political cohesion. The symbols respond to inconsistencies and contradictions of everyday life in ways that reassert traditional authority and patterns of control. To recognize the role of the research in this social and political context is also to direct attention to the intellectual as an element in the dynamics of social reproduction and transformation.

Notes

1 The use of history in this paper is related to the belief that there is a dynamic relation between social change, social commitments, and the discourse in the social disciplines. The purpose of using history in discussing science is to suggest that human understanding requires consideration of the development and interrelation of social ideas, customs, traditions and social practices.
2 The invention of new symbolic forms to replace the 'old' without altering the conception of human relationships is discussed in Becker (1932). He focuses on the shift from religious thought to science as a source of social authority.
3 The relation between initial setting of problem and conclusions should not be startling to anyone involved in research, be it symbolic, empirical or critical. One of the major difficulties of research is its tautological character (see Rose, 1967).
4 There are other attempts to make field-study a critical endeavor; see, for example, Reid (1973).
5 Criticism of ethnomethodology and symbolic interaction as 'liberal' is found in Sharp and Green (1975) and Gidlow (1972).
6 The relations between community and individuality, sociality and individuality, self and external world are embedded in epistemology and social theory. Thoughtful discussions of the implications of these relationships are found in Lukes (1973) and Wood (1972).
7 An interesting example of the use of negotiation is Martin (1976).

References

BACHRACH, P. (1966) *The Theory of Democratic Elitism: A Critique*, Boston, Mass., Little, Brown.

BECKER, C. (1932) *The Heavenly City of the Eighteenth-Century Philosophers*, New Haven, Conn., Yale University Press.

BELL, D. (1976) *The Cultural Contradictions of Capitalism*, New York, Basic Books.

CAGAN, E. (1978) 'Individualism, collectionism and radical educational reform', *Harvard Educational Review*, 48, 2, pp. 227–66.

CICOUREL, A. *et al.* (1974) *Language Use and School Performance*, New York, Academic Press.

CUSICK, P. (1973) *Inside High School: The Student's World*, New York; Holt, Rinehart and Winston.

DREITZEL, H. (1972) 'Social science and the problem of rationality: Notes on the sociology of technocrats', *Politics and Society*, 2, 2, pp. 165–86.

FRIEDRICK, B. (1972) *A Sociology of Sociology*, New York, The Free Press.

GIDLOW, B. (1972) 'Ethnomethodology — A new name for old practices', *The British Journal of Sociology*, 23, 4, pp. 395–405.

GOULDNER, A. (1970) *The Coming Crisis of Western Sociology*, New York, Basic Books.

HEYL, J. (1975) 'Paradigms in social science', *Society*, 12, 5, pp. 61–7.

KUHN, T. (1970) *The Structure of Scientific Revolutions*, 2nd ed., Chicago, Ill., University of Chicago Press.

LUKES, S. (1973) *Individualism*, Oxford, Blackwell.

MARTIN, W. (1976) *The Negotiated Order of the School*, Toronto, Macmillan.

MEHAN, H. (1978) 'Structuring school structure', *Harvard Educational Review*, 48, 1, pp. 32–64.

MERELMAN, R. (1976) 'On interventionist behavioralism: An essay in the sociology of knowledge', *Politics and Society*, 6, 1, pp. 57–78.

OLIVER, D. (1976) *Education and Community: A Radical Critique of Innovative Schooling*, Berkeley, Ca., McCutchan Publishing.

REID, H. (1973) 'American social science in the politics of time and the crisis of technocorporate society, towards a critical phenomonology', *Politics and Society*, 3, 2, pp. 201–43.

ROSE, A. (1967) 'The relation of theory and method', *Sociological Theories, Inquires and Paradigms*, New York, Harper and Row, pp. 207–19.

SHARP, R and GREEN, A. (1975) *Education and Social Control: A Study in Progressive Primary Education*, London, Routledge and Kegan Paul.

SMITH, L. (1978) 'An evolving logic of participant observation, educational ethnography and other case studies', *Review of Research in Education*, Chicago, Ill., Peacock Press.

WILLIS, G. (Ed.) (1978) *Qualitative Evaluation; Concepts and Cases in Curriculum Criticism*, Berkeley, Ca., McCutchan Publishing.

WOOD, E. (1972) *Mind and Politics; An Approach to the Meaning of Liberal and Socialist Individualism*, Berkeley, Ca., University of California.

2

*Roles of the Intellectual
in Contemporary Society*

Chapter 5

Social Science and Social Amelioration: The Development of the American Academic Expert

The previous chapters focused upon the discourse of educational research. Conflicting social values, visions of order and principles of authority are carried in the patterns of communication and ritual of research. To talk about the social assumptions of the discourse of research, however, requires that we look not only at discourse but also at the social location of the intellectual. The social scientist is a social type that exists as an element within the general dynamics of reproduction and transformation in society. This position in contemporary, industrial society provides for the establishment of the moral direction and will. The political scientist, economist, sociologist and educational researcher are called upon to give coherence to our institutional conditions and their possibilities.

The reformist tendency of social science is obscured by general folklore and ideology. The movement of social science into the university at the beginning of the twentieth century capitalized on the general belief that the university serves the civil society as a whole and is not bound by interests of the polity. This image was proposed by Max Weber to free the German university chairs of their partisan politics and incorporated in the American context to create an institutional setting that makes the academic intellectual seem free from particular interests of the state or the economy. This theme is perhaps best exemplified in Jencks and Reisman's (1968) study of the academy, in which they argue that professors rule the university.

When examined historically, social science has been and is involved in the general problem of social reform and amelioration. Three historical themes give focus to this social role. One is the shift in cultural sensibilities among the middle class which defined science as a means to emancipate the individual. The independent self-governing individual no longer had to appeal to God for solving questions of social affairs but to the qualities of rational thought. By the late nineteenth century, individual achievement and competence were no longer assessed by one's personal contributions to worldly affairs. The status and worth of one's contribution were to be determined by professional communities which provided the means by which democratic persons could free their creative energies.

Two, there was the development of the intellectual as a social type concerned with agitation as well as understanding, a purpose which can be traced back to Plato's *Republic* but whose strategy towards reform is altered as social science American is incorporated into the university. The tradition of social science prior to the early twentieth century was established by spokespeople and protagonists in social affairs. Social science was to educate the masses and provide direction for moral and social progress. The new social science moves from social agitation to expertism as a shift in the strategy to bring about reform.

The third element involves the movement of social science into the universities to legitimate the efforts of social amelioration. The image was of an expert-community that served civil society as a whole. The social science of the university, Offe (1981) suggests, involves a 'relationship of a secret transfer between the academic and non-academic systems of knowledge' since the topics, theories or criteria of relevance are not generated by the disciplines themselves, but by the agendas of the political process (p. 32). In its desire to believe itself devoted to depoliticized research, social science loses sight of its involvement in the creation and definition of the political process.

The purpose of this chapter is to explore historically the reformist tendencies of social science. In the next two chapters, the contemporary role of educational research in institutional reform will be considered. The relation between social movements and the research of the scientist-qua-expert is still evident although masked by the formal rhetoric and imagery of 'objective' science.

Social, Culture and Economic Change in Occupational Formation

To understand the role of the academic intellectual as a social type, there is a need to consider the transformations of cultural sensibilities and economics that gave rise to the professional expert in the late nineteenth century. The ideology that reform and change are brought about through expert-neutral knowledge and that the university serves the civil society as a whole emerges and takes root during this period. While this section cannot fully explore the transformation in cultural and occupational structure that gave direction to contemporary social science, the intent is to provide a sense of that history.

Underlying the formation of professional communities was a fundamental redefinition of individuality among the American middle class. A new corporate view was established in the late nineteenth century. Having roots in political, economic and religious theory of seventeenth and eighteenth century England — that of Hobbes, Locke and Mill — Americans emphasized the primacy of the individual. It was believed that the individual had an active ego which could be emancipated through competition with others. The notion of the sovereign individual was originally embedded in the economic theory of *laissez-faire* capitalism and a political theory of democratic liberalism. The theologies of the reformation also contributed to this emphasis on individualism, for people were to work for salvation through their contribution to the material world. By the late nineteenth century, though, the individual's good works and self-development were thought to occur in structured communities. The emancipated, sovereign person was to perform sanctioned activities within organized spaces. Self-development and fulfilment were to be tied to participation in communities of the competent. These communities of competent professionals, however, widened their mission. Their task was to guide social reform and progress.

These changes in the relation of individual to community were accomplished in a context of broad changes in the material structure and cultural consciousness of the American middle class. Substantial demographic shifts and changes in capitalism in American society occurred after the American Civil War (1865). At this time, American society was becoming interdependent in its material organization. Drastic changes had occurred in the nature of the market, transportation systems, and occupational specialization (see Haskell, 1977; Bledstein, 1976). Goods moved faster and rates for transportation were cheaper than prior to the War. In 1794 it took ten days to move goods from western Pennsylvania to New York City; by 1841 goods moved from western Wisconsin to New York in the same time. Industrial growth and great capital accumulation also became part of the American landscape, giving credibility to corporate organizations.

These material changes were accompanied by drastic modification in cultural sensibility and awareness of the middle class. One of these cultural changes was related to the perception of causation

(Haskell, 1977). As changes in markets and transportation indicate, the interrelation of people to production outside their community tended to be minimal into the 1800s. A community had both a material and, as important, a cultural sense of being an island. Individuals could depend upon the personal understanding of their milieu to identify cause. The reasons or causes of events seemed to be in the sight of the actors. Lay opinion and common sense seemed adequate to define social reality and to become self-reliant. Professionals of the island community — the minister, doctor or lawyer — could attribute causation close-at-hand and, where necessary, mediate between the island and larger community.

The complex social and economic changes that followed the American Civil War supported a new cultural view of an interdependent universe in which personal milieu was devitalized. Change was seen as pervasive and ceaseless, in which there is *no* independent variable. Subtle causal links were sought to explore deeper causes or 'laws' of society. Necessity began to underlie the new style of explanation. What were once seen as causes in the island communities were now believed to be symptomatic reflexes of some deeper causes which devalued autonomous action and self-reliance.[1]

The way in which people were to interpret the interdependent world was through theories provided by communities of professionals. The professional was to re-establish intellectual and moral authority that was being threatened by the cultural and material changes. Middle-class cultural beliefs had begun to accept the notion that specific occupations had responsibility to define and interpret specific ranges of social affairs. These communities of the competent provided structured spaces by which individuals could interact, communicate and achieve, and establish authority in society.

Important to the structure of these professional communities was the use of words. The late nineteenth century middle class thought words liberated the nature of the individual by bringing that nature to consciousness. Words became part of a person's cultural capital. To be able to categorize social relations was to have the power to define, to organize and, possibly, to control those social relations.[2]

The idea of career charted one's movement in a professional community. Career comes from the word carry, which in 1819 meant 'ground on which a race is run' (Bledstein, 1976). By the end of the century, career had acquired a cultural meaning to describe a person's course or progress through life. It described a pre-established, total pattern of organized professional activity. To have a career was to have scheduled mobility. The decision for a career was a decision about identity, about self-image and material prospects in the expanding social universe. Self-improvement occurred through the application of one's trained judgment, and active control and confidence over one's situation. To make a decision about a career was to make a decision about character and about an inner self that would be realized in the struggle of a progressive professional activity.

These transformations in economic conditions and cultural awareness provide a background against which we can understand the emergence of social science as a dynamic of society. The crisis in authority that emerged in late nineteenth century America called forth the need for interpreting and reasserting coherence in the new social situation. The changing notions of causality, sociability, space and words redirected how particular strata of society — the middle class and gentry — reconsidered their role in the establishment of moral will and value. The role of the intellectual was tied to political ideology of the independent, democratic person. Each person could be emancipated through hard work and disciplined character. The independent, self-governing individual, however, was no longer located in an island community but dependent upon communities of competent others, the professionals. The communities provided for the development of expertise to understand and explain the laws of the world to the public-at-large.

Communities of the Competent: Movement towards the Professionalization of Social Science

The belief that society as well as individuals could be emancipated through communities of competent professionals initially appeared outside the university. The first social scientists were members of the older professions of the ministry or journalism. Their task was to reassert the authority of gentry in reforming society. These men rejected the social determinism of Spencer and Marx by asserting a voluntaristic and spiritual view of human affairs. It was only later, as the social scientists became incorporated into the academy, that a more deterministic view dominates and more rigorous procedures of data collection emerge.

The American Social Science Association: The Reform of Society through Professional Knowledge

The American Social Science Association (ASSA) reflected the interest of the gentry in reasserting authority by guiding the reform of society.[3] The men who originally adopted the name of social science in the late nineteenth century were members of the older professions who had mediated between the island community and society. The position of the professional as the culture expert had existed since the Renaissance as Western culture had allocated questions that surpassed common sense and tradition to the classical professions. As the theme of interdependence and complexity seemed to threaten the basis of social and cultural authority, these older professionals sought to reassert authority through social science. Science was to provide the underpinning of esoteric advice that the professional could dispense to the lay public.

The ASSA was founded in 1865 by men of science, university reformers and a triparite of ministers, lawyers and physicians. By the time it disbanded in 1909, the Association had been involved in the organizational development of historians, economists, and sociologists. The ASSA helped to create communities of inquiry through its professional journals, media of communication, professional associations and periodic gatherings. The transformation into more specific academic disciplines illuminates how the purpose of social science to bring about reform was maintained while strategies shifted.

The members of the ASSA were concerned not merely with understanding society but with improving it. As genteel reformers (Hofstadter, 1963), ASSA members felt a moral obligation of their class to educate the masses to the nature of good and evil and to guide the evolution of the society. The Association's leaders were involved in the abolitionist movement and supported John Brown. The Association was formed to work with the Massachusetts Board of Charities to reform the state's charitable and correctional institutions. The call for social science was to publicize the abuses and to coordinate a decentralized system of almshouses, hospitals, and *ad hoc* relief.

The founders of ASSA adhered to the idealism of Emerson and Hegel and reacted to the determinism of European positivism. The task of the organization was to create ways of thinking about the reorganization of social affairs that would re-establish the authority of tradition and value among the mass public who, the members of the association believed, had withheld deference. The association organized into four divisions that responded to the existing professional patterns, with the exception of ministers. The study of human affairs was divided into Education, Finance, Health, and Jurisprudence.

The ASSA drew upon the mantle of science to give its mission legitimacy. Its meaning of science, however, had no stringent boundaries. Anyone who wished to join the ASSA could. The varied nature of its intellectual base is exemplified by its secretary for most of its years, Franklin Benjamin Sanborn. Sanborn viewed social science as a convenient rubric for inquiry. Inquiry, however, involved two dimensions. One was to increase understanding and explanation. But inquiry also involved the activity of reform in which scientists had no edge over the novelist. Sanborn was a teacher, poet, journalist, radical and political reformer, government bureaucrat, philosopher, classicist, propagandist, and philanthropist.

The eclectic style of the ASSA was reflected in its meetings and *Journal of Social Science*. Papers involved journalistic discussions, inductive styles of reasoning about social issues, as well as discussion of topics such as cholera. The underlying theme of papers and of the association was a rejection of positivism, an unwillingness to admit limits of human freedom, and the maintenance of the theological distinction between people and nature.

The reformist strand and gentrified notion of ASSA social science came into conflict with the emergent structure of the university. In the early twentieth century, the Association sought to merge with the newly created research university, Johns Hopkins. The university was created in the 1880s to provide an independent research institution. It was to be a place where research and analysis of social questions could be conducted as a full-time occupation by men of science.

The first President of Johns Hopkins, Daniel Coit Gilman, was a charter member and former president of the ASSA. Gilman recognized, however, that the acts of investigation and agitation could not coexist and only the former could be professionalized. This recognition was based upon a number of social and intellectual elements of the world at the turn of the century. A university President had to account for the pressures of the University Board of Trustees, and public criticism and agitation might challenge the interests of the trustees who were typically members of the business community. Further, the underlying belief in causation held by members of the ASSA, that human affairs involved moral agents who were autonomous and masters of their own fate, no longer dominated the cultural outlook. Thought had shifted to a determinism to be uncovered by inductive reasoning. Without university backing and a general shift of the *weltanschauung*, the ASSA lost membership and had not enough money to continue. It disbanded in 1909.

The failure of the ASSA illustrates the transformation of social science. The new professionals valued sociability, careers, and organized space in which to practice their work. But the volunteeristic and spiritual view of self-help that underlay the ASSA was no longer appropriate. In the place of ASSA emerged the specialized academic disciplines, populated by professional social scientists who acted as paramount expert authorities on the nature of people and society. These experts sought the institutional arrangements of the university to maintain their reform tendencies but adopted different strategies to influence policy. That strategy, as argued in examining the formation of economics, was for them to become the expert advisor to policy-makers.

The Movement of Economics into the Academy: The Shift from Reform As Mass Education to Expertism

The professionalization of economics provides a forum for understanding the shift to expertism as a strategy of social science to bring about reform. The initial meeting of the American Economics Association was informally sponsored by the ASSA at its annual meeting in 1885. The history of the American Economic Association is one of professionals moving into the university as a separate discipline of study while maintaining the original desire of the ASSA to make professional knowledge influential in reform. The difference between the two organizations was in their strategies to achieve that influence (see Church, 1965, 1974).

Prior to the Civil War, discussion of economic and political issues was an afterthought in moral philosophy and subordinate to religious concerns. The early members of the economic profession focused upon moral issues and reform. Many members were related to the 'mugwumps', descendants of social elites and committed to civil service reform. In part, the 'mugwumps' reacted to the values threatened by social and economic movements of the 1870s and 1880s.

While the emphasis of economists was upon reform, there was no one voice speaking for the nature and direction of that reform. Some economists were trained in British evolutionary thought. These men sought to apply learning to the immediate improvement of politics and social mores. Another group of the German historical school of economics, were advocates of labor and protectionism. Richard T. Ely, a principal founder and publicist for the American Economic Association, was a professor of political economy at Johns

Hopkins and later the University of Wisconsin. Ely sought to combine economics and religious reform. At the organizational meeting of AEA in 1885, Ely said; 'One aim of our association should be the education of public opinion in regard to economic questions and economic literature' (Church, 1974, pp. 586–7.) He and other 'historical' or inductive economists argued that only an activist government could solve America's social and economic problems and that the association was 'to loosen *laissez faire's* hold on the public and political mind' (Church, 1974, p. 587).

The reformist tendency to influence the masses, however, created tensions. Economists, as did other social scientists, found that their incursion into public education had created strains within the business community and in the university. Trustees, alumni and administrators reacted strongly when academic social scientists spoke against existing policies or for socialism. University administrators did not want to risk offending trustees or the middle range of public opinion. When economist Henry Carter Adams failed to teach economics as the issue of free trade versus protection, trustees at Cornell became angry. Adams' professional competence was questioned. In moving to Michigan and in the wake of the Haymarket strike hysteria of 1886, President Angell of Michigan hesitated to promote Adams because of the negative 'public' reaction to his book advocating moderate state regulation of industrial capitalism and working people's rights (Bledstein, p. 294). Only after Adams shifted his work away from the subject of state action and disavowed his 'socialist' views did his professorship become approved.

The older tradition of popular education to obtain the allegiance of the masses was dropped as a strategy of social science by the early 1900s and a strategy to influence policy-makers was adopted. Leading economists of the time rejected the notion that the social scientist could combine both investigation and popular education. The public airing of disagreement was seen as hindering efforts to affect public policy. Academic debates were to be internal to the professions, aired at professional organization meetings and in scholarly writing. The more efficient means towards reform was through the role of the expert-advisor to policy-makers.

The role of expert was emphasized by the appropriation of the styles of argument and practice seen to characterize the physical and biological sciences. The belief that rationality can be used to control and manipulate the natural order was transposed to include the control and manipulation of social affairs. Much of the early economic research, for example, was to discover the universal truth that could harmonize society. As important, the attributes of scientific practice were considered to reflect the general American democratic beliefs in openness and fairness. Science was a potential authority that transcended the favoritism of politics, the corruption of personality, and the exclusiveness of partisanship.

The movement towards expertism is reflected in both the perceptions and organization of thought in economics. The classical notion of theory was one of a negative science. Theory was to trace the probable effects of a proposed policy and to warn against evils likely to flow from some policy adoption. The new theories of economics were, in contrast, to provide a positive guide. Theory was to be tested against the facts and amended (Church, 1974, p. 594).

The social role of the intellectual to provide direct advice to the policy makers is illustrated in the 'Wisconsin Idea'.[4] Developed during the progressive era at the turn of the twentieth century, the University of Wisconsin faculty were to provide usable intelligence in the service of the state, commerce and industry. As one of the many land-grant universities created in the mid-nineteenth century, the original university charter made reference to the practical importance of knowledge 'to commerce, industry, mining and agriculture' (Curti and Carstensen, 1949, p. 6). The 'Wisconsin Idea' was a normal and reasonable extension of this charter. Faculty from the University of Wisconsin headed and staffed major state government agencies, drafted the nation's first civil service laws and established the Legislative Reference Service to provide expert advice to the state law-makers. John Commons, a Professor of Economics at the University of Wisconsin who drafted the new Civil Service Law and then served as its Commissioner, said of the role of the economist, 'I learned ... that the place of the economist was that of advisor to the leaders, if they wanted him and not that of propagandist to the masses' (Church, 1974, p. 608).

The role of expert-advisor, however, did not occur without debate, conflict, and modification. Conservatives in Wisconsin reacted against the progressive policies of regulation that emerged from the collaboration of state and university. The commitment of the university to progressivism, as well, was never completely accepted within the institution (Hofstadter, 1963). Many university faculty were conservative. As important, there was a belief that the practical emphasis betrayed the ideals of classical scholarship, a tension that still exists within the university.

Academic Freedom and the Legitimacy of the Social Scientist As Expert

Establishment of the social scientist as expert to policy-makers required an institutionalization of the image of science serving the universal interests of the civil society. The principle of academic freedom provided one such mechanism. Emerging as a principle during the formative years of the modern American university, academic freedom represents a myth of the university as a 'market place of ideas' where different intellectual traditions can debate freely the major social, political, and economic ideas of a time, untrammelled by outside interests and pressures.

The idea of academic freedom received social prominence from social scientists who had studied in German universities. Many of the early and influential social scientists had received degrees from German universities and had been encouraged to consider the issue of academic freedom as a cornerstone of higher education (Herbst, 1965). The founding members of the social disciplines looked with favor on the independent existence that the natural sciences had established within European and American universities.

The American academics sought to modify the issue of academic freedom in light of certain differences between the American and German social systems. In German theory, academic freedom referred to freedom to teach the results of investigations free from interference from the outside. In return, professors were expected to give their services freely to the state. The German university was a state organ. Professors were civil servants bound by oath to support the state and its government. When professors engaged in partisan politics, it was often as apologists for national policies. German-trained American academics, such as Ely, rejected this stance. They accepted their role as educational reformers. The cornerstone of whatever they achieved, they believed, rested with their academic status and claim to scholarly, 'objective' rather than political knowledge.

The image of the scientist as serving the society as a whole and not particular interests is expressed by President Angell of Michigan in 1871. Angell defined the university as responding to the comprehensive needs of the civil society. Angell's inaugural address stated that there was a 'vital relation' between the state and the university in which the academy 'contemplates civil society as charged not merely with the negative work of reprocessing disorder and crime, but also with the higher positive office of promoting by all the proper means the intellectual and the moral growth of the citizen' (Bledstein, 1976, p. 324). The university was seen as serving the civil society; its knowledge was to be universal and neutral.

To accept this idea of 'untrammeled inquiry', no matter how noble, is to ignore the historical context in which the idea of academic freedom emerges as a viable principle in the social affairs of the university. The idea of academic freedom assumes importance in the late nineteenth century to reflect the argument that science was not a matter of opinion and belief but of research and investigation and that the institutions in which these efforts occurred would provide for the betterment of society as a whole.

It is also a context in which the social scientist as expert-to-policy-makers was seeking legitimacy. The professional expert wanted freedom to serve as a non-partisan advisor and mediator in public affairs. Academic freedom gave license to the professions to serve the politicians without fearing changes in the political parties that controlled government. Academic freedom is given credence by another dynamic. It is a period in which university administrators and faculty sought to establish their semi-autonomy in the social structure.

A function of academic freedom to give legitimacy to the expert-reformist tendency of social science and to the semi-autonomy of the university can be illuminated in the development of the University of Wisconsin. In the period following the American Civil War, the university sought to establish its autonomy in hiring, promoting and firing of professors. John Bascom, President of the University of Wisconsin between 1874 and 1887, sought to establish an autonomous institution of academic learning by asserting the role of the President over the Regents in appointment, promotion and dismissal. He came into conflict with orthodox religion, the business community and professional politicans. Bascom was forced to resign as a result of this conflict but set in motion a principle of administrative and faculty semi-autonomy.

The principle of faculty semi-autonomy received one of its most famous tests in the charge against Richard Ely, a nationally known professor of economics discussed earlier in relation to the formation of the American Economic Association. In 1894 Ely was charged by a Regent for believing in strikes and boycotts and, in his teaching and writing, for supporting socialism and anarchist doctrine. Ely denied these charges to a Regent committee established to investigate. He said that he had become more conservative and was explicitly anti-anarchist. The committee found Ely not guilty of aiding a local printers' strike or of boycotting a firm using non-union labor. Ely, however, never argued the right to teach free from outside restraint. Further, Ely was a close friend of the University President who sought to protect his colleague and friend.

One irony of the situation was that John Olin, who was denied promotion and tenure in the Law School because of his prohibitionist activities, suggested, with the approval of the University President, that the committee might indicate support for an instructor's right to teach what he believed to be true about the issues of the day. The report, adopted by the Regents, stated, in part:

> In all lines of academic investigation it is of the utmost importance that the investigator should be absolutely free to follow the indications of truth wherever they may lead. Whatever may be the limitations which trammel inquiry elsewhere we believe that the great state University of Wisconsin should ever encourage that continual and fearless sifting and winnowing by which a long truth can be found (University of Wisconsin Regents, 18 September 1894).

An independent existence would free the social scientist from the conflict that the partisan role had created and provide the authority necessary to influence policy. The claim to impartiality and an independent existence, according to historian Fredrick Jackson Turner, would enable the expert to:

> disinterestedly and intelligently mediate between contending interests. When the word 'capitalistic classes' and 'the proletariate' can be used and understood in America, it is surely time to develop such men, with the ideal of service to the State, who may help to break the force of these collusions, to find common grounds between the contestants and to possess the respect and confidence of all parties which are genuinely loyal to the best American ideals (in Hofstadter, 1963, p. 200).

The independent location of the university professor was to provide a vantage point to mediate between political groups and find harmony. In that sense, the university academic would be non-partisan. But it is also clear from the debates at the turn of the century that such independence did not mean a role that challenged vested interests.

Once established, however, the principle of academic freedom had unintended consequences of helping dissenting traditions. While enabling the expert to serve as a mediator to the powerful, it also served to legitimate, to some extent, dissent and critical social science. The legitimation of intellectual traditions critical of capitalism was supported by liberal-capitalist ideology in which competition and pluralism are important.

The legitimacy of dissent also became part of the folklore of universities and assumed significance in the development of intellectual traditions in America.[5] A plaque quoting the 1894 University of Wisconsin Regent report on 'sifting and winnowing' stands on the building housing the administration of the university and is quoted in times of challenge to legitimate expression of dissenting views within the academy. The University of Wisconsin was, for example, one of the only universities in America that Senator Joe McCarthy did not attack during the strident anti-communist rhetoric of the 1950s. McCarthy, a Wisconsin senator, was responsive to the powerful lobby that had developed in the state: almost every state governor, legislator and congressperson had graduated from the University and the 'Wisconsin Idea' created a strong constituency through state business, agricultural and professional stratas. As a result, 'dissenting' social scientists and thinkers of the period were able to find refuge at the University of Wisconsin, with the language of 'sifting and winnowing' used to legitimate the semi-autonomy of the academy.

The extent to which dissent and 'alien' ideologies can exist, however, is limited. Regents 'give' the prerogatives of academic freedom and do withdraw them from time to time (Smith, 1974). A large Eastern state university's Regents, for example, recently refused to hire a Marxist political scientist to the chair of its political science department after the faculty voted to offer the position. Further, indirect means to limit 'radicalism' exist. Out-of-state tuition was raised by the Wisconsin State legislature during the turmoil of the campus in the 1960s. The public argument was to make out-of-state students pay their 'fair share' since they were not tax-contributing members of the state-subsidized university. But underlying the 'fiscal debate' was a political one. The legislature sought to make it financially difficult for people from Chicago and New York to attend the university. These out-of-state people were visible leaders to the student protests of the 1960s. During this same period the Regents also sought to deny a salary raise recommended by the sociology department to one of its distinguished but politically active professors. With the 1894 Regent declaration providing a background to the debate, the pressure was for the Regents not to interfere and they rescinded their vote not to give the salary raise. The debate and power of the Regents, however, was not lost in the general university community.

New elements in the university have emerged to limit politically charged dissent. The pressure for conformity to formal and instrumental rationality today comes from administrators who use terms like 'fiscal crisis' to deny tenure to dissenting faculty who have otherwise received approval from the collegial structure of the university. Academic freedom is also restricted by the 'norms' of the community which delegitimate value-oriented knowledge and substantive rationality.

Arguments about universal knowledge, the interests of 'civil society' and academic freedom obscure the particular social and economic interests that are historically embedded in the social organization and research programs found in the university. The invention of academic freedom as an American principle was related to the legitimation of the new reform strategy of the social scientist, that of expert to the state. An unintended consequence was to legitimate the dissenting academy.

The Philanthropist and Usable Knowledge

The reformist element of social science has been considered in relation to changes in cultural and social sensibilities and occupational movements towards professionalization of knowledge. The role and location of the social scientist also need to be accounted for by considering the particular interventions of the new corporate capitalist. Prior to the late eighteenth century, the university was an elite institution. It trained the gentry and the ministry. Its ideal was classical education in which the individual was to be trained for intelligent service to society. The professional was conceived as one best trained in character and tradition rather than in useful knowledge (see, for example, Rothblatt's, (1976) discussion of Cambridge University). By the beginning of the twentieth century the American university gave focus to the production of 'usable' knowledge for the improvement of the commercial, industrial and governmental interests in society. Professional schools developed within universities to give further emphasis to this change. This movement towards practical university education was brought about through the philanthropy of businessmen (Curti and Nash, 1965).

Following the Civil War many businessmen saw the university as hostile to business interests. The new business elites had achieved their success with little schooling. They viewed the academy as having little immediate relation to the practical tasks central to life. The economic view was supported by views of the polity. The dominant perception of the citizen placed a premium on the judgment and common sense of the common man. The evangelical spirit in American religion also fostered an anti-intellectualism. Personal experience and revelation were to supersede the road to salvation offered by the rational, educated clergy (Hofstadter, 1963).

With the sponsorship of the philanthropist, education in the universities became more practical after the Civil War. Many nineteenth century enterpreneurs sought to transform existing institutions or to establish new ones that were responsive to the demands that these entrepreneurs defined. These demands were related, at first, to the technical complexity and sophistication of industry, later to production and distribution of products and, following World War II, more directly to corporate-state interests as the university became the central institution for research and development.

Many of the earlier philanthropists did not have a formal education and wanted to advance standards based on ability in practical affairs (Curti and Nash, 1965). In 1847 Abbott Lawrence, a wealthy textile manufacturer, sponsored a scientific school to teach practical sciences at Harvard. In a letter to Samuel Eliot, Treasurer of Harvard, Lawrence pointed out that the existing system of higher education in America was well suited to train theologians, doctors and lawyers, but there was no place to 'send those who intended to devote themselves to the practical applications of science ... the engineers, miners, machinist, mechanics.' He recognized that 'the application of science to the useful arts has changed ... the conditions and relations of the world.' Peter Cooper, an ironworks and telegraph magnate in New York City, established Cooper Union to provide night instruction for those who wanted education but could not obtain it through day instruction. Cooper's vision embodied the ideas and spirit of the Enlightenment to produce a superior human being who used reason and had a chance to realize his full potentiality. Educational opportunities would help an individual live a moral life. The proper means of this education, Cooper believed, lay in the practical rather than classical curriculum (Curti and Nash, 1965, p. 77).

Philantrophic foundations were created in this period to produce reform and innovation in the entire higher education system. The foundations sought to improve existing institutions and had a special-ized staff whose task was to 'give' the money. Rockefeller, for example, established the General Educational Board in 1902 to bring order and efficiency in education. Another purpose of the board, to which Rockefeller gave high priority, 'was to show socialists that capitalism was capable of promoting the greatest "general good"' (Curti and Nash, 1965, p. 215). The Board was able to shape specific policies and programs in higher education through its grants, such as the implementation of the Flexner recommendations in medical education. The Carnegie Corporation, the Ford Foundation and, in more recent years, corporate foundations have become vital in the continual reshaping that has marked the development of colleges and universities.

The influence of philanthropy was utilitarian. Training students for intelligent participation in society meant providing useful know-ledge. The movement towards practical instruction influenced the movement of social science into the university. The behavioral sciences received philanthropic support during their formative years as these sciences of social affairs seemed to offer the efficiency and practicality deemed so valuable.[6] These sciences were also deemed as useful in solving the social problems of industrial production (Noble, 1977).

The emphasis given to useful knowledge helps one to understand the rise of professional schools within the university. During the later part of the eighteenth century law, teaching and social work be-gan to appear as schools within the university. There seemed to be no contradiction between the practical orientation of research, the teaching of the helping occupations and the mandate of the university.

By the beginning of the twentieth century a shift in the meaning of professor had taken root. Prior to 1865 college professors did not monopolize the subject of individuals and society. The new pro-fessors, however, claimed social science was able to do this. Further, the problems of society were increasingly seen as related to providing useful knowledge.

The movement of utilitarian thought into the university was not straightforward and unidimensional but involved the tensions be-tween the older humanities and science, conflicting paradigms, and political interests outside the university.[7] The formation of the Wisconsin Alumni Research Foundation illustrates both these par-ticular interests that dominate and compete within a university setting. The Wisconsin Alumni Research Foundation (called WARF) was incorporated in 1925 as an independent organization to raise money to support research at the University of Wisconsin-Madison campus. The creation of the Foundation occurred in relation to two events (see Fred, 1973). One was the General Education Board giving a $12,500 grant to the University. The Progressive Wing of the Republican Party questioned and protested the grant as 'tainted' money because the Board was funded by John D. Rockefeller. The Regents rejected this money and then made a decision that the university would reject all outside donations. (These actions were rescinded in 1930.)

The second event in that year was a discovery of a method to prevent and cure rickets in animals. The professor who made the discovery sought to assign the patent to the University but the Regents rejected the idea as they had no mechanism to assign the royalties. The Regents then voted to create a non-profit sharing corporation from the capital given by alumni and friends of the university. The purpose of the foundation was to encourage scientific investigation and provide means to develop, apply and patent discoveries for public and commercial uses. Today WARF has an income of $33 million and distributes $6 million each year to faculty research and for building on the campus. In addition to patent royalties, the alumni association receives large donations from its business and professional members.

The Wisconsin Alumni Research Foundation illustrates the complex relationship between university, state and business. The trustees of the Foundation are major corporate and banking leaders in the country. Many of the funds of the Foundation go towards science and technology. Yet the means of distributing these funds are determined by a faculty committee that has no direct contact with the Foundation. The allocation of funds in the social sciences and humanities, some have argued, favors the humanities because of the composition of the committee; the social sciences are favored over the professional schools. In the everyday world of university life, the mandate of the Foundation to 'useful' research is mediated by the internal politics of university life.

The Social Location of the Academic: Intellectual to Intelligentsia?

The argument to this point is that academic disciplines have a strong reformist tendency which has evolved as the outcome of multiple transformations and traditions in society. This chapter has focused upon the interplay of cultural, social, and economic elements that influenced the professionalization of social science. The tradition of the university served to legitimate the social sciences as there was a shift in strategy from agitation to expertism to bring about social reform. The idea of academic freedom is seen within this social and cultural context. While it protects dissent, it also legitimates the new role of the social scientist as expert/reformer. Embedded in these themes is the view that the academic social scientist is a social type within the general dynamics of reproduction and transformation of society.

The university provided a plausible place for the state, business and the professional middle class to express their interests as those of the society as a whole. The academy captures the general social faith that one rises in life and career through merit, competence, discipline and control — elements basic to the American conceptions of achievement, success and democracy. The intellectual tradition of the university moves attention away from class structure as influencing observable diversity in standards of living and world view, focusing instead upon individual self-importance and individual attainment.

For the professional, the university provides a particular cultural sphere. In a society where there was no effective tradition of apprenticeship and no significant gentry, the university certifies spheres of cultural authority and autonomy through attention to prolonged disciplined schooling. The university is believed to be a source of non-partisan expertise and technical know-how. The theoretical base implied by university education makes the professional seem worthy of independence, respect and power. The professionals can use the sanctity of the university 'to define a total coherent system of knowledge with a precise territory, to control the intrinsic relationship of their subject by making it a scholarly as well as applied science and to root social existence in the inner needs and possibilities of documentable worldly processes' (Bledstein, 1976, p. 88).

The academic intellectual must also be viewed as involving a transformation of role. That role is that of the intelligentsia rather than intellectual. The concern is with service and production of 'useful' knowledge. The neutral researcher's strategic requirements and division of labor are adjusted to the official categories of demand and definition. While not monolithic and without tension, the ideology of neutrality has been successfully internalized into the consciousness of our research communities. The linkages between political agenda and research or between political reform movements and institutional practices are ignored. This uncritical subordination of research to the logic of rational authority is illustrated in contemporary efforts to study change and to evaluate educational programs. The story of these two occupational endeavors is the establishment of the priorities and constraints set by the general political process. It is to this new role of intelligentsia and its implications that we now turn.

Notes

1 In some ways, the cultural shift in causation was captured in the European Tonnies' (1887/1963) *Gemeinschaft* and *Gessellschaft*: community vs society. In communities, men and women were bound together by personal obligation, sacred values and patriarchal authority. Social relations and kinship relations were ends in themselves. The material and cultural shift to 'society' involved a reaction by Tonnies to the *laissez-faire* capitalism and liberalism and the promise seen of corporate capitalism and liberalism. Relations in societies were bound by their utility, an expression of 'rationality' and private individualistic ends. The shift from community to society involved new problems for political and social integration (see, for example, Schwendinger and Schwendinger, 1974).

2 See Bledstein (1976) for a discussion of the importance of structured space in America. Rothblatt's (1976) discussion of cultural change in England provides a backdrop to the emergence of sociability as a conception of culture.

3 I am only providing a sense of the dynamics and debates that underlie the work and challenges to the ASSA here. My intent is to point to the plural elements that helped to give rise to social science. (For a discussion of the ASSA, see Haskell, 1977.) These elements involve an interrelation of cultural, ideological and economic themes.

4 The University of Wisconsin-Madison is used as an example throughout this essay for two reasons. One, it has a special place in the development of the American university. Second, as a Faculty member I am acquainted with the university folklore and practice. For discussions of the history of this university, see Curti and Carstensen (1949) and Bogue and Taylor (1978).

5 I am not sure that the role of dissent is an established principle except in the major American research universities.

6 In contrast was the development of British empiricism as a policy mechanism of the state (see Abrams, 1968).

7 For an insightful discussion of this tension in one of the British elite universities, see Rothblatt (1968).

References

ABRAMS, P. (1968) *The Origins of British Sociology, 1834–1914*, Chicago, Ill., University of Chicago Press.

BLEDSTEIN, B. (1976) *The Culture of Professionalism, the Middle Class and the Development of Higher Education in America*, New York, Northon and Co.

BOGUE, A. and TAYLOR, R. (Eds) (1978) *The University of Wisconsin, One Hundred and Twenty-Five Years*, Madison, Wisc., University of Wisconsin Press.

CHURCH, R. (1965) 'The economists study society: Sociology at Harvard 1891–1902', in BUCK, P. (Ed.), *Social Science at Harvard, 1860–1920. From Inculcation to the Open Mind*, Cambridge, Mass., Harvard University Press.

CHURCH, R. (1974) 'Economists as experts: The rise of an academic profession in America 1870–1917 in Lawrence Stone', *The University in Society, Europe, Scotland and the U.S. from the 16th Century to the 20th Century*, Princeton, N.J., Princeton University Press, pp. 571–610.

CURTI, M. and CARSTENSEN, V. (1949) *University of Wisconsin, A History, 1848–1925*, Vol. 1. Madison, Wisc., University of Wisconsin Press.

CURTI, M. and NASH, R. (1965) *Philanthropy in the Shaping of American Higher Education*, New Brunswick, N.J., Rutgers University Press.

FRED, E. (1973) *The Role of the Wisconsin Alumni Research Foundation in the Support of Research at the University of Wisconsin*, Madison, Wisc., Wisconsin Alumni Research Foundation.

HASKELL, T. (1977) *The Emergence of Professional Social Science: The American Social Science Association and the Nineteenth-Century Crisis of Authority*, Urbana, Ill., University of Illinois Press.

HERBST, J. (1965) *The German Historical School in American Scholarship: A Study in the Transfer of Culture*, Ithica, N.Y., Cornell University.

HOFSTADTER, R. (1963) *Anti-Intellectualism in American Life*, New York, Alfred A. Knopf.

JENCKS, C. and RIESMAN, D. (1968) *The Academic Revolution*, New York, Doubleday and Co.

NOBLE, D. (1977) *America by Design, Technology and the Rise of Corporate Capitalism*, New York, Alfred A. Knopf.

OFFE, C. (1981) 'The social sciences: Contract research or social movements', in MCNALL, S. and HOWE G. (Eds) *Current Perspectives in Social Theory*, Vol. 2, Greenwich, Conn., JAI Press, pp. 31–9.

ROTHBLATT, S. (1968) *The Revolution of the Dons: Cambridge and Society in Victorian England*, New York, Basic Books.

ROTHBLATT, S. (1976) *Tradition and Change in English Liberal Education, an Essay in History and Culture*, London, Faber and Faber.

SCHWENDINGER, H. and SCHWENDINGER, J. (1974) *The Sociologists of the Chair: A Radical Analysis of North American Sociology, 1883–1922*, New York, Basic Books.

SMITH, D. (1974) *Who Rules the Universities? An Essay in Class Analysis*, New York, Monthly Review Press.

Chapter 6

Motion As Education Change: The Misuse and Irrelevancy of Two Research Paradigms

A belief in reform is a consistent and powerful theme underlying our culture. Its strength lies, in part, in the image of reform which synthesizes a commanding social belief that institutions and societies grow, change and progress in some orderly and continuous fashion. Reform suggests the responsiveness, benevolence and control of change in our social institutions. This belief in reform and change is a continual theme of Western thought, emerging from ancient Greece, reinterpreted in the Christian view of social order, and secularized by social science. As argued in the previous chapter, the theme of reform is embedded in the organization of American social science.

The processes by which social and political commitments to change are realized have undergone a drastic transformation since the mid-twentieth century. Reform and change have become the pre-rogative of the professionals who seemingly possess the technical knowledge to control the movement of social affairs. In the past attempts to alter social institutions in America were due to the combined efforts of lay, business, political and professional interests. In recent years the problem of reform has increasingly become a problem of the expert who, with the tools of science, identifies problems of institutional life, designs the programs to solve those problems, and evaluates and prescribes the remedies. This new social style in redressing problems has professionalized reform, taking on a characteristic of an enterprise that has 'a self starting capacity of its own ... the machinery began to think for itself' (Moynihan, 1969, pp. 21–2). The strategy of reform by a depoliticized social science has become so much a part of our tradition that we often lose sight of the social roots of our customs and theories.

The role of the professional expert has a dual and conflicting social interest when focusing upon the problem of change. There is the activity to define and find solutions to the problems of institutional life. Many believe that the scientific expert creates the knowledge and conditions that harness the uncontrollable events of our lives. The knowledge of science is seen as providing for a social reconstruction of institutional life. At the same time, the professionalization of reform gives status and privilege to a number of converging social interests. The intellectual qua expert maintains his position by the continual effort to find the errors of our ways and to offer the routes to salvation for a people who can never obtain perfection. The science of institutional change also calls forth a mechanism of legitimation: the 'sciences' project images of responsive, modern and efficient institutions.

The promise and pathologies of the sciences of change need to be placed against the actual assumptions and organization of knowledge. If we focus upon explanations of social and educational change, we find a particular cognitive style and range of assumptions from those who adopt the professional-expert strategy. The styles of thought are borrowed from the empirical-analytic and symbolic sciences. These styles of thought, it will be argued, misappropriate those sciences in ways that enable social order and stability to become paramount.

How general paradigmatic assumptions are transformed in educational practices to reform is the concern of this chapter. Two approaches to change will be considered. One draws upon a conception of change as management, sometimes called the 'center-to-periphery' approach. A second focuses upon people negotiating to identify appropriate courses of action — the problem-solving approach to change. In each instance, limitations and assumptions specific to the approaches will be discussed. After examining each approach, however, I will argue that the surface differences in the two change orientations in fact hide similar assumptions about expertise, social structure and consensus. Each restricts change by organizing bias to legitimate priorities, status, and privileges within existing institutions.

Underlying this study of change models and the following chapter on evaluation is a historical concern. The early twentieth century social science strategy of understanding and mass education has shifted to one of the professional-expert to policy-makers. That change in reform strategy has been so internalized into the folklore of science that the relation between the intellectual and social movements is lost. It is accepted as common-place that studies of change and evaluation are 'neutral'. Yet these models respond to the agenda set by the political process and the particular publics that have the power to give definition to problems of social amelioration. The notions and assumptions of the center-to-periphery, problem-solving approaches and evaluation 'make sense' when placed in relation to these larger social conditions.

Center-to-Periphery: Change As the Adoption of Research

The most important concept of change in American political decision-making has been the center-to-periphery approach. It assumes that universal, logical and efficient procedures exist for the defining and organizing of change. These procedures can be identified through some centralized research and development effort. Once identified, the procedures are provided to schools for adoption. Advocates suggest that the approach can close the gap between research and practice as well as improve relationships between the research community and schools.

The center-to-periphery approach is generally defined as having four distinct stages (Havelock, 1970).

1 Initial *research* identifies, conceptualizes and tests ideas without any direct concern for practice;
2 *Development* moves the research findings into problems of engineering and 'packaging' of a program that would be suitable for school use;
3 This is followed by *dissemination* (diffusion) to tell, show and train people about the uses and possibilities of the program;
4 The final state is *adoption/installation*. The change becomes an integral and accepted part of the school system.

The Research, Development, Dissemination and Adoption (RDDA) approach assumes a rational sequence that accounts for all phases of the change process. Further, the procedures are deemed appropriate for any group or for any purpose. As one author argues, this approach provides 'a classification scheme of processes related to, *and necessary for*, change in education' (Wronski, 1969, p. 278, my emphasis). In a different context, it is said, 'The principles of planned change are applicable to the adoption of any new ideas, practices or product' (Hahn, 1975, p. 135).

The approach suggests neutrality and universality. Flow charts are constructed to give apparent precision to the logical characteristics of the organization. Engineering words are borrowed from cybernetic theory or organizational language to suggest an orderliness and tidiness to the process. Modules, inputs/outputs, dissemination, diffusion become part of a language that suggests a schema of order, precision, and clarity.

Research efforts have developed to assess the factors influencing implementation of and impediments to the center-of-periphery approach. These include teacher surveys to assess knowledge and commitment to the proposed innovation, data about financial allocations and time provided by a school district to learn about the reform program, or assessment of the actual use of materials to determine degree of implementation. The emphasis upon the degree of implementation is exemplified by the Levels of Use instrument developed at the University of Texas (Hall *et al.*, 1975). Six levels of use are identified: from non-use (where the user has no knowledge of the innovation), to integration (combining existing efforts with innovation), to renewal (level 6 in which the user re-evaluates the quality of the use of innovations and seeks major modification). The Levels of Use instrument is to enable the planner is to determine whether the innovation is used with fidelity. While research has suggested that there must be some situational flexibility to account for adaptation as well as adoption, the Levels of Use implies a continuous pattern of use and adaptation, as well as adoption.

The language of implementation and impediments suggests that a problem of institutional change can be regulated through rational thought. There is a belief in science as a means to organize and control social and natural phenomena. This belief emerged strongly in the late 1960s to guide the newly formed initiatives of the federal government to improve schooling. A former associate commissioner of education, Leon Lessinger (1970), argued that engineering techniques can make school *managers* operate efficiently and effectively. Hendrik D. Gideonese (1968), of the same Office of Education and writing for a newly created federal educational research and development center, spoke of the need to apply scientific and technological knowledge to educational practice. Drawing on analogy to agriculture, space, medicine, and industrial research and development, Gideonese believed that 'the degree to which the policy questions arise in educational research can, must, or ought to be considered as a subset of those which arise for science as a whole.' Science, he continued, is to develop a model that could coordinate theory and practice into a total research effort.

The conception of science that underlies the center-to-periphery approach is borrowed from the paradigmatic commitments of the empirical-analytic sciences (see Chapter 2). The borrowed belief is that a science is concerned with the appropriate application of technique to realize defined goals under given conditions. Theories of change, as theories of learning, are to be oriented towards appropriate means for achieving some pre-established criterion. The purpose of the science of change is to explain, order, and analyze the components without judging their final normative appropriateness. *Change theories assume a neutrality towards the 'product' being introduced or the organizational goals.* The professional-scientist is to provide 'objective' knowledge to be used by policy-makers. With this assumption of purpose are other paradigmatic commitments, such as seeking universal and formalized knowledge, adopting the notion of social system in which interacting variables can be studied as distinct and independent entities, and the disinterest of science to the goals of the system.

While the empirical-analytic sciences have offered a valuable perspective to social and psychological research, their incorporation into planned change creates a new set of dynamics that the empirical-analytic paradigm was not developed for. The empirical-analytic sciences are best suited to direct attention to rules by which social order and stability are achieved. Creating taxonomies that give the appearance of change (such as the steps of RDDA model) does not alter the assumptions or purpose of the paradigm but creates its own irony. It is no longer to understand basic human behaviors or regularities but to serve organizational purposes to manage our social conditions. The resulting analyses of change are at best of motion and activity within stable, unchanging systems. This can be illustrated in the evolution of one of the educational research and development centers sponsored by the federal government during the 1960s and 1970s.

To the Periphery: An Example

During the mid-1960s and under a grant from the US Office of Education, one of seven national research and development centers was created at the University of Wisconsin-Madison. The purpose of the centers was to coordinate theory and practice in ways that would make a substantial and lasting impact upon schooling. Through proper administration and effective organization, it was believed that institutional goals could be efficiently achieved. The particular focus of the center in Wisconsin was 'to improve the efficiency of cognitive learning and translate that knowledge into instructional material, and procedures.'[1] A variety of curriculum experts, behavioral scientists, communication specialists, and school district people met to develop plans for research and programs. The direction of the center was to provide for school change by increasing efficiency through the application of a science of management. As did the early twentieth century social scientists, the center's scientists conceived of the reformer's role as providing useful knowledge to those in policy-making positions.

The center's planners proceeded to develop a comprehensive plan by identifying logical and hierarchical aspects of learning and school organization. One center task was to identify and order a hierarchical scheme by which children could learn concepts and skills efficiently. The rationale and instructional schemes took for granted the existing definitions of what should be taught — the goals of the system. For example, it did not consider why certain concepts should be learned by children but concentrated on the ways of organizing and sequencing concepts that have already been chosen.

The science of instruction was behaviorism, focusing upon knowledge and skills that had a clear and measurable definition of mastery. The science of organization was drawn from the application of 'systems' thought. Systems analysis came into vogue in the late 1950s as a mechanism to systematically organize complex phenomena into logical and controllable variables. Borrowed from military and business planning, schools were 'seen' as interrelated organizational variables that are functional to school outcomes (see Romberg, 1968). The idea of systems was to provide a logical framework for identifying and interrelating objectives and groups of variables thought to be effective in learning. Such a system involved identifying goals and a management procedure that would guide student interaction with materials, equipment, teachers, and physical facilities of the school, and to monitor the abilities of students to achieve the appropriate behaviors through assessment procedures.

The search for a mechanism to identify efficient methods of learning led to the center's first instructional innovation, the unitized school. The school was divided into larger groups (units) of 100–150 children, four to five teachers and teacher-aides. The ideas of units emerged from the methodology of the psychology-based educational researchers. The researchers were interested in individual differences and the problem of inquiry was to identify how to group pupils effectively to manage their progress towards predetermined curriculum objectives. The means of research was to create a large enough sample so variables could be manipulated adequately and controlled. The unit organization responded to this experimentation approach. *Thus, what was created as a research procedure to gain understanding became an assumption for organizing social relations in schools.*

Later, the unit organization was combined with other administrative elements. In addition to the unit, there was an instructional programming model, which provided seven steps or procedures to organize and evaluate the efficiency of children's mastery of concepts and skills; a differentiated staff (headteacher, teachers, aides, principal) to monitor more efficiently children's progress; and external support groups for the program, such as state educational agencies and teacher education programs.

The justification of each element of the system was to offer efficiency to the system. Klausmeier, the leading advocate of the program, argued that the Instructional Unit '[m]ore vigorously than would be expected in the usual classroom teaching situation,... to get each child to learn as fast and as well as he can, to remember what he learns and to use it in achieving individually and socially, useful goals' (1966, p. 3).

By the late 1960s outside pressures brought the center to pull together the different research and development projects into a single program called *Individually Guided Education*. The name was chosen after much discussion: it emphasized the importance of individual differences and the word, 'Guide', suggested that the Wisconsin program was different from the Individually *Prescribed* Instruction developed at the University of Pittsburgh Research and Development Center, a center with which people at Wisconsin felt they were in competition. The choice of name also reflected a relationship that the center had with the Individually Guided Education program sponsored by the Kettering Foundation. Originally the two groups worked together but soon found that the ideological differences were too great. The Kettering Foundation work focused upon strategies of problem-solving to increase teacher and student participation in decision-making, adopting a version of the progressive rhetoric of the previous years for curriculum reform. The Wisconsin Research and Development Center gave more attention to outcomes, learning mastery, and social efficiency for educational reform.

The crystallization of Individually Guided Education into a specific reform system for elementary schools occurred for a variety of reasons. One was the desire of the center researchers to make their knowledge accessible to schools. While the rhetoric of social science had shifted from reform to technical advice, and this later usage is clear in the formulation of problems of the Wisconsin center, the reform purpose was still important. Individually Guided Education, according to one of the leading developers of the program, is to alter the conservative inhibiting conditions of school that prevented teachers from adapting instruction to the needs of individual students (Klausmeier, 1977, p. 3). The reform, while in essence moral, ethical, and social, was to seem technical, a shift that represents the general rhetoric of contemporary social science.

Other factors external to the center influenced the crystallization of the program. Federal agencies that sponsored research and development argued that the knowledge be usable. Federal agencies wanted tangible outcomes that could be submitted as evidence of the success of federal expenditures to congressional committees and to accounting officers in the Office of Management and Budget. By the early 1970s the work of the centers could no longer be presented as 'in progress'; products had to be created to meet the accounting criteria of the federal agencies. These accounting criteria, it needs to be noted, were often procedural: how many reports were completed and on time, or what were cost overruns.

The center's response to school implementation was to design a four-phase strategy: *awareness* of Individually Guided Education (for example, a regional coordinator or center person would come to talk to school staff to gain commitment to the program); *changeover* to Individually Guided Education in which technologies of the program become incorporated; *refinement* of practices in schools using the program and *institutionalization* or acceptance.

While the logic of change seems straightforward and rational, one must realize that the actual development of the change program did not proceed in a clear, logical manner. The unit organization, for example, evolved not for pedagogical reasons but to provide university researchers with a large enough sample for their studies. The curriculum reading project used in the program originated not from research but from teachers' requests for the development of a management scheme to order the numerous objectives that they were told were important. The development of an implementation procedure, as suggested earlier, emerged from pressures external to the project. The name of the project, Individually Guided Education, was created amidst a competitive setting between centers. By the 1980s the name and emphasis of the center shifted as different pressures from Washington and within the center emerged, with a current focus on school and psychological diversity. The shift, however, was not a shift in its utilitarian mission.

The Individually Guided Education example maintains central assumptions of the center-to-periphery approach. Change is defined as a rational, logical sequence, subject to analysis and implementation through a science of management. There is a consistent faith that a systems approach can be applied to the principles of educational psychology, curriculum objectives, and school variables in ways that can identify and arrange an appropriate sequence for efficient learning. The elements of order and change are believed to be clear, distinct, and taxonomical in nature. The reform program, however, introduced a certain sophistication into the approach: it provided mechanisms for working with local districts and some flexibility in the manner of adoption. This sophistication was introduced as a problem of management engineering: the process is believed to be a neutral, non-ideological intervention appropriate for all elementary schools. Further, the research program was tied to the problem of development: the fundamental assumption was that useful knowledge for decision-makers could be contributed.

Some Uses and Abuses of the Metaphor of Center-to-Periphery

The center-to-periphery approach views schooling metaphorically as an organism with certain patterns of growth and development. This metaphor underlies Western thought from the Greeks through modern, social-evolutionary theory (Nisbet, 1969). The attributes of the metaphor are that change

1 has directionality,
2 is cumulative,
3 is irreversible,
4 has stages (birth, growth, decay), and
5 has purpose.

The power of the metaphor is that it synthesizes several complex units of thought into one commanding image of change. Its limitation is that the metaphor was developed to provide broad sweeps of history in which there is no time or space. One can talk about the movement of societies from less complexity to greater complexity focusing upon changes in transportation, religious conceptions, or government in a taxonomic fashion as if time and place are not important.

The taxonomies of change, however, are irrelevant when applied to particular places and specific times. The seeming clarity of the imagery of change in the taxonomy of RDDA or the Research and Development models, in fact, obscures the actual conduct of the situations in which change is to be applied. The development of the Individually Guided Education program is a case in point.The research effort was to be organized free from the constraints of practical considerations. In fact, the early research efforts of Individually Guided Education were tied to cooperative ventures with teachers in schools. The categories of innovation, improvement and change were more often defined in relation to existing categories and agenda in the school than by any outside consideration of what was to be changed. The development of a management reading curriculum, for example, originated with teachers confused with all the different objectives and tasks associated with the teaching of reading. The teachers asked the researchers to develop a logical order to those tasks to make their job manageable. The reading program was a response to the teachers' request, creating a management system which included ordering reading instruction into hierarchical and measurable tasks. As the program became used, however, the purpose of using the management as a tool for instruction shifted subtly as many teachers defined taxonomies as the task of reading itself. Labeling the initial phase as 'research' filtered out the dynamics, implications, and consequences of the process.

Focusing upon taxonomic qualities imposes a different limitation when one considers the meaning of the reform program as it was realized in schools. The social world does not exist as purely logical or rational actions as envisioned in the change models. Schools are dense social situations in which different values and interests compete. There is no correspondence between the panorama of evolutionary change (awareness, changeover, refinement) and the empirical world. As programs such as Individually Guided Education are brought into schools, their technologies are realized in ways that contain important elements of randomness, struggle, and situational persistence. A study on the Oregon R & D Center's attempt to introduce a rational management scheme into a school district is replete with examples of the non-rational, chaotic and political aspects that influence the meaning of the reform effort (Wolcott, 1977). The manner in which the technologies of Individually Guided Education were incorporated into the ongoing institutional contexts of schools suggests that the reform was given priorities and values different from the reformers' intent (Popkewitz *et al.*, 1982). The reform technologies gave credibility and legitimacy to schools which had different patterns of work, conceptions of knowledge, and professional ideologies. The taking-for-granted of systems goals worked to legitimate the very institutional arrangements to be changed.

To apply abstract taxonomies to historically situated problems is to reify the social situation. The dynamics of interaction, social communication, and institutional values are obscured. The abstract principles of change have no concrete meaning or particular bearing. As important, the model takes for granted the structure of the institution by declaring itself neutral to a system's goals and purposes. There is no conception of social structure by which one is to relate the possibilities and effects of change. In its place, the procedures of reform/change are considered as change itself. One does a survey of perceptions or use of the technologies. Observations are made to assess levels of use. Change becomes the implementation of procedures to make established procedures more efficient. Motion and activity become a substitute for change.

Problem-Solving: Democratization of Change?

Partially in response to research which focuses upon the local school district adaptation of innovation and partially in response to a political belief in the importance of local participation and control, a 'problem-solving' approach has emerged recently to organize American federal and local efforts for change. It is argued that the center-to-periphery approach cannot provide the best solutions to improving school. The identification and development of innovation should lie with the people who are involved in the concrete situations. Lois-Ellin Datta of the National Institute of Education (1980), for example, notes that there is a rapid shift to 'local problem-solving and mutual adaptation as the dominant metaphors for educational change' (p. 101). This shift, she continues, is related to federal funding policy in which most dissemination money in the US Office of Education and National Institute of Education supports problem-solving approaches.

The shift to local problem-solving is advocated in a much heralded four-year study of 'change-agent' programs, the Rand study of *Federal Programs Supporting Educational Change* (Berman and McLaughlin, 1978). The research focused upon factors influencing the acceptance or rejection of the innovations in a school system. The evaluation sought to understand organizational processes that were related to adaptation, continuation, and institutionalization of change. The last was technically defined, referring to the incorporation and acceptance of projects' goals at both classroom and district levels after outside support ended. The research suggests that the content of the project is less important for success than mutual adaptation (in which both the project and setting were changed) and a broad-based support among district and teachers.

These conclusions led the researchers to argue that federal efforts focus upon the *process* of change and not its outcome. They note that the educational method (individualization, curriculum revision, general enrichment) or outcome seems less important than the nature and quality of involvement at each stage of the change process.

> [f]ederal efforts to improve the change process within school districts should take precedence over their past concerns with improving educational products; that federal evaluators should expect and encourage the adaptation of programs to suit local needs; that the federal government should promote local institutional development in addition to more targeted project approaches; and that federal legislation should establish ways to provide more differentiated and flexible support to school districts. In short, these premises suggest a shift in the federal role toward the process of educational change (Berman and McLaughlin, 1978, p. x).

This process approach involves a 'problem-solving manner'. Federal change efforts are to enable local districts to 'identify their needs and then seek solutions to them'. Teachers, it is believed, are closest to the problems and the process and therefore in the best position 'to suggest remedies for perceived deficiencies' (p. 29).

The problem-solving approach assumes neutrality as to the direction, purpose, and outcome of change, focusing instead upon the process of change. The school staff is to identify problems within their specific context, design solutions to those problems and, in the process, become trained in procedures for future problem-solving. As with the center-to-periphery approach, there is a deliberate and sequential order or stages to the problem-solving process. Paul and Lipham (1976) identify a seven-stage model guided by a change agent which includes:

1   developing a need for change which includes becoming aware that there are problems and the desire for external help;
2   establishing relationships with an outside organization, such as a curriculum consultant or state educational agency; a

good collaborative arrangement is considered essential for the success of a project;

3 diagnosing the problem which suggests a basis for alternative solutions;

4 examining alternative goals and establishing plans of action;

5 transforming plans to change efforts;

6 generalizing and stabilizing the change, including gaining organizational consistency and providing tangible benefits;

7 achieving a terminal relationship where the outside expert is no longer needed (Paul and Lipham, 1976, p. 234).

Another interpretation of the problem-solving approach is provided by Goodlad (1975). Goodlad suggests that we should view a school as a natural system in which the change agent helps develop the system to become 'self-renewing', that is, sensitive to its own needs for productive survival and capable of utilizing resources effectively to that end (p. 96). The process of self-renewal is described as DDAE: 'a staff process of engaging in *dialogue* about school issues and problems, selecting certain specific and making *decisions* regarding *actions* to be taken, and then taking these actions, with subsequent *evaluation*' (p. 97, my emphasis). While recognizing that no process is content-free, the model does not promote any innovation. The process of reform is 'essentially apolitical, seeking to define a better life in a better world.'

Problem-solving relies upon a change agent as does the center-to-periphery approach. The change agent, however, is now located within the organization. Its purpose is to interest those within the school to promote change. The wise change agent, suggests Goodlad, reduces anxiety about the change by recognizing that the innovation be designed and explained as a way of performing the basic functions of the school better. Stressing of the 'new' as tied to better ways of doing established things is to maintain support and stability.

A research program is used to support the efficacy of problem-solving change (as with the center-to-periphery model). In the high DDAE schools, for example, there is high professionalism, high teacher sense of efficacy, and high teacher morale. More cooperative teaching arrangements, more friendship networks among teachers, and more task-oriented communication networks among teachers seemed to exist in high than in low DDAE schools (Goodlad, 1975, p. 135).

The assumptions of the problem-solving approach can be understood more clearly by considering its assumptions as related to the paradigmatic commitments of a symbolic science. There is a recognition that the social and political dynamics of a situation influence the manner in which change is to be designed and implemented. Negotiation, face-to-face interactions, and language are seen as essential to how people define expectations about appropriate and plausible behaviors. The problem-solving approach draws upon this view of science, placing emphasis upon the development of a consensus of rules that govern and direct the use of social categories. The shift in focus from the center-to-periphery model does not mean a rejection of the procedural and neutral role of the change process. There is an assumption that discourse can be treated independently of the institutional norms, beliefs, and patterns in which the language is embedded. Rather than making organizations more efficient, the purpose of a change model is to improve the conditions for communication.

The Theme of Problem-Solving: An Example

The empirical functioning of a problem-solving approach can be explored through a study of a middle school effort to develop an individualized instructional program (Popkewitz, 1978). The program emerged out of a collaborative arrangement between a middle school and an R & D Center. Where the Individually Guided Education program developed along a center-to-periphery approach, this program sought a participatory 'process' approach. The project researchers, school administrators, and teachers jointly planned to implement and to evaluate a school-wide effort to individualize instruction. The project called for the school staff to think critically about alternative educational experiences for secondary schools.

The project designers considered their change model as neutral to outcome. The process of involvement, participation, and communication seemed as essential as the identification of a problem. In the development of the school problem-solving approach, for example, the definition of individualized instruction was kept ambiguous. This was done to permit the school staff to develop their own definitions and organizational pattern. It was assumed that school reform must be based upon a staff competent to initiate and sustain a dialogue about instruction. Further, there was a commitment to an 'interactive model' in which teachers, administrators, parents, and students participated in the making of decisions.

The implementation of the problem-solving process began with a workshop prior to the start of the school year. The workshop was designed to have the staff obtain a consensus on the educational purpose of the change process. A 'hierarchy of purpose' was constructed in which specific purposes ('to develop communication channels between parents and staff') were placed at the bottom and abstract ones at the top. From these different levels of purpose, the staff chose one abstract purpose to guide their school-wide individualization strategies. That purpose was: 'to develop a school program which develops specific competencies based upon individual needs and interests.' The agreement on a single, general purpose was to provide a collective commitment and criterion for later decision-making.

After discussing possible alternative strategies, five tasks related to the general purpose were identified by the staff, time lines constructed for the school year, and groups organized to implement the reform. The task forces were: creation of an Uninterrupted Sustained Silent Reading (USSR) period; a flexible schedule to provide greater individualization; a club period in which students could pursue their own interests; improvement of parent-teacher conferences; and a teacher-advisor system in which closer personal relationships could be developed in school. During the first two-thirds of the year each task force of four to six teachers and one or two parents met after school to discuss procedures for implementation. Towards the end of the year most of the task forces had implemented their projects.

Institutional Bias and Limitations in Problem-Solving

The substantive meaning and implications of the change tasks need to be considered within the institutional structure of the school. The activities existed within certain norms, beliefs, and patterns of conduct that gave definition to teaching, childhood, and learning. The background assumptions of the change model posited biases for decision-making. To understand the social function of the various task forces is to relate the reform activities to the underlying rules and beliefs that guided school conduct.

As in the center-to-periphery approach, there is an assumption that change is a neutral activity brought about through the application of efficient procedures. The procedures are thought of as universal, devoid of any reference to the specific goals and purposes of organizational life. While one may want to argue that the planners' intent is to give attention to central issues of schooling, there is no guidance to distinguish between issues that confront institutional life and those which have only administrative potency. In the everyday world of social conduct, this procedural focus has important consequences. The density of institutional life makes it unlikely that substantive issues about priorities, values and beliefs will be made problematic.[2] The biases of school communication and work limit decision-making to an administrative arena in which consensus and stability assume importance.

The conservative quality of the problem-solving approach is evident in the functioning of the middle school task forces. The strategy to maintain consensus was built upon a fragile sense of commitment. The workshop purposes were abstract statements that provided emotive symbols to condense the general feelings, hopes, and desires of many associated with school. The abstractness, however, permitted teachers with diverse beliefs and practices to accept the task forces without feeling contradictions. As the task forces began their actual work, teachers recognized ideological divisions within the school and chose strategies that did not challenge the ongoing priorities and relationships. The activities of the task forces, contrary to the project designers' intent, maintained consensus by reducing substantive dialogues and possible conflict.

The activities of change became procedures to make existing practices seem reasonable. The advisor groups were to help teachers develop better student attitudes towards 'what teachers were doing, to try harder, to do better.' They were also to help create greater psychological satisfaction, while reducing vandalism, disregard for authority, and violations of school rules. The groups' activities did not involve rethinking the nature of interactions in school or developing any sustained dialogue between teacher and students. The emphasis on consensus also left unchallenged existing school organizational biases in which order and control took precedence over educational goals. No individualization occurred.

The teachers' acceptance of the reform program had little to do with the program's goals. The district had declining enrolments. Administration and teachers saw the change process as giving evidence of the innovative quality of the staff and thereby providing arguments against possible cutbacks. The program also provided the middle school with an identifiable focus and credibility with the district administrators. This was important as the teachers saw themselves as not having the same programatic coherence and esteem as the senior high school and thus not being able to marshal the same force of argument in crucial budget and allocation discussions. The task forces were to legitimate the school program to the larger professional community.

While teachers publicly expressed certain general sentiments about improving the quality of life for students in school, the situational language and practices of the reform indicated a specific, institutionally related interest. Change could be administrative. It would provide mechanisms to improve the psychological satisfaction of students to the established school priorities and to serve to legitimate the staffing arrangement and personnel within the larger school district. The issue to emerge from the problem-solving process was how to reduce strain and tension within the organization.

Some Uses and Abuses of a Metaphor: Problem-Solving

The institutional effects of the problem-solving approach direct attention to certain limitations of the model. The approach is drawn from a commitment to a democratic political process in which people are involved in decision-making. The irony of the problem-solving approach, however, is its depoliticization of that process. Management and procedures become central. The problem is redrawn as 'technical' assistance to provide the expertise to enable a school to 'start where it is'. Ignored are the underlying patterns of belief and value that give organization to a school. Bachrach and Baratz (1970), for example, argue that all organizations are a 'mobilization of bias' which allows certain types of decisions to be considered legitimate while others are filtered out as potential arenas of choice. Some teachers in the middle school, for example, did want to focus upon student alienation as a curriculum problem but realized that the background assumptions of the school's 'problem-solving' gave credibility only to problems of student control and to a professional perspective that defines the child's mind as a receptacle to be filled. As a result, concerns about existing priorities in curriculum and organization become muted and non-issues.

The problem of 'problem-solving' does not distinguish between subjective and objective interests (Popkewitz, 1979). Subjective interests refer to a psychological state in which people express preference or opinion. The rituals of committee meetings, the use of a 'needs assessment', or political elections ostensibly provide a mechanism for people to express their subjective preferences and interests. These subjective interests exist in relation to objective interests. Our beliefs, feelings, and preferences are, in part, formed in relation to the horizons in which we live. Our participation in institutional settings creates ways of 'seeing' our daily situations. The meanings attached to our subjective interest lie in the feelings and attitudes generated as people engage in institutional patterns of conduct. Problem-solving emphasizes the subjective interests without providing any means for linking the subjective feelings to the rules, meanings, and power-relations that underlie our objective conditions.

The subjective interest of the problem-solving approach is related to perspectives in industrial psychology and sociology. It is interesting to note that the purpose of these subdisciplines was to coordinate the advances in scientific technology with the human elements of the technological enterprise (see Noble, 1977). Human relations approaches evolved, at first under the leadership of Harvard Business School Professor Elton Mayo, to bring a stable correspondence between the forces of production and social relations. By drawing from these industrial disciplinary perspectives, the problem-solving approach maintains a dichotomy between the work employed and the processes of production. The dichotomy obscures those relationships and leads to a surface identification of problems and solutions. One could compare the 'problem-solving' approach to that of Paulo Friere in which there is explicit recognition of institutional elements which give definition to issues to be entertained in the dialogue. The problem-solving approach provides no direction for defining an issue or problem except subjective feelings.

The belief that school staffs can identify and plan to alter their own assumptions and power arrangements through a focus upon process seems to belie experience. Schools are complex social contexts. There is little time for critical reflection. Their social and political values are often anti-intellectual, anti-democratic and anti-educational.[3] These values are built into the way curriculum is defined, the social organization of classrooms, and administrative theories of schooling. Because of the implicit quality of these values, they are psychologically compelling to participants and the publics of schooling. To consider change as process without form is to lose sight of the substance that underlies reform and to conserve what is to be changed.

The Coming Together: Technical Change As Ideology

The center-to-periphery and problem-solving approaches seem to be different paths to school change. The problem-solving model shifts from the logical considerations of the organization to the systems of communication. It is to provide a process that is to enable people to judge what is worthwhile and to be changed in a situation. Both approaches recognize that change may not be linear, sequential, and rational, but assumes that rational models 'may be highly useful for identifying potentially critical issues for encouraging change, for starting a change process and for establishing points during the change process' (Paul, 1977).

The differences in approach disappear as the underlying assumptions of the two approaches are examined. The center-to-periphery and problem-solving approaches rely upon a belief that change is a managed process to be organized by a change agent. The role of the problem-solving change agent is 'helping and training' through 'a face-to-face basis in order to promote two-way communication'. The approaches also rely upon an assumption of a 'system' which defines the ongoing social relations in schools as an entity that exists outside political, cultural, and social processes. The center-to-periphery and problem-solving approaches assume a neutrality as to systems goals that in fact obscures the values and implications of schooling as a social institution. In both instances, the structure of institutions is left unscrutinized as procedures for change become central. This obscuring of social conditions and relationships introduces elements of ideology into the science of change.

Change As Motion within a System

Underlying the center-to-periphery and problem-solving approaches is a view of the world as a 'system'. The notion of system contains a set of assumptions and presuppositions that provide background rules for the development of change models and their subsequent analysis and interpretation. It assumes that any social field can be subdivided into constituent elements and that each element can be viewed as an independent 'system'. For example, one can look at the classroom 'system' as separate from the school and social/political system, or at the teaching system as analytically separable from learning. Once isolated, the idea of system directs attention to the placement of all structures, elements, and practices into some conceptual or intellectual place that contributes to the harmony and stability of the system. The idea of system involves a research assumption of neutrality towards the goals and purposes of the organization. The task of identifying and analyzing system elements is to increase the efficiency of function in the organization.

The assumptions of 'systems' have certain implications for the consideration of change. Change is the manipulation of the internal mechanisms of the systems to ensure continual consensus and legitimacy of the organization; for example, change becomes a way of increasing the efficiency and functionality of teaching or learning. As the boundaries of inquiry are prescribed to the boundaries (and assumptions) of the existing system, the act of change becomes motion and activity within the ongoing relationships of the school. The social outcomes are to conserve the *status quo* by creating an illusion that activity is change.

The implications of 'systems' thought become apparent when we examine discussions of change. Wronski (1969, p. 278), for example, explicitly adopts a systems perspective by posing the following questions to guide people in considering school changes: 'In what ways are changes generated in a social system?' 'What forms of social organization facilitate or impede change?' 'What kind of personal factors dispose one to accept or reject change?' The strategy for answering these questions is to illuminate how the parts interrelate to maintain the ongoing consensus or equilibrium of the whole.

Conflict, within this perspective, becomes 'tension-management' (Wronski, p. 278). The words suggest harnessing disagreement to allow the managers of change to control the directions and rate of change. Put somewhat differently, conflict is to be channeled to make sure that those in control do not lose their power over the situation. The concern is with how to modify a social organization so as not to disrupt the orderliness and stability of the total system.

The search for alternatives within this perspective is defined within the existing boundaries, premises and beliefs of the ongoing system and its power arrangements. For example, Jwaideh and Marker (1973) identify four elements to estimate the rate and direction of future change: These are

1   persistency of social institution;
2   the continuation of orderly trends;
3   the recuperation of experiences with the institution; and
4   planning that is a deliberate effort to effect change in a consciously determined direction.

The management of change, by definition of its elements, is tied to the history of the established social order. There are no questions about whether the persistency or continuation of the institution is 'good' or ethically warranted. The planning exists with a 'system' whose dispositions are already constituted and seemingly unchallengable.

The definition of 'system' can be viewed in relation to a major role of social scientists in contemporary society. That role is to organize reform by being an expert to policy-makers. The idea of 'system' screens out questions of the values and priorities of the political process and focuses upon the elements internal to the system and how those elements can be placed in greater efficiency and harmony. It is interesting to note that the nineteenth century notion of system gave attention to *both* the internal and external elements that influence the functioning of the system. By the mid-1960s the idea of systems gave focus only to its internal elements. The symbotic relation of those in power and social science to produce social amelioration constituted a limiting factor regarding the conception of system and its dynamics of change.

Expertism: The Change Agent

In significant ways, both approaches to change involve the scientific expert, the change agent, as bringing deliverance to the social world. The role of the change agent can be summarized in the following fashion: social affairs are defined for the purpose of change as occurring in a linear, sequential order. Individuals tend to be passive or at least willing converts to these social patterns. The task of the change agent is to identify the proper methods or procedures to get participants to accept the call for change. Central to change is the expert who defines the situation and manipulates the clients/groups to acquiesce in the predefined decision or path.

Implementing change entails, in part, the change agent 'uncovering' forms of resistance which prevent people from accepting the expert's decisions. This entails the change agent's use of psychological techniques to gain participants' acquiescence in the proposed change. Audience acceptance of reform is viewed not as a problem of the change program but of the client's motivation. The unaccepting are not prepared psychologically for the change and many, it is reported, have a fear of the unknown. 'The change agent should keep in mind that innovations that arouse feelings of insecurity and fear are unlikely to be adopted unless he takes some action or prepares carefully designed messages aimed specially at reducing fears' (in Jwaideh and Marker, 1973). The change agent's task, therefore, is to make the client feel secure and non-anxious about the expert induced changes.

One approach to the management of people is to hire a change agent who can obtain a 'degree of similarity between agents of change and members of a target system'. To develop trust and acceptability by the 'target group', the change agent is to exhibit characteristics of those who are already in the organization: for example, s/he is to have similar characteristics, such as education and past experience.

The manipulative character of the expert is illustrated further in the view taken of organizations. One variation of change models, called a normative re-educative approach, has the change of a group's attitude and relationships as its explicit purpose. Groups are viewed as audiences which are to accept the change agent's definition of the situation. Groups are (1) the *media* of change, or (2) the *targets* of change, or (3) the *agents* of change. The language of the model reveals the power relationships between people in a group and the change agent. People who do not accept the change agent's definitions are laggards, authoritative, dogmatic, dependent, non-risk-taking — bad people. The good person accepts the innovations, risk taking, and 'independence' defined by the change agent.

Thus the good or healthy organization is one whose members accept the priorities of the expert. The most amenable organization to change is 'modern'. Its characteristics are a positive attitude towards change, a high value placed on science and education, and social relationships that are rational and businesslike rather than emotional and affective. The rejecting organization is traditional. The lack of a favorable orientation is due, it is said, to a less developed technology, social enforcement of the *status quo*, a low level of understanding of scientific methods, and a social organization which facilitates personal relationships. The modern is called a healthy organization and presumably the traditional is ill.

We can extrapolate from these categories that 'modern' means more anonymous social relationships, less communal ties, and more technological, 'scientific', and detached perspectives. One can apply a different name to this notion of modern — alienation. The healthy, modern organization makes reasonable the social forms in which the scientist/expert applies technologies to control social relationships.

The expert management of human affairs leads to an attempt to provide precision in the internal functioning of the organization. Barriers to change are thought to occur because of lack of clarity and consensus about goals and methods of evaluation. This concern for explicitness must be placed within a context of control. To rationalize and make 'real' only that which is explicit has an ideological function: the rationalization makes those events subject to the control of those who create the definitions.

The stance of the change agent is, at best, modelled after a nineteenth century conception of the physical sciences. As the variables of the physical world are treated as 'things' or 'objects' to be manipulated, the change agent conceives of his/her world in a similar manner. People become dependent and independent variables subject to the control of the expert qua scientist.

Change, Motion and Ideology: Conclusions

While the center-to-periphery and problem-solving approaches seem different, their underlying assumptions to institutional life are similar. There is a lack of consideration of the structural elements that give meaning and interpretation to school life. There is also an acceptance of the motion of administrative aspects of schooling as the definition of change.[4] More frequent use of an innovation, continuation of use of a technology, or teachers' satisfaction over participation, however, are only indications of motion not change.

Part of the problem of the change approaches is its limited theory towards social life. The change agent 'facilitates' by providing the procedures for activities. But this movement and activity takes for granted social structure by focusing on the 'system' as an entity in and of itself. The neutrality towards the goals of the system removes questions about how institutional norms and beliefs filter into and intervene in the daily life of the system.

The incorporation of the two paradigms into change models offers a way of considering two central problems of contemporary science. One is the relation of the work of intellectuals to practices of our institutions. Our notions, commitments and traditions of research are continually brought into our everyday life. That introduction involves transformations that no intellectual tradition can ever completely foretell or direct. The empirical-analytic and symbolic sciences have specific cognitive interests. Those interests are related to order and stability of our social world. It is an irony of change models that they are designed to conserve. Without understanding the history and interests of our sciences, we become trapped by our metaphors and limit our possibilities.

A second issue of contemporary science is the social location of the researcher. Both center-to-periphery and problem-solving models need to be considered in relation to their publics. Studies of change are given impetus through contract research and are to offer expertise to policy-makers for social amelioration. The agenda is formed by the political process but obscured by the rhetoric of apolitical research.

One can argue at this point that any model of change must contain an understanding of the reproductive dimensions in a society; that order and change are tied intricately as the two sides of a coin. What occurs in the consideration of change, however, is a borrowing of elements from two paradigms which focus upon mechanisms of order, legitimacy, and stability. In the context of social research, these two paradigms (empirical-analytic and symbolic) are important for understanding regularities and patterns that underlie our human condition. As a means for considering the elements and dynamics of change, they are misplaced and create a contradiction. Order is accepted as change and no adequate theoretical perspective to change is provided.

Whereas the purposes of the social sciences are to illuminate and explain, the sciences of change have ideological qualities. Change as management defines school and society as autonomous things that have laws of their own which operate apart from the intentions and plans of people. All human activity is to be brought under the realm of 'rational' thought, that is, thought that can create administrative control. At the same time, the 'non-rational' and 'irrational' elements (institution, personal autonomy and aesthetics) are eliminated from consideration. This form of rationalization denies the deep ethical and political choices to be confronted. Educational problems seem to be problems of technical know-how. These technical problems are to be resolved by experts. A consequence is to limit our conceptions of possible alternatives for ourselves and our youth.

The rational conceptions of educational change serve those who manage and control an institution. Gouldner (1970) argues that the 'rationalization' of public affairs defocalizes the ideological dimensions of decision-making and diverts attention from differences in ultimate values and ethical consequences of our social policies. A framework is provided for resolving limited differences among the managers of the organization who have little conflict or value. Models of change help to conserve those who benefit from the existing arrangements.[5].

The promise of the professional and of science in our society is one which the old, established churches once provided. The focus of the expert is to lift people above their captivity in the ordinary and to provide redemption of their hopes and expectations. The dramaturgy of reform, in particular, provides such a vision of redemptive transformation — it enables people to believe social institutions are responding and are benevolent. Modern institutions, whatever their current faults, are made to seem capable of providing salvation.

The power of the professionals to create and shape the nature of that redemption dominates our modern world. That power, we have argued, is not neutral. Our officially sanctioned change models make the assumptions, priorities, and patterns of existing actions seem reasonable and justifiable. The social, communal, and political dimensions of human struggles are denied. In their place is a process that involves acquiescence in decisions of the expert who manages emotions, facts, and people.

Notes

1 This discussion is drawn from a study of the reform program, Individually Guided Education, Popkewitz *et al.* (1982).
2 These conclusions have also been explored in a different context: an effort to increase American Indian participation in school policy-making (see Popkewitz, 1976).
3 These elements of schooling are discussed in Jackson (1968) and Hofstadter (1963).
4 The Rand Study, cited earlier, defines institutionalization of reform as the incorporation of behavioral or organizational elements of an innovation. For a critique of the distinction between organization and institution, see Meyer and Rowan (1977).
5 For a discussion of this issue, see Bates (1981).

References

BACHRACH, P. and BARATZ, M. (1970) *Power and Poverty*, New York, Oxford University Press.
BATES, R. (1981) 'Educational administration: The technologization of reason and the management of knowledge; towards a critical theory', Paper presented at Annual American Educational Research Association Meeting, Los Angeles.
BERMAN, P. and MCLAUGHLIN, M. (1978) *Federal Programs Supporting Educational Change, Vol. 8: Implementing and Sustaining Innovation*, Santa Monica, Ca., Rand Corporation.
DATTA, L. (1980) 'Changing times: The study of federal programs supporting educational change and the case for local problem solving', *Teachers College Record*, 82, 1, p. 101.

GIDEONESE, H. (1968) 'An output-oriented model of research and development and its relationship to educational improvement', in KLAUSMEIER, H.J. and O'HEARN, G.T. (Eds), *Research and Development Toward the Improvement of Education*, Madison, Wisc., Dembar Educational Research Service, pp. 157–63.

GOODLAD, J. (1975) *The Dynamics of Educational Change: Towards Responsive Schools*, New York, McGraw-Hill Company.

GOULDNER, A. (1970) *The Coming Crisis of Western Sociology*, New York, Basic Books.

HAHN, C. (1975) 'Eliminating sexism from the schools: An application of planned change', *Social Education*, 29, 3, p. 134.

HALL, G. *et al.* (1975) 'Levels of use of the innovation: A framework for analyzing innovation adoption', *Journal of Teacher Education*, 26, pp. 52–6.

HOFSTADTER, R. (1963) *Anti-Intellectualism in American Life*, New York, Alfred A. Knopf.

JACKSON, P. (1968) *Life in the Classroom*. New York, Holt, Rinehart and Winston.

JWAIDEH, A. and MARKER, G. (1973) *Bringing about Change in Social Studies Education*, Boulder, Colo., Social Science Education Consortium, Inc. and ERIC Clearinghouse for Social Studies Education.

KLAUSMEIER, H. *et al.* (1966) *Project Models: Maximizing Opportunities for Development and Experimentation in Learning in the Schools*, Occasional Paper, Madison, Wisc., Research and Development Center for Learning and Re-Education, p. 3.

KLAUSMEIER, H. (1977) 'Instructional programming for the individual student', in KLAUSMEIER, H. *et al.* (Eds), *Individually Guided Education*, New York, Academic Press.

LESSINGER, L. (1970) 'Engineering accountability for results in public education', *Phi Delta Kappan*, 52, pp. 217–25.

MEYER, J. and ROWAN, R. (1977) 'Institutional organization: Formal structure as myth and ceremony', *American Journal of Sociology*, 83, 1, pp. 55–77.

MOYNIHAN, P. (1969) *Maximum Feasible Misunderstanding: Community Action in the War on Poverty*, New York, The Free Press, pp. 21–2.

NISBET, R. (1969) *History and Social Change: Aspects of the Western Theory of Development*, New York, Oxford University Press.

NOBLE, R. (1977) *American by Design, Science, Technology and the Rise of Corporate Capitalism*, New York, Alfred A. Knopf, Ch. 10.

PAUL, D. (1977) 'Change processes at the elementary, secondary and post-secondary levels of education', in NASH, N. and CULBERTSON, J. (Eds) *Linking Processes in Educational Improvement*, Columbus, Ohio., University Council for Educational Administration, p. 16.

PAUL, D. and LIPHAM, J. (1976) 'Strengthening facilitative environments', in LIPHAM, J. and FRUTH, M. (Eds), *The Principal and Individually Guided Education*, Reading, Mass., Addison-Wesley, p. 234.

POPKEWITZ, T. (1975) 'Reform as political discourse: a case study' *School Review*, 84, pp. 311–36.

POPKEWITZ, T. (1978) 'The social structure of schools and reform: A case study of IGE/5', *Qualitative Research for Education*, Berkeley, Ca.,: McCutchen Publishing.

POPKEWITZ, T. (1979) 'Schools and the symbolic uses of community participation', in GRANT, C. (Ed.) *Community Participation in Education*, Boston, Mass., Allyn and Bacon, pp. 202–23.

POPKEWITZ, T. et al. (1982) *The Myth of Educational Reform: The Study of School Responses to Planned Change*, Madison, Wisc., University of Wisconsin Press.

ROMBERG, T. (1968) 'The development and refinement of prototypic instructional systems', in *Research and Development Strategies in Theory Refinement and Educational Improvement*, Theoretical Paper No. 15, Madison, Wisc., pp. 14–18.

WOLCOTT, W. (1977) *Teacher vs. technocrats: An Educational Innovation in Anthropological Perspective*, Eugene, Oregon., Center for Educational Policy and Management, University of Oregon.

WRONSKI, S. (1969) 'Implementing change in social studies programs; Basic considerations', in FRASER, D. (Ed.) *Social Studies Curriculum Development, Prospects and Problems*, Washington, D.C., National Council for the Social Studies, p. 178.

Chapter 7

Educational Evaluation As a Political Form

As argued earlier, science has a particular sacred quality in Western industrial societies. It is believed that science provides society with the knowledge and expertism that can bring a better life. The quality of the better life is not restricted to the physical and biological world. An innovation of the past century is the application of scientific thought to social and political institutions. The assumptions, implications and consequences of this innovation are the concern of previous chapters.

One consequence of the sacred quality of science is the adoption of the form of its argument by the knowledge-based 'helping' occupations. I use the word 'form' in this context to focus upon an occupations's adoption of the overt procedures and rituals of scientific discourse. This adoption occurs often without the concomitant use of the substantive processes and content of scientific discourse. Social work, law, teaching, psychiatry have made formal, logical and evidential-based rhetoric of science a cornerstone of their position in society. It is problemmatic, however, whether the actual status and privilege of the professional occupations are founded upon scientifically valid knowledge.

The symbolic power of science in the professions makes reasonable an occupation's expanding control and administration of sectors of institutional life. Theories and procedures of science are part of our commonplace to counsel individuals about family, school, or work roles. Common-sense wisdom and everyday knowledge are to be denied, replaced by professionalized knowledge which defines a special authority relation between the expert and the client.

The legitimating value of science explains the increasing professionalization of universities. The knowledge occupations use the universities to increase their social accreditation and to expand their realms of competence through increased specialization and research located in university settings. While some may argue that the increased specialization of knowledge is necessary and indeed helpful in dealing with the complexities of industrial societies, the argument here is to make the question of who is 'helped' problematic, giving attention to the interests involved.

The capacity of science to legitimate occupational mandates provides an account for the development of the evaluation field. Spinning off from educational psychology in the past twenty years, the specialization developed under a renewed federal mandate for social amelioration. That mandate involved the control of new expenditures in social programs and the belief that social institutions could be managed to bring about social change. The newly created discipline of social auditing has an intent different from science. The evaluator is to determine the usefulness of program intervention. The explicit audience is those who make policy. Borrowed from science, the techniques of evaluation give plausibility to the auditing: social problems are to be solved on the basis of rational and efficient approaches.

This chapter concerns the evaluation and the evaluator as expert. Evaluation as was change is viewed as an occupational endeavor which has social location and cultural significance. The practice of evaluation emerges from certain larger social pressures of an active state policy of social amelioration. That policy involves the incorporation of a particular form of rationality which defines policy change as utilitarian, linking scientific procedures to social administration. This utilitarian focus separates scientific procedures from the substantive concern of science and introduces a particular set of dynamics and value. As before, I call this ideological as it offers a style of discourse for establishing the well-being and progress of individuals without offering a complementary theory of social context for self-reflection and criticism.

To understand the style of discourse, ideological quality and the social location of evaluation, the chapter proceeds in the following manner. The cultural belief in science as progress is considered. Evaluation maintains a belief that people can control and manipulate the social world as one does with natural phenomena. The idea of progress, however, receives a particular definition as it is incorporated into work that responds directly to the political agenda. Science is no longer conceived as a means of enlightenment and understanding. Science is procedures to serve the administration of social affairs. As inquiry is transformed to technology, so is the intellectual transformed into a strata of the intelligentsia whose tasks are fundamentally administrative rather than critical (see Gouldner,

1976, for discussion of this distinction). This new role is found in three types of evaluational practices: accountability, decision-making and case study approaches. While a surface appearance of these approaches is a response to different social interests, an exploration of the assumptions reveals an interest in legitimating institutional arrangements, a professionalization of knowledge and a particular role for the 'scientist' qua reformer.

Evaluation As a Sine Qua Non of School Improvement

While our common-sense notions of evaluation have roots in nineteenth century social and political thought, evaluation was given a new and more specialized definition during the 1950s and 1960s.[1] Following World War II many believed that the same energy used to defeat our enemies could be turned inward to solve pressing social problems. Solutions to problems of starvation, material production, education and poverty were to be viewed from the same perspective: the application of scientific methods to understand, explain, and manipulate towards the desired social purposes. As science had solved problems of material well-being, social science and human engineering techniques could provide direction for solving problems of the psychological and social well-being of people.[2] This was a period in which many social scientists believed there was an end to ideology and the problems of society were technical in nature.

Schooling was an essential part of the federal program for social intervention. An expanding economy made it plausible to consider the school as an instrument for altering social and economic inequities. Compensatory programs were to provide the poor and minorities with access to an expanding middle class and professions. Head Start, tutorial programs, affirmative action, Teacher Corps, to name a few, were created to establish school conditions and opportunities for social mobility for those who were socially and economically disadvantaged.

The direct and massive federal involvement during the 1950s and 1960s marks both a continuation of previous trends towards centralization as well as a departure in American educational policy (see Kaestle and Smith, 1982; Ravitch, 1982). Policy and funding of education have always involved a tension between local, private, and federal concerns, with the major school funding coming from local real estate taxes.[3] Prior to the National Defense Educational Act of 1958 and the 1965 Elementary and Secondary Education Act, the federal government had less involvement and impact upon day-to-day activities in schools. Past educational reforms received impetus from combined efforts of business leaders, civic reformers, private foundations, university lecturers, and professional educators. The legislation beginning in this period made the federal government's role in educational policy more direct and pronounced. That policy was based upon a belief that professionals within institutions could effectively bring about the necessary reform. Title I of the 1965 Elementary and Secondary Education Act designed to 'break the cycle of poverty and equalize lifetime opportunities' (McLaughlin, 1976, p. 397) through school intervention, was built upon the following two assumptions.

1 Schoolmen knew what to do with the new resources and would be able to use them to design and implement special compensatory programs.

2 The infusion of new resources into the nation's local school districts would lead to educational reforms *from within* and through the existing system (McLaughlin, 1976, p. 397).

Faith in the expert guided the social amelioration efforts. The idea of rational, systematic evaluation was a part of the national mandate to make schools a viable instrument for responding to economic and social change and for creating incentives for change. Legislation included evaluation as an essential part of the effort to improve the conditions of the poor and to produce curriculum that responded to changing economic conditions. A newly created National Science Foundation, for example, turned attention to curriculum problems and sponsored a host of projects concerned with improving science teaching. Project directors were asked for formal evaluations to help schools in deciding whether to use the new curricula and to provide evidence to Congress for the success of its expenditures (Cronbach, 1980).

Evaluation was also considered by Congress as a possible means of control. The Elementary and Secondary Education Act of 1965, for example, required that school districts offer an evaluation plan and a summary report to state agencies which allocated the funds (Cronbach, 1980). Designed to provide additional services for children of the poor, the Elementary and Secondary Education Act demanded data that set forth, in the language of the legislation, 'the effectiveness of payment under this title and of particular programs assisted under it in improving the educational attainment of educationally deprived children', including 'appropriate objective measures of educational achievement' (in Cronbach, 1980, p. 32).

The call for change involved a particular view of rationality and efficiency. It was drawn from logical-positivism and a particular style of thought which used the general rules of empirical-analytical sciences to argue for the *management* of social problems. Budget planning and systems analysis provided the way of analyzing effects of policy in social programs. The evaluations tightened managerial review, verified the worth of innovations, and ensured that programs were efficient. Planners assumed that organizational activities could be logically organized in a clear and unambiguous manner, modified by more efficient management, and the results of a planned change (the outputs of a system) defined and measured against costs (monetary and social).

Evaluations had a second purpose. They could testify to the need for federal educational aid and the commitment of the government and school professionals to 'self-renewal'. The statistics collected by the National Assessment project 'on educational accomplishments and shortcomings would make it easier to obtain more generous appropriations for schooling' (Cronbach, 1980, p. 34).

The emergence of evaluation studies was a cultural response to social issues. It was to assess and direct an active state policy of amelioration. The organization of assessment captured a prevailing belief that social problems were soluble by making institutions more efficient and rational and hence controllable by the state. 'Being rational' meant a particular way of thinking and planning associated with systems analysis and budget planning. It was to define social and organizational elements as having conceptually distinct and ordered properties. These properties could be controlled and manipulated towards some desired end. The problem of change and reform was to better coordinate and administer the means or processes of institutional life. If we think back to the earlier discussion of paradigms, each intellectual tradition contains different methods of thinking or of 'being rational' about social affairs. While state planners did consider conflict theories in early planning, the emergent policy adopted only empirical-analytic rules for practice and defined these rules narrowly as the administration of program planning and evaluation (see Rose, 1972). The data of evaluative studies have the dual purpose of managing government business and providing 'objective' criteria that could win political acceptance of new program proposals.

Legitimating Evaluation As Science

The rapid acceptance of evaluation as a means of control and legitimation has occurred in relation to a cultural belief in science. For many, science is the means of progress. This belief posits that the future is built upon planned, rational thought in which people are the masters of change. Science is seen as an autonomous form of discourse by which to plan for change. The practice of science is to rationally analyze social conditions so causes could be known. The knowledge of science is that of the social order, social consensus, and social reconstruction. In this respect, science and ideology are interrelated as part of people's active construction of their social worlds. The ideology has specific groups assuming responsibility for assessing the status of current worlds in order to give direction to future possibilities.

The relation between the positive appreciation of *what is* and the creation of a collective identity that mobilizes for future projects is lost in much current discussion of contemporary social science and evaluation. If one looks at the work of Comte, Durkheim, or early American sociologists, the relation between science and progress is clear. Lester Frank Ward, one of the founders of American sociology, argued that society could determine its own future and great and rapid progress could be attained artificially by clear and accurate foresight (Ward, 1906). By the 1950s Ward's faith in science was transformed to involve the belief that science is an important instrument governing social processes and those processes could be evaluated and planned for in an enlightened manner (see Lundgren, 1979). The notion of evaluation capitalized on this assumption of science as progress, making the endeavor both prophetic and dogmatic.

To understand the fundamental shift in assumption and practice that accompanies the movement of science into evaluation, we need to focus for a moment upon the meaning of progress.[4] In part, our views of change, growth, and progress are inherited from the Greeks. The Greeks saw change as part of the nature of each living thing, having its own inherent patterns or laws of cause, mechanism and purpose. The purpose of inquiry was to contemplate the marvels of *nature*, not to manipulate them. It is here that the meaning of theory originates in contrast to praxis; the latter is concerned with the non-law-like negotiations, interests and exigencies of the social and political world. The Romans transformed change and progress to include the physical aspects of man and society, creating a dichotomy between the social and physical worlds. Christianity fused progress with the moral idea that includes the belief in the power of people to create and plan society. Indefinite progress became a part of Western consciousness, theologically joining historical necessity and historical inevitability. St Augustine, for example, drew upon the ideas of divine necessity from the Old Testament and of the internal, self-perfecting necessity found in Greek thought.

The shift in meaning was profound: no longer was the idea of progress seen as adapting to circumstances of what is conceived as the nature of things. Progress was an ideal type on which to build schemes for social reform or revolution. People were to assume an important place in the determining of their world.

It is in the eighteenth century that the idea of indefinite progress becomes secularized. The belief in progress included all social institutions and human happiness, human manners as well as knowledge. This view was modified in the following century as people looked to natural evolution and laws of societies, as in the development of governments, economics, and culture. The underlying assumption was that progress was a linear, sequential development of human affairs which science could illuminate and guide more efficiently.

The eighteenth and nineteenth century view of progress underlies the active state policy following the 1950s. The perception was that education is decisive to an individual's prospect for social position and scientific management could bring about broader political and economic goals. A national network of research and development centers were to provide the 'knowhow' to make substantial and lasting reforms in the schools. Sidney Marland (1972), of the then US Office of Education, argued that schools can apply management procedures to ensure 'the *smooth operation* of our contemporary educational institutions' (p. 340).

This belief in science as ameliorating our human condition took a narrow, technological meaning as it was translated into practice. The new occupation of evaluation took its perspective from 'the rational/empirical/behavioral frame of reference, which induces pragmatic assumptions such that education can become a scientifically ordered enterprise and that it should develop definite curriculum and instruction that can stand the test of cost-effectiveness' (Yee, 1973, p. 299). Evaluation is to manage and make more efficient, therefore enlightening the process of change and social amelioration. Whereas Lester Frank Ward defined progress in a broad, wholistic manner, the new scientific progress was narrow in conception. The focus was upon particular institutional elements unrelated to social and economic transformations.

While the view of progress implicit in state policy was built upon a nineteenth century deterministic view of physics, that view of growth and progress is no longer viable in the field from which it is drawn. Contemporary science views the scientist as a participant involved in the processes of theorizing, people in an interactive process with natural phenomena, and ethics as an integral element in the practice of science (Toulmin, 1982).

Our contemporary notion of progress must also be considered in the context of the professionalization of social science discussed in Chapter 5. Where the early social scientists were concerned with the interrelation of social, economic, and historical questions, the modern professional-expert focuses upon discrete elements of institutional life. This change in social science is related to the accommodations deemed necessary to serve as expert to the policy-maker.

Techniques As Ideology: Separating Science from Its Procedures

The belief that science brings progress underlies the occupational organization of evaluation. Evaluators establish ties to scientific procedures while, at the same time, distinguishing evaluation as a particular expertise which has a special claim to status and privilege. The privilege is based upon adopting the formal logic of science in which techniques of data collection and analysis become paramount. This emphasis makes technique a moral domain in which the existing ethos and practices of institutions become non-problematic. The notion of disciplined inquiry to emerge in the field of evaluation, as I will argue, involves the adaptation of the public *form* of research without incorporating the self-correcting, self-reflective mechanism of scientific discourse.

We can understand the use and transformation of scientific discourse in professions by focusing upon the development of symbolic canopies that provide linguistic coherence and interpretability to institutional patterns. Theories, folk-wisdoms, and myths about an occupation emerge as institutions develop a history and respond to social transformation. Medicine becomes health care and wellness education. Schools are defined as education and as treating children's *needs*. Theories of need and ministry are created to explain, interpret, and justify the expanding importance of an occupation's definition and control of its clients. The special language of the helping occupations thus has dual meanings: to direct and organize the help given to clients while, at the same time, making the professional activities seem reasonable and credible.

The form of scientific practice can be viewed as a part of the symbolic canopy of evaluation. With specialization emerges a series of 'theories' to define the distinct purpose, character, and relationship of evaluation to other academic and practical activities. The success of evaluation canopies is that they complement and legitimate policy-making imperatives and, at the same time, permeate practical discourse in classroom curriculum development and instructional planning.

One of the major tenets of the emergent canopy is the disciplined form of evaluation. The purveyors of evaluation wisdom tie evaluation procedurally to science: evaluation gives rigorous attention to the detail of the world, systematic discussion of procedures, and training for practitioners in the procedures of data collection and analysis. This tie to science, however, involves an important distinction in purpose and, hence, substance from science.

Evaluation is seen as fundamentally different from research. This is most prominently discussed in a major edited collection of essays by Worthen and Sanders (1973). These articles argue the distinctive quality of the evaluation endeavor. As social fact, the text illustrates a way in which 'theory' and reflective writing become useful in creating a symbolic canopy for occupational practice. The articles are thoughtful and insightful about the demands, diversity of thought, and sources of conflict confronting the creation of a new occupation. The text, however, does not question the social fact itself.

In the introductory essay to the volume Worthen and Sanders argue that evaluation is a form of disciplined inquiry. Evaluation places a premium on objectivity and evidential tests. Emphasis is on immediate value questions of social worth and utility, with little interest in generalizing across time.[5] Research, in contrast, 'is the activity aimed at obtaining generalizable knowledge by continuing and testing claims about relationships among variables or describing generalizable phenomena' (p. 19). It is 'mission oriented . . . providing knowledge relevant to providing a solution [generalizable] to a general problem. Evaluation is focused on collecting specific information relevant to a specific problem, program or product' (p. 23).

The authors continue that the evaluator's role is largely that of a methodological expert. Methodology is defined narrowly as a concern with the procedures by which data are collected and analyzed. The evaluator is to apply research techniques to the solution of a particular practical problem. To be adequately trained in methodology, the evaluator is to give emphasis 'to such topics as statistical analysis, measurement and psychometrics, survey research methods and experimental design' (p. 36). The approach is eclectic, that is, to incorporate concepts and approaches that contribute to the answer to the practical problem.

Making evaluation a methodological problem drawn from science but distinct from that endeavor has certain consequences. If we view science as a community of discourse, its statistical techniques or survey research methods are part of that dialogue. They develop within a paradigmatic context that involves communal norms, beliefs, visions, and tensions. The procedures of inquiry take on meaning, direction, potency, and value within the discourse of science. Factor analysis and field methods, to cite examples discussed in earlier chapters, maintain values and visions of social order associated with its disciplinary development and use. That is why one cannot talk about *the scientific method*, but scientific methods which evolve as people respond to the curiosities, issues, and phenomena of a field.

In fundamental ways, scientific procedures are context-bound, dependent upon their disciplinary field of use. Reusch and Bateson (1968) point to only four ways people have invented to obtain data about human phenomena. We can talk with people, observe events as a neutral observer, participate in ongoing life, and read the generalizations a culture makes about itself. The importance, definition, and potency of these procedures are in relation to the intellectual traditions, problems, and curiosities that give meaning and self-criticism to the practice of inquiry.

To remove scientific procedures from their self-correcting communities and to give them a life of their own is to unwittingly crystallize the procedures *and their values*. To borrow procedures without giving attention to the substantive assumptions of their use is to make the enterprise technical in quality.

This technical quality is evident when one focuses upon the meaning of 'value' in evaluation. Worthen and Sanders (1973) state that evaluation is different from research because it is 'to judge worth or social utility' (p. 12) and place 'emphasis upon immediate value questions' that draw upon philosophical inquiry (p. 15).

As one looks at the meaning of value or worth, it is narrow and utilitarian. The notion of value as utilitarian, developed in the nineteenth century by John Stuart Mill (see Hamilton, 1977), contains the beliefs that principles of conduct can be obtained from the canons of experimental inquiry and that social behavior can be judged unequivocally against a one-dimensional, ordinal scale that defines goodness and badness. Value, according to Worthen and Sanders (1973), is to measure the success of a program, product, or procedure, such as whether a curriculum produces adequate standardized test results or whether a textbook is superior to competitors. Higher test scores or more use are operationally defined as value.

The utilitarian assumption posits a dichotomy between goals and practice. Worthen and Sanders note 'that in this [evaluation] process there is no assessment of the worth of the objectives themselves' (p. 21), thus separating the process of evaluation from the problem-at-hand. Goals and interests served are made part of administrative process and seem not open to scrutiny and debate.

This separation of goal and practice reinforces the value of technique and administration of social affairs. Ideally, practice emerges from the interrelation of purpose with situated actions. To separate the two is to deny that interrelationship and the interplay of thought and action. Ignored are the rhetorical quality of goal statements in institutions and the assumptions about social values that underlie programs. The rhetoric assumes a consensus by obscuring the conflict and political debate important to goal setting. The assumption that consensus and harmony exists is a false assumption in social affairs and serves those interests that have power in institutions.

Rationality As Interest-Bound

Another type of value is ignored when problems of social affairs are made technical: how arguments are framed and categories selected to organize practice contain value. Underlying curriculum development and program selection are ways of reasoning and acting that have implications for questions of social order, legitimacy, and authority. This order of 'value' is ignored as procedural problems determine worth.

Let me provide a brief example of the social implications and consequences of a reform program, Individually Guided Education

(Popkewitz *et al.*, 1982). The goals of the program were placed in a language to capture a variety of American beliefs: institutions should be responsive to individuality, merit, and efficiency. The language of the program condensed a feeling and general cultural value but by itself conveyed little of the assumptions that underlay the practices upon which Individually Guided Education was built. To understand the effect of the program is to delve into the assumptions about social world and individuality that informed the concrete proposals (systems analysis and management theory) and how these assumptions were realized with the social and political complexity of school life. We found, for example, conflict among the program designers about the epistemology to organize curriculum and teaching. This conflict, however, was muted as the research for the program was translated into models of change. Change was a problem of correct organization and efficient ordering of ideas and people. Classroom analysis suggested that to define school change as a management problem deals only with the public face of school life (Popkewitz, 1982). The existing patterns of conduct had different criteria of success and failure and these were left unchallenged. The reform was part of the ritual of schooling and helped to maintain the legitimacy of the enterprise as modern and benevolent.

One might consider the view of evaluation offered by Cronbach and Associates (1980) as different in assumption and approach from a management orientation. The discussion is premised upon a belief that evaluators have become too enthralled in technique, that much that purports to be theory of evaluation is scholastic and involved in endless categorizations and 'debates over numerological derivations from artifical models' (p. 2). Evaluation, it is argued, should give attention to conceptual problems and the relation of technique to concepts: 'We reject the view that "design" begins *after* a research question is chosen, as a mere technical process to sharpen the inquiry' (p. 14). Questions and facts are inseparable, with political consideration as well as substantive and technical ones influencing inquiry. The concern is with the relevance of information rather than form of inquiry.

Further, the relevance of information is considered as political and normative rather than technical. The mission of evaluation 'is to facilitate a democratic, pluralistic process by enlightening all the participants. Evaluation should not serve to strengthen the hands of the commissioning authority'; 'program evaluation is the process by which society learns about itself and should contribute to enlightened discussion of alternative plans for social action'; 'An open society becomes a closed society when only the officials know what is going on. Insofar as information is a source of power, evaluations carried out to inform a policy maker have a disenfranchising effect' (pp. 1–2).

What is not offered in this argument is the analytic posture by which evaluation is to be oriented. By that I mean that the intellectual traditions, concepts, and underlying assumptions of social affairs to guide a critical inquiry are not discussed. As the previous chapters illustrate, not all knowledge has enfranchisement as its interest, and science has its antagonistic qualities. Not to argue the substance of inquiry is to make a formal plea that does not have the necessary sustained argument to consider what are appropriate concepts to organize data, insights, and generalizations. That is, the argument is made without exploring the conceptual and metatheoretical assumptions that are to illuminate conditions of schooling.

This is not to say, however, that Cronbach does not affiliate with a tradition. While rejecting a technical approach, an underlying assumption is that of an equilibrium model of social systems. 'Evaluation is a handmaiden to gradualism; it is both conservative and committed to change'; 'Ideally, every evaluation will inform the social system and improve its operation' (p. 2). By adopting this vision of order, a particular pluralistic political theory is adopted that is never made explicit — that theory, derived from Hobbes and Locke, is individualist and views social structure as groups of varying interests which government mediates. A consequence of this theory is that certain contradictions do not receive expression. Morality is technically defined as the ability to organize as an interest group. Social issues receive legitimacy only when supported by organized groups in society. Social value and ethics do not transcend the elements of interest-group politics; thus they provide a restrictive view of morality and politics.

The contradiction in evaluation as determining worth and as a neutral technical enterprise offers a certain ideological posture. To do an evaluation suggests that the public will is expressed through the balanced weighing of needs of interested groups and rational choice based upon expert counsel. Actions and policies are justified by the dramaturgy. In fact, the language of evaluation often creates terms of classifying the merit, competency, pathology, or authority of groups and individuals. It implicitly defines the interests to be favored and handicapped. These political implications can be illustrated with three approaches to evaluation: 'accountability', decision-making and case studies.

Evaluation As Accountability: Technique As Value

One prominent approach of school evaluation is called 'account-ability'.[6] This term captures a variety of techniques that draw upon human engineering and management theory. Schools are defined as production-oriented institutions to be managed by precise standards and techniques that direct, predict, and control all the activities of the organization. Leon M. Lessinger (1970), a former associate commissioner of education, argues that 'the development of engineering techniques in systems analysis, management by objectives, contract engineering (including bids, warranties, penalties, and incentives), logistics, quality assurances, value engineering, and human factor engineering' make it possible to set behavioral standards that can be measured to determine the efficiency of instruction (p. 218). The techniques of accountability are based upon an assumption of certainty. Evaluation as accountability is to determine the degree to which social and psychological elements can be made isomorphic with predetermined 'objective' models.

An innovation of the accountability movement is the creation of social organizations to implement instructional management schemes. The idea of social management in American education can be traced back to people such as Bobbitt, Charters and Snedden. But these ideas do not involve the necessary practical technologies until the late 1960s and early 1970s. Following use in war and business, systems analysis provided a technical device for considering practical problems such as the application of behavioral principles to coordinate curriculum and instruction. Personnel sorting devices and computers became available for use in schools. At the same time, school specialization became more pronounced. Federal grants, for example, supported the creation of full-time reading specialists and development of management designs for reading programs. Reading became a distinct subject-matter for behavioral curriculum reorganization in elementary and secondary schools.

The emphasis upon engineering technology takes two distinct but interrelated dimensions for evaluating schools. One concerns the specification of precise objectives that are measureable. Called behavioral or performance-based objectives and criterion-based measures, these statements describe what a student will do after completing a prescribed unit of instruction. ('A student will list four causes of the Industrial Revolution.') The student is held accountable for obtaining competency in performing the task, with emphasis on a demonstrated product or output.

A second dimension of accountability is to improve efficiency and control of school organizations to achieve the objectives. Operational definitions and ground rules of the system are set to obtain control of all elements in the system. Planning Programming Budget Systems, instructional management systems, systems analyses, and computer-assisted instruction provide procedures to be used to place all the known structures and practices into some conceptual scheme. (The commonly used flow-chart illustrates this tendency to define all the parts of a system and their relationship.)

In accepting management as the basis for evaluation, a value system is tacitly accepted. This view defines efficiency of action as the most important standard of educational judgment. Attention is shifted from intrinsic value of action to the internal orderliness and rationality of school activity. Procedure or utility of action is the goal of accountability. There is no discussion of the network of social and political rules that underlie classroom activities. Rather the focus is upon the expertise of educators to identify the most efficient modification procedures.

By focusing upon only that which is observable and quantifiable, accountability obscures and trivializes our view of life by creating a one-dimensional lens. To consider history as 'a list of three major factors causing a war' is to mystify the process of *doing* history — the human drama and adventure involved in cross-examining documents and the *conflict* that exists within scholarship about the interpretation of events and people. Intellectual, social, and political life does not have a high degree of consensus and measurability when problems of quality or issues of human welfare are at stake. Nor do inquiry, problem-solving, critical thought, and creativity have specified outcomes or measurable elements. To add new technologies to the classroom is not to just *add on* to existing arrangements but is to alter the quality of relations as well. Certain values and interests are accepted.

There is a substantive meaning to educational accountability. It is to reduce curriculum to discrete, particular units of observable behavior that can be controlled and predicted. The function of education becomes one of techniques to apply the most rational, technically efficient form to some predefined standard.

The irony of the accountability approach is that it is conservative to existing authority relationships and knowledge. Here we must consider school as teaching children not only objective statements about the world but also dispositions about what it means to know. The focus on measurable, definable units of behavior can teach children that the only legitimate questions are those formed according to predefined standards. Tentativeness, skepticism, and a playfulness with ideas important to our contemporary epistemologies are obscured. The criterion of competency assumes stability and harmony in the social world. Predefined knowledge puts emphasis upon order and control as the goal of teaching and instruction. To be educated is to have a fund of learned responses that fit into the established scheme of things.

Accountability creates a map of the world that seems to provide an interpretation of everyday life. This interpretation assumes consensus and diverts attention from the struggles, strains, and contradictions that underlie institutional practices. Reliance on management procedures ignores inequities and inequalities, problems of social conditions and social differentiation except as problems of administration. The emphasis on making current objectives more concrete and measurable rigidifies existing content, structure, and value.

The 'science' of accountability is ideology. It mobilizes social action and social solidarity by assuming that action is built upon impersonal rhetoric provided by experts. The logic and rationality of this ideology comes not from the scientific community but from the transformation of the labor process in US industry (Clawson, 1980). The idea of management was created to gain control over labor and production. There was a separation between the conception and the execution of work. Prior to the industrial revolution and its reorganization of labor, we could think of work as having a craft quality. The individual worker had the conception of the work found in production. This conception contained the creative power by which people shape and fashion the object of the world. This craft quality was found in the contract system used in the early American factories. By 1920, though with much resistance, management emerged as an element in production to gain greater control over the labor processes. The systems of control involved reordering both the physical and social processes of labor. It is from this social and economic history that the assumptions and practices of accountability are derived. Accountability separates conception from execution — each element of school work is defined separately by a manager who controls the process of the person to learn.

In reflecting on these changes from a social-historical perspective, Braverman (1974) argues that management perspectives destroy the self-organized and self-motivated quality of community. Work becomes dehumanized and new forms of control are introduced. Labor is subdivided so that the individual no longer has a conception of how the separate elements of the work process relate to the total product of labor.

Evaluation As Decision-Making: The Administration of Power

The centrality of administration and the expertism is captured in the focus upon evaluation as serving 'decision-makers'. Stufflebeam (1973) suggests that the focus of evaluation should be upon variables over which administrators have control: 'Evaluation is the process of delineating, obtaining and providing useful information for judging decision alternatives' (p. 129). While suggesting an alternative 'naturalistic approach' to evaluation that relies less on survey and outcome measures, Guba (1978) recognizes utility as a central value. Evaluation 'has come to be widely viewed as the handmaiden of decision-making and social policy development' (p. 1). Cronbach and Associates (1980) seek to broaden the notion of decision-making to include the disenfranchised while accepting the utilitarian purpose of evaluation in aiding policy-making. A general consensus seems to exist that evaluation is performed in the service of decision-makers and should provide useful information.

Both the broad and narrow definitions of evaluation for decision-making have a strong symbolic appeal. They point to the value placed upon participation in institutional life while, at the same time, directing attention to the need for impersonal knowledge and rationality among those in authority to make choices. Decision-making modifies the certainty of the accountability approach while maintaining the need to organize reform with the expert advice of social scientists. In condensing these two contradictory values, the idea of decision-making establishes a relationship between authority and social order that is rarely explored.

In order to evaluate adequately the function of decision-making as a purpose of evaluation, we must consider decision-making theories as part of a value commitment to liberal democracy.[7] There is a belief that individuals should assume responsibility for decision-making in institutions that affect their lives on a day-to-day basis. This commitment to decision-making has two different but related emphases: to obtain a more equitable allocation of goods, services, and knowledge; and to involve individuals in public affairs as a means of maintaining the vitality and creativity of a society. Democracy is to provide concrete forms for individual growth and self-development.

Once said, however, we are left with little to understand the nature *and* interest of the decision-making process. Decision-making focuses upon the surface aspects of choices made in organizations. It does not consider that many of the wants, values, and priorities of 'decision-making' are determined by the structural and historical conditions of our institutions. All organizations have a 'mobilization of bias'. Certain values and rules are taken for granted, becoming background assumptions which orient participants towards definitions of problems and ways of 'thinking' and challenging institutional discontinuities (Schattschneider, 1960). Student alienation, dropouts, or failure in school are defined and responded to in relation to organizational biases which define:

1   that it is good to be in school;
2   that the failure involves lack of effectiveness in existing programs, such as a student's not learning to read, or lack of individual ability, and
3   success or failure as related to some achievement measures.

These preferences are mediated and legitimated within horizons established by the history of schooling and those interests which have struggled for control and dominance over its ongoing affairs. Not to consider the ethos and structures that give organization to the categories of institutional life is to ignore the interests that shape and fashion the contexts of decision-making.

This relation between structure, history, and decisions can be pursued by considering how our preferences are formed in social worlds. While we can react to these worlds with conviction, detachment, or revolt, we cannot ignore the relationship between biography and sociality. Satisfaction, competence, or a 'healthy' self-concept have meaning only with reference to the socially organized context in which one's 'personality' is expressed. Psychology and sociality are inextricably related: there is no psychology of individuals without a sociology of institutions.

The relation of history and subjective feeling is essential to the problem of decision-making. To understand what is a decision, a theory of the context in which decisions are made must be considered. In the ongoing events of our daily life are multiple 'decisions'. Some of these decisions are 'caused' by preceding events; some are made in order to effect some desired state; some respond to the exigencies of daily life, some are designed to challenge the ongoing nature of that life. Decision-making without a theory of context does not enable us to distinguish these different intents, purposes, and outcomes.

Evaluation as decision-making denies the political base to which it appears to respond. Critical thought, observation, and analysis of the conflict of values that underlies politics are filtered out. Administration is substituted for politics. The problem of policy is one of rational, secular logic and evidence. In fact, policy-making is a political activity in which there is rarely a consensus of objective and interests. Floden and Weiner (1978) argue, for example, that decisions involve roles, relationships, sets of beliefs, values, and commitments that are a dynamic part of the process in which the evaluation provides only short-run information.

Evaluation As a Case Study: Responsive to Whom?

In response to the expert/elite orientation of both accountability and decision-making approaches, some evaluators have advocated evaluation as case study methods (see Guba, 1978; Stake, 1980; Parlett and Hamilton, 1972). The case study method or naturalistic inquiry gives attention to the perceptions and ongoing activities of the people involved in the program being evaluated. The language and perceptions of various participants are used to portray the ongoing dynamics and interests of the program. This approach is believed to be more democratic and less elitist in orientation. The people involved in the program are also involved in the creation of the evaluation, the telling of the story, and the assigning of value to the endeavor.

To express these concerns, Stake (1980) suggests evaluation should be responsive. He argues that the style of data collection and reporting should involve references to the satisfaction and dissatisfaction that 'appropriately selected people feel towards it'. The description of the program should have illustrations of the value perspectives of the people involved and their reports of successes and failures.

The case study method explicitly rejects the assumptions of accountability and rational decision-making. These latter, 'preordinate', evaluation plans emphasize statements of goals, use of objective tests, standards held by program personnel, and research-type reports (Stake, 1980, p. 76). The formal communications of 'preordinate' evaluation, Stake believes, do not respond to the needs of the persons for whom the evaluation is being done.

The starting point of a responsive evaluation is the issues of the program. Stake suggests that after getting acquainted with a program, an evaluator should 'acknowledge certain issues or problems or potential problems' (p. 79). The issues become central to the formation of the evaluation. They structure the continuing discussion with clients, staff, and audience.

With surface appearances and interest different from the decision-making approach, the case study method coincides with the previous approaches by maintaining a notion of subjective interest.[8] The issue of program evaluation is personal feeling, satisfaction, or uneasiness. The psychological states of participants are paramount. The horizons within which these states are established receive no scrutiny. No guidance is provided for understanding what is an issue. C. Wright Mills (1959), for example, suggests that there is a distinction between personal troubles and issues. An individual may feel alienated from a job or lack enough money to fulfil basic family needs. When many people have such troubles and these troubles point to institutional contradictions, Mills argues that the troubles become issues. In the case study approaches, personnel problems and institutional issues are not distinguished. A problem could be one of improving the efficiency of the very context which produces alienation or dealing with structural issues. As no theory of context is provided, the evaluated and evaluator have no way to judge what is an issue.

House (1978), in reviewing different models of evaluation, argues that the case study method, as do all existing approaches, maintains a liberal utilitarian ethos. The case study method maintains a relativistic view of truth. Its ultimate criteria of what is good and right are individual feelings or apprehensions. A reductionist's view of knowledge is maintained by focusing upon individualistic psychologies. Political pluralistic theory is maintained which does not require the representation of a view unless there is an active involvement of the group in the process. Finally, it is believed that increased knowledge makes people happy, better, and, in some ways, more satisfied.

Implicit in case studies, then, is a social and political theory. The difficulty of the political stance is that it does not come to grips with the limitations of that theory; that is, the relation of the subjective conditions of people who participate in the ongoing historical conditions. If our ways of reasoning, thinking, and feeling are intricately related to social formations that have history and interest, the consummation of subjective interest as the only interest makes evaluation one-dimensional and distorting of processes and outcomes.

In certain ways, the case study approach does respond to contemporary epistemology of science. It seeks to establish an interactive model between researcher and context and recognizes the ethics of science by locating the task of evaluation in democratic theory. What is ignored, however, is the relation of the specific 'case' to the larger social context in which meanings, values, and actions are made credible and 'normal'. This relational view is essential to the development of political theory. In the 'case' of evaluation, the political theory is denuded of its politics and transformed into a technical study of situations.

As with the other approaches to evaluation, case study is to be considered as related to the social location of the evaluator. Tied to policy and the administrative organization of institutions that seek social amelioration, the reliance upon subjective interests posits a relativism that neither threatens nor challenges the objective interests which underlie our institutional conditions. Case study accepts uncritically the existing perceptions, communications and categories offered by the agenda set in the political process.

Conclusions

Evaluation is a social phenomenon. It is a system of thought and practice of a particular occupational group. The mandate of that group is given by an active state policy for social amelioration and institutionally appropriated as essential to the task of school planning. The form of evaluation is borrowed from a nineteenth century conception of physics in which the purpose of inquiry was to control nature and the theoretical and practical location of the scientist was believed as one of disinterest. While these assumptions of physics have changed in contemporary research, evaluators maintain the nineteenth century view. Disinterest is combined with a separation of purpose from the procedural rules of science. The resulting rationality is neither scientific nor disinterested. The technique of evaluation becomes a moral domain by which to judge social worth.

The procedural logic, impersonal rhetoric, and rules of evidence of science form a basis to argue for the administrative control of social life. Utility of actions is the purpose of evaluation. What is not maintained is the substantive content of scientific endeavors which have the potential of a self-critical, reflective dialogue. The symbolic canopies of this occupation are to explain and justify its status.

There is an irony in the view of knowledge as utilitarian

(Buchmann, 1982). Relegating all knowledge to utility makes virtual-
ly everything by which people determine and decide problems
seemingly irrational. Practical actions, however, are more compli-
cated than providing assertions of utility. They involve, among other
aspects, moral values and political considerations. To impose utility
as a constraint of knowledge is to actually devalue knowledge by
making use paramount. It is to impose a narrow bias towards
individualism and an interpretation of human action as economic
activity.

The utilitarian focus on evaluation introduces an ideological
element into practices. We can pursue this implication by considering
science as a form of discourse as well as practice (see Edelman, 1977).
The formal language of science is based upon roles of evidence, logic
of argument, and conceptual development that seeks to place concrete
social affairs in a wider context for scrutiny. The language of
evaluation has a different function. While its syntactic structure and
grammatical order are drawn seemingly from science, the style of
expression is a public language. It creates an image of efficiency in
which facts are tied to visions of the social order. The visions are
more often than not defined by the categories and prescriptions of
those who contract for the evaluation, generally government agencies
or administrative bodies of schools. Accountability and evaluation as
decision-making, for example, locate practice in some transcendent
sphere that is removed from the concrete conditions and experiences
of people. Behavioral objectives, budget planning or 'needs assessment' make our social conditions seem objective, impartial, and fixed.
In fact, these situations are products of changing power constellations. By borrowing the form of science, evaluation bolsters authority by evoking the belief that science sanctions the status, distinctions,
social norms, and role structures. What exists in flux is seen in unity
and universality.

The problem of the case study approach, we argued, is different
at one layer of understanding but may have similar ideological
qualities. The focus upon subjective interest ignores a theory of
context that can enable people to consider the interrelation of self to
social world. The issues of schooling and social location are relati-
vized and individualized. As with accountability and decision-
making, the case study approach may preserve and promote the
existing order of power in events. The relationship of the world and
their connections is obscured.

Consideration of evaluation as a public language enables us to
understand a political function. Floden and Weiner (1978) suggest

that the act of requiring and commissioning evaluation provides a ritual of participation and affiliation. Evaluation can create an impression that government is serious in its commitment to pursuing public goals while the actual interests served are obscured. The language of evaluation encourages a sensitivity to a particular pattern of social interaction, thus creating a posture of political loyalty. Conflict is managed by suggesting problems are open to negotiation and compromise. The display of technical expertise also demonstrates that occupational prerogatives and status deserve support. An evaluation can calm the anxiety of the citizenry and 'perpetuate an image of governmental rationality, efficiency and accountability' (Floden and Weiner, 1978, p. 16).

To treat evaluation as a problem of ideology is not to suggest that approaches do not exist which have potential for self-criticism and reflectivity. Work in England and Australia has sought to incorporate theories of context into the task of evaluation. These theories of context seek to define pedagogical problems as containing issues of social, philosophical, and political import. Often called action research, the evaluation involves teachers and researchers in reflecting about the assumptions, implications, and consequences of day-to-day life in their institutions. Barry McDonald at the University of East Anglia, for example, has sought to consider the implications of liberal political theory to school evaluation (see McDonald and Norris, 1981). Stephen Kemmis (Carr and Kemmis, 1983) at Deakin University in Australia is working to incorporate the perspectives of the Frankfurt School of Social Theory into methods by which people in schools can become reflective. Jack Whitehead (1982), University of Bath, focuses upon dialectical logic as a way of considering the possibilities and limitations of school life.

These approaches place great demand upon teachers' reflectivity because of the institutional arrangements found in schools which work against such practices. Yet without placing evaluation within an adequate political theory of context, evaluation remains solely a symbolic canopy that legitimates occupational and institutional authority and control.

Notes

1 See Hamilton (1977) for discussion of the social and philosophical roots of our contemporary concern for evaluation. For a discussion of the ties of our present to the past, see Kaestle and Smith (1982).

2 It is important to note that the original planning of state intervention involved conflict theories. These sought to involve the poor and disenfranchized in public institutions and policy-making. This intent, however, was modified in practice as the reforms of the 'War-on-Poverty' became administratively oriented (see Rose, 1972). There were also counter-hegemonic social movements towards change. These movements had a similar lure of a promising and splendid future but this vision focused upon *avante garde* art and socialist politics (see Barrett, 1982). These counter-moments receive only a partial hearing in histories of social change.

3 This observation about the organization of education is not to argue that American schools have not maintained hegemonic dispositions. Rather, it is to argue that the direct relation between hegemony and the organization of schooling is more diffuse and subtle than organizational charts might convey.

4 For discussion of the idea of progress, see Nisbet (1969) and Becker (1932).

5 This belief in the context-bound nature of evaluation is not universal. Cronbach, for example, believes that evaluation should generate knowledge that extends beyond the immediate situation. Cronbach's position, however, is not the favored one.

6 This section is drawn, in part, from Popkewitz and Wehlage (1973).

7 See Popkewitz, 1979 and House, 1978, for arguments concerning the political commitments underlying educational and evaluational projects.

8 Parlett and Hamilton (1972) raise a caution about not situating inquiry but this caution is lost in the more recent literature on evaluation.

References

BARRETT, W. (1982) *The Truants, Adventures among the Intellectuals*, Garden City, N.Y., Anchor Books.

BECKER, C. (1982) *The Heavenly City of the 18th Century Philosophers*, New Haven, Conn., Yale University Press.

BRAVERMAN, H. (1974) *Labor and Monopoly Capital: The Degradation of Work in the Twentieth Century*, New York, Monthly Review Press.

BUCHMANN, M. (1982) *Knowledge Utilization: Second Thoughts about the Second Coming*, East Lansing, Mich., Institute for Research on Teaching.

CARR, W. and KEMMIS, S. (1983) *Becoming Critical: Knowing Through Active Research*, Geelong, Deakin University Press.

CLAWSON, D. (1980) *Bureaucracy and the Labor Process: The Transformation of U.S. Industry, 1860–1920*, New York, Monthly Review Press.

CRONBACH, L. and Associates (1980) *Toward Reform and Program Evaluation: Aims, Methods and Institutional Arrangements*, San Francisco, Ca., Jossey-Bass.

EDELMAN, M. (1977) *Political Language: Words That Succeed and Policies That Fail*, New York, Academic Press.

FLODEN, R. and WEINER, S. (1978) 'Rationality to ritual: The multiple roles of evaluation in governmental processes', *Policy Sciences*, 9, pp. 9–18.

GOULDNER, A. (1976) *The Dialectic of Ideology and Technology: The Origins, Grammar and Future of Ideology*, New York, Seabury Press.

GUBA, E. (1978) *Toward a Methodology of Naturalistic Inquiry in Educational Evaluation*, Los Angeles, Ca., Center for the Study of Evaluation, University of California.

HAMILTON, D. (1977) 'Making sense of curriculum evaluation: Continuities and discontinuities in an educational idea', in SHULMAN, L. (Ed.), *Review of Research in Education*, Vol. 5, Itasca, Ill., Peacock.

HOUSE, E. (1978) 'Assumptions underlying evaluation models', *Educational Researcher*, 7, 3, pp. 4–12.

KAESTLE, C. and SMITH, M. (1982) 'The federal role in elementary and secondary education, 1940–1980', *Harvard Educational Review*, 52, 4, pp. 384–408.

LESSINGER, L. (1970) 'Engineering accountability for results in public education', *Phi Delta Kappan*, 52, pp. 117–225.

LUNDGREN, U. (1978) 'Educational evaluation, a basis for, or a legitimation of, educational policy', *Scandinavian Journal of Educational Research*, 23, pp. 31–45.

McDONALD, B. and NORRIS, N. (1981) 'Twin political horizons in evaluation fieldwork', in POPKEWITZ, T. and TABACHNIK, B. (Eds). *The Study of Schooling: Field-Based Methods of Research and Evaluation*, New York, Praeger.

McLAUGHLIN, M. (1976) 'Implementation of ESEA Title I, A problem of compliance', *Teachers College Record*, 77, 3, pp. 397–415.

MARLAND, S. (1972) 'Accountability in education', *Teachers College Record*, 73, pp. 340–5.

MILLS, C. (1959) *Sociological Imagination*, New York, Oxford University Press.

NISBET, R. (1969) *Social Change and History: Aspects of Western Theory of Development*, London, Oxford University Press.

PARLETT, M. and HAMILTON, D. (1972) 'Evaluation as illumination: A new approach to the study of innovatory programs', Occasional Paper No. 9, University of Edinburgh, Centre for Research in Educational Sciences.

POPKEWITZ, T. (1979) 'Schools and the symbolic uses of community participation', in GRANT, C. (Ed.), *Community Participation in Education*, Boston, Mass., Allyn and Bacon.

POPKEWITZ, T. (1982) 'Reform as the organization of ritual', *Journal of Education*, 164, 1, pp. 5–29.

POPKEWITZ, T. and WEHLAGE, G. (1973) 'Accountability: Critique and alternative perspective', *Interchange*, 4, 4, pp. 48–62.

POPKEWITZ, T. et al. (1982) *The Myth of Educational Reform: A Study of School Responses to Planned Change*, Madison, Wisc., University of Wisconsin Press.

RAVITCH, D. (1982) Response to Kaestle and Smith, *Harvard Educational Review*, 52, 4, pp. 412–14.

REUSCH, J. and BATESON, G. (1968) *Communication: The Social Matrix of Psychiatry*, New York, W.W. Norton and Co.

ROSE, S. (1972) *The Betrayal of the Poor: The Transformation of Community Action*, Urbana, Ill., Schenkman Publishing.

SCHATTSCHNIEDER, E. (1960) *The Semi-Sovereign People: A Realist's View of Democracy in America*, New York, Holt, Rinehart and Winston.

STAKE, R. (1980) 'Program evaluation, particular responsive evaluation', in DOCKRELL, W. and HAMILTON, D. (Eds), *Rethinking Educational Research*, London, Hodder and Stoughton.

STUFFELBEAM, D. (1973) 'Educational evaluation and decision making', in WORTHEN, B. and SANDERS, J. (Eds), *Educational Evaluation: Theory and Practice*, Worthington, Ohio, Charles A. Jones.

TOULMIN, S. (1982) 'The construal of reality: Criticism in modern and postmodern science', *Critical Inquiry*, 9, September, pp. 93–111.

WARD, L. (1906) *Applied Sociology: A Treatise on the Conscious Improvement of Society by Society*, Boston, Mass., Ginn and Company.

WHITEHEAD, J. (1982) *A Dialectician's Guide for Educational Researchers*, mimeo, Bath, School of Education, University of Bath.

WORTHEN, B. and SANDERS, J. (Eds) (1973) *Educational Evaluation: Theory and Practice*, Worthington, Ohio, Charles A. Jones.

YEE, A. (1973) 'The need for a broader perspective and dialogue in education', *Educational Leadership*, 30, pp. 229–301.

Chapter 8

The Researcher As a Social Actor: Possibilities, Pathologies and Notes of Caution

This book has been concerned with the contradictory character of social and educational research. In an important sense, social theory enables us to look at our particular contexts and beyond the ordinary limits of our lives to understand their possibilities and their constraints. This transcendent quality of knowledge involves tensions. The languages of social affairs are human inventions and, as such, contain assumptions, values, and priorities that respond to institutional arrangements, historical developments, and the contradictions of our social conditions. No theory is neutral or unattached.

The paradoxical nature of social research poses a particular problem for social and educational researchers. Reason and rationality provide a hope for a more humane reconstruction in society. Yet to acknowledge that knowledge systems are related to particular historical groups in society is to recognize that our forms of reason and rationality embody limits and pathologies. The knowledge of inquiry is always socially and culturally bound. The position of researchers is defined by their affiliation with other groups and interests in society. This relationship is illustrated in the previous chapters by examining the reform tendencies of the academic expert, the assumptions of the study of change, and the formation of educational evaluation. These previous discussions point to an important function: the researcher renders disparate interests cohesive by presenting particular interests as those of the society as a whole.

In this chapter the contradictory role of educational science as promise and pathology will be pursued. Educational research is considered as a particular case of the intellectual in society. While the inherent relations of theory, practice, and praxis are argued, the difficulties they present are by no means easily resolved.

Research and Social Practice

This century has witnessed a change in the nature of authority and the manner by which authority is legitimated.[1] In particular, intellectuals as a social group have changed from sacerdotal personages to secular experts, independent of the patronage of the church or aristocracy but dependent upon the state or the competition of the 'market'. The currency of the new secular expert is the production of knowledge. The validity of knowledge is based upon rules of logic and reference to the empirical, rather than to the social status of the speaker or to the authority of God. The change in the nature of authority contains an illusion of the separation of thought from practice. The intellectual is not considered as an actor in our social conditions.

The separation of thought and practice is expressed in a paradox of the intellectual's work. The knowledge of the intellectual is seen as having a cross-contextual validity: social and psychological theories provide an order and system of classification that seem independent of historical age and social relations. Theories of learning, teacher behaviors, or the political economy of the classroom are thought of as universally applicable. Theory, it is believed, identifies rules that transcend particular and historically situated contexts. The belief in transcendence, however, is in conflict with the historical nature of social knowledge. Our understandings and explanations of social affairs are never separate from social location, cultural circumstances and human purpose.

The relation of science to social practice occurs in a number of different ways. One is in the various cognitive interests that shape and fashion our research. As argued in earlier chapters, there are multiple paradigms to guide our attempts to understand and explain the events and people of the world. Empirical-analytic sciences, for example, contain a cognitive interest in the correct application of technical rules, seeking the most efficient means to achieve stated goals. A second science and interest is symbolic, focusing upon how meaning and interpretation are formed in patterns of communication. A third science is critical. Its cognitive interest is to understand the sources of domination in one's society. Each paradigm imposes a form to rationality that guides thought, reason, and inquiry. Each approach contains its own internal tensions and strains as these sciences are worked out in social affairs.

To be rational and reasonable, then, is not something that we should presuppose as being unidimensional and ahistorical. Empirical-analytic, symbolic, and critical sciences contain particular sets of assumptions about what is logical, thoughtful, and reasonable. Nor are these social and educational sciences monolithic or free-floating elements in a social and political world. The idea of cognitive interest enables us to consider the social sciences as particular and conflicting ways in which cohesion and consent are established in modern, technological societies.

A second aspect of the relation of science and practice lies in the direction given to will and possibility. To adopt any intellectual tradition is to adopt a way to challenge social arrangements. Each 'rationality' provides a logic to frame problems *and* their solutions. To select and organize schemes for analysis and interpretation has consequences beyond 'descriptive' reporting.

The question of 'how do things work' is also a question of how to change those things, as the two questions are intertwined. This relationship was shown embedded in the origin of social sciences. It is also analytically tied to the nature of language in the disciplines. To 'see' problems from the perspective of empirical-analytic sciences, for example, is methodologically to accept structural arrangements as viable and naturally evolving. Research is to identify how to modify and make more adaptable the evolutionary workings of the ongoing social system. This position towards existing interests is 'built into' the science through the underlying assumptions, commitments, and concepts of the paradigm itself. Symbolic and critical sciences, as well, orient and prescribe a world by interpretive schema. We need to recognize, therefore, that all human knowledge is just that — human knowledge which contains dispositions that have reference to both cognitive interests and social practice. The study of 'what is' has reformist as well as descriptive qualities.

This role of the intellectual in social transformations and repro-duction is argued by Gramsci (1971). The intellectual serves to mediate or transform the relationship of the rulers and ruled into a single dynamic entity. The mediating role, Gramsci argues, is not through coercion or force but through persuasion and consent. This occurs as a specialized group assumes responsibility for defining conceptual and philosophical notions that are to give organization to social life. The intellectual becomes the expert in legitimation, influencing moral conduct and direction of will by controlling the communications through which a society establishes purpose and describes and evaluates its institutional conditions.

Intellectual and Social Movements

The relation of theory practice can be considered by recognizing that there exists a complex set of interrelationships among social movements and intellectual groups. The history of social and educational sciences is related to discontinuities, strains, and struggles that exist in the larger society and which are drawn into institutional domains as people seek to resolve the uneasiness and contradictions that confront them.

The behavioral sciences are a case-in-point. During the 1920s and 1930s behavioral science emerged as an alternative to the dominant legal and organizational analysis which took for granted the formal definitions of government, organization, and policy. The methods of behavioral study made official definitions problematic by examining how people behaved, how policies were formulated and implemented, and how groups interacted to form social and political practice. The behavioral sciences used mathematics and behavioral analysis to model social sciences upon the perceived procedures of the natural sciences.

Behavioral sciences responded to at least three conditions external to their disciplinary context. One was a search for ways to give coherence to the discontinuities and strains of the particular historical time. The 1930s was a period of world-wide depression and revolution and behavioral theories were a conservative response to these conditions. Their presuppositions gave reference to structural evolution, harmony, and stability. Second was the legitimacy provided by 'science' to the academic expert in the new relationship to policy-makers. The detached stance and use of mathematics made these social sciences seem related to the high-status physical and biological sciences. Third, behavioral sciences were organically attached to the emerging corporate bourgeoisie. They were concerned with the administration of production. Behavioralism and behaviorism could be used to socially organize labor processes as well as for understanding.

In our contemporary situation the location of behavioral science is no longer contested. Its position is tied to traditional authority in society. The analytic posture of research accepts dominant structures, patterns, and dispositions. A social implication of behavioral research is to provide for the uninterrupted continuity of institutional relations. From time-on-task research to studies of school 'system', change or learning, the messages of behavioralism in educational research are of coherence, legitimacy, and stability.

The movement of behavioral science towards traditional social interests has not occurred without counter-movements. New groups of intellectuals emerge to give symbolic coherence and direction for alternative or oppositional social structures.[2] The sociology of knowledge in the United States has emphasized elements of the past that are still active and viable in the experiences of the culture, while concerning itself with the creation of experiences, meanings, and values which do not receive expression in current institutional arrangements. The sociology of Berger (1976) and the arguments of 'progressive' education, with its emphasis on community and developmental psychologies, assume that there are alternatives to the dominant patterned ways of life.

Scholarly traditions that give attention to the emergence of new social relations also have been revitalized. Often associated with socialist politics and Marxist analysis, these traditions stand in opposition to existing dominant culture. These intellectuals seek to establish an organic relationship with the working class, seeing this class, as Marx did, as an oppressed class to be freed from domination by other interests in society. This class is thought to provide the leadership for a formation of more just and humane social patterns. Much of the oppositional literature about schooling seeks to identify ways in which teachers can use pedagogical relationships to work towards socialism and can create enabling strategies for working-class people (for example, Apple, 1982; Giroux, 1983; Whitty, 1981).

These three elements of the academic intellectual (traditional, residual, and emergent) exist as part of a dynamic of institutional life. The interaction and conflict among paradigms provide conditions in which science itself evolves.[3] The cross-currents of ideas are also part of a nexus of more general issues of social reproduction and transformation. As discussed in earlier chapters, models of equilibrium or conflict underlie the various paradigms. The models are related to visions of social order and to values that are cherished and threatened by institutional contradictions. This dynamic is a moment in the work of social science. It is embedded in discussions of pedagogical theory.[4]

In considering the researcher as part of an occupational group and within larger complexes of institutional interests and relations, we must recognize that the position of the intellectual developed from the movement of feudalism to a market economy in which there were shifting values and room for intellectual subcultures. Intellectuals were relatively free to choose the content of their work. Eastern intellectuals, in contrast, emerged from an Asiatic mode of production in which land was given for service and was not inheritable. This Eastern system was transformed into one of rational redistribution. The intellectual was a civil servant who claimed a key role in the process of social reproduction and distribution of surplus value. The Eastern intellectual's position has become that of exploiting the relative monopoly of complex knowledge as a means for achieving state goals. Tied to the state distribution system, alternative values play a lesser role. Intellectual conflict and ideas of 'academic freedom' do not receive legitimation. This relationship was illustrated in the discussion of Soviet pedagogical research and the distinction between the Marxism of those in power and those who seek power.

The situation of the contemporary intellectual is seemingly in direct contrast to the earlier ideological and moral mission of the intellectual associated with the priestly estate and the nineteenth century intellectual. The contemporary Western intellectual articulates the intelligence of particular social groups and the institutional sectors to which they affiliate. In this position, their knowledge is defined as transcendent. The shift from priest to scientist, with its related change in the function of intelligence from explaining the ways of God to explaining nature, poses an irony. The theological mission once assumed by the priestly class is still present but in a new form. The movement is from an explanation of a heavenly order to a discussion of nature's rules, but the new explanations are to give purpose and meaning to a world that is otherwise deemed purposeless.

Professionalization of Knowledge: A New Intelligentsia?

The problem of the role of the intellectual is noted throughout history. Marx and Bakunin debated the role of the intellectual and the vanguard. Gramsci (1971) pointed to the contradiction in the position of the intellectual in society: intellectuals' status outside social movements, their tendencies toward reform, and their membership in a new educated class. A possible tension is posited as the intellectual seeks to postulate what is good for others in society. The tension evolves around whose good and interest is articulated.

The reformist role of the intellectual takes on a particular historical form with the emergence of the professional 'helping' occupations, such as teachers, psychologists, and social workers. The label 'professional' gives these expanding occupations status and legitimacy. The professions make jurisdictional claims upon major sectors of private and public life (Bledstein, 1976). Special occupations assume public administration of the domains of family life, education, law, marriage, sex, medicine, and welfare. Their mandates are concerned with moral formation and the control of the culture, language, and daily practices within institutional arrangements. These particular occupations are seen as having license to translate personal problems into categories defined and controlled by the profession. The role of the helping professions is not only to provide symbolic canopies for social relations in society (for discussion of the class location of these occupational groups, see Wright, 1978). The professional combines scholarly work with applied procedures for controlling the meanings and relationships within its institutional territory. The knowledge of the lawyer, teacher, and social worker is to describe, organize, and prescribe the scope and boundaries of possible social relations and meanings for their clients. As such, the mandate of the professional occupations involves techniques of social manipulation as well as symbols that are to influence moral conduct and direction of will. This relation to control was explored in the discussion of models of change and evaluation. Each emerges in relation to a state agenda for social amelioration. The social scientist assumes a major role as expert-to-policy maker, providing technical knowledge to make the administration of institutions efficient and effective. This function, it was argued, is ideological and has implications to the dynamics of cultural and social reproduction and production.

The moral authority of these occupations is grounded in the authority of science. The formal language of science calls attention to things in the world rather than to the processes by which ideas and activities occur. The reliance upon procedures, rules of evidence, and impersonal knowledge posits a world of efficiency and rationality. There are explicit and distinctive qualifications built upon factual support. There are rules to justify assertions as well as a self-conscious and self-critical attitude. The formal language contains elements of cognitive playfulness and promotes a consideration of the possibilities of our human condition. The promise of science to professional life is to seek closer relations between the mandate and everyday practices.

The authority of science is important to institutional legitimacy. By affiliating occupational work with the ritual and ceremonies of science, institutional life seems 'objective'. Images of inner control, respect for rules and proven experience are projected. The credentials establish the competence and trust in those who are to have the special power over worldly experience. The professional occupations seem to transcend politics, the corruptions of personality, and the partisanship and capriciousness of the everyday.

The establishment and maintenance of trust is important to institutional conduct because of the ambiguity and controversy that underlie our institutional conditions. The mandate to 'educate', for example, can never be straightforward or unidimensional. In part, schooling involves goals of 'citizenship', understanding, or learning that have no clear outcome or direct process. But just as important, there are the predicaments of schooling. Our world is one of social differentiation in wealth, status, power, and sensibilities. It is a world in which our noble acts and heroic deeds to improve social conditions have unanticipated and sometimes unwilled consequences as the ideas of people are acted upon in practice. It is a world of historical continuity, where the assumptions and presuppositions of the past provide us with dispositions towards the permitted and unpermitted of the present. These ambiguities of our social life interweave with the mandate and practices of schooling.

At this point, we must recognize that the formal language of science never exists away from a public language. The words and practices of research are situated in institutional patterns. Occupational language and practices are not simply formal instruments for describing events but are themselves part of the events, helping to create beliefs about the nature, causes, consequences, and remedies for institutional practices (Edelman, 1977). The syntactic structure and grammatical order not only create a structure for inquiry, skepticism, and experimentation; the public language also creates a structure for loyalty and social solidarity.

In institutional contexts it is sometimes difficult to distinguish between the formal language of science and the public languages of professionals. The terms of research are often drawn from social relations and contain the normative assumptions of the context. To label someone as disabled, gifted, talented, or presenting a disciplinary problem is to bring to bear social values and socially cued perceptions about 'good' and 'evil'. Each category of schooling classifies what is to be considered educated or deficient. A category orients us to the sensibilities and awarenesses to be valued in individuals. Gifted or disabled are not categories rooted in science *per se* but definitions arrived at through cultural negotiations among competing interests in schooling and society. While these definitions are inserted into scientific discourse to give explicit and distinctive qualifications, the formal language does not remove the cultural biases and institutional origins of the words.

This merging of formal and public language is a part of contemporary research. Recent research efforts in America, for example, have been directed towards 'engaged-academic time'. The focus of the research is the relationship between time spent in classrooms studying subject-matter and achievement. Such research, however, is not merely a scholarly pursuit. Questions about 'engaged-time' or 'time-on-task' begin with the acceptance of the official definitions about what is academic and learning. Further, the discourse about that research is brought back into institutional contexts in a manner that ascribes value and meaning different from the purpose of science itself. The question of how much time spent on mathematics and reading validates pre-existing beliefs about the importance of children being kept busy without reference to the content of school learning. The separation of process from content reinforces the importance of the control mechanisms of classrooms, such as timed tests and worksheet assignments.

'Engaged-academic time' research directs attention to a relationship between research and our patterns of social conduct. As research becomes a part of an institutional context, there is a merging with ongoing beliefs and priorities. Reason is confused with conclusion, affect with meaning. The consequence is not self-reflection of existing patterns. Rather, the authority structure of the organization is strengthened by the research. Professional folk wisdom about the 'gulf' between theory and practice obscures this social function of the intellectual. Theories do act back upon the situation that they were to explain.

The Pathology of Science: Bureaucratic Conceptions

The acceptance of school categories as the basis for research directs attention to another aspect of professionalization in the helping occupations. Often the language of inquiry is one of bureaucracy rather than science. It is a language that creates a view of human activity that is highly specialized, fragmented, and impersonal. It is a language filled with jargon and banalities, such as needs assessment, teaching/learning styles, modules, competencies, criterion-referenced testing, and so on. The language of bureaucracy dulls our critical facilities by its fascination with procedure and rules.

We have already witnessed the form and imagery of bureaucratic language in the study of planned school change and evaluation. For the most part, the image of social affairs is one that is devoid of human involvement and social interaction. (An exception here is the case study and critical action research discussed in Chapter 7.) Knowledge is seen as distinct from method, content as unambiguous and hierarchical in quality, and rational thought as logical, technical, and predefined. The problems of thought, action, and value are reduced to logical and psychological states or qualities (see Popkewitz, 1983). Social affairs are then to enact our taxonomies, flowcharts or 'systems' of social events. Actions are no longer expressions of people but symbolic performances used to define people in general. This conception of knowledge and process devalues what is human. What are essentially social and human activities are made to seem thing-like facts separated from their human source.

These assumptions of research fit assumptions of bureaucratic thought more than those of science. Good science becomes the proper management of institutional affairs and its clients. The purpose of the research, evaluation, or change is the application of appropriate techniques to realize defined goals under given conditions. The procedure is to treat the social world as impersonal. Its elements exist as static entities that have objective qualities. The movement of the elements is seen as hierarchical and linear. The self-criticism and cognitive playfulness associated with science are lost as the purpose becomes rationalization and codification of existing procedures. The demands for exactness enshrine stability and regularity by disregarding the political and moral considerations of our institutional forms.

It is an irony of such research that the conclusions of 'study' are nonsensical. In a review of teacher 'effects' research in teacher education (Popkewitz *et al.*, 1979), the findings were found to have little potency for understanding or explaining the events of schooling, teaching, or learning. For example, some findings suggest that it is good to talk about a lesson taught or plans to teach. Further, it is better that such talk be with a person rather than a tape recorder. Another study tells the reader that you are more likely to do something if you spend time practicing it. Research on 'affective' aspects of teaching tells us that a teacher should talk clearly, be enthusiastic but not necessarily warm, varied but not necessarily flexible. The research makes sense only, if at all, when placed in a context of bureaucratic language and interests, as the 'explanations' obscure more than they reveal of our social conditions, practices, and interests.

The use of bureaucratic thought in professional science may have consequences for the capacity of individuals to provide for themselves (Lasch, 1977; Donzelot, 1979). Individual ability and personal competence are redefined through rational schemes which reify our social conditions. These rational schemes are controlled, disseminated, and evaluated by particular occupational groups. As the psychologists define and prescribe marital and family relations, the urban sociologists issue guidelines for living together in cities, and educators counsel children about why they are not learning and being 'responsible' for what the school defines as learning, a form of dependency is introduced. Skills and knowledge, previously developed by individuals are reconstituted in ways that mystify our social conditions. The individual is no longer responsible for the construction of reality but has it characterized, maintained, and certified by licensed groups. These schemes make the trivial seem consequential and focal while obscuring the dynamics between individuals and their social world.

Possibilities of the Intellectual

While this book has maintained a debunking motif towards the practices of research, it has also suggested that science can offer forms of knowledge that have 'corrective' possibilities. Those possibilities, however, are not contained in the common belief that science provides specific guides for the organization of the present and future. Science, as any form of knowledge, is not able to provide such positive guidance.[5] Rather, the possibilities of the intellectual are in taking a negative stance towards our social conditions. The strength of our inquiries lies in the creation of different and critical webs of meanings for judging the appropriateness of our cultural circumstances and in assuming a skeptical attitude towards our words, customs, traditions, and institutions.

Social and educational sciences are dialects of language and, as language, provide us with only a partial vision of what exists. Science abbreviates and orders the scattered data of one's biography as conceptual perspectives give people a proximate vision of our human condition. To conceptualize is to perform a transitive operation on reality which neither mirrors nor copies experience but allows people to suppose that things are happening after a fashion. What appear to be acts of discovery are inventions.

Understanding that science is linguistic invention is to understand its limitation. Science enables us to suppose that things are happening. It does not tell us what things are. Nor is science immune from the values of its theorists and from the theorists' relation to, and position in, a particular society. The languages of science are embedded in culture, history, and social relations. While seeming to decontextualize and transcend our social conditions, the languages of science pose their own irony.

The possibility of a science of our human condition emerges from making problematic what is accepted as normal and natural. Society has many different layers of meaning, not all of which are part of the consciousness of everyday reality. To engage in study of our social situations is to scrutinize the facades of the apparently self-evident and self-validating assumptions of our world. Understanding our pretensions, deceptions, and self-deceptions enables us to find holes in the order of causality and reduce our collaboration with the accidents of birth and circumstances. Our perception of the whole and our relationship to it can be changed and enlarged with such vantage points.

The importance of a critical posture emerges, I believe, from the forms of domination that typify contemporary society. Power and control are exercised through patterns of communication that establish particular social relations. This control involves hegemonies in which particular interests in society are made to seem universal. We need to take seriously Berger's (1976) admonishment about those who call for brave new worlds: 'The world today is divided into ideological camps. The adherents of each tell us with great assurance where we're at and what we should do about it. We should not believe any of them' (p. 1). Berger continues that debunking is not an end in itself. The skepticism of inquiry can open up new avenues of understanding, policy, and, although Berger does not mention it, practice. The most promising element of science is a 'trust yet skepticism' towards our human condition. We need to recognize what traditions and customs are important to maintain while being able to make what seems normal in our world an object of scrutiny and transformation.

To engage in critical inquiry requires a multiple and complex conception of causality. Historical processes, regularities in social action, structural conditions, and the actions of particular individuals contribute to persistence and change in social situations. Each chain of events has, as its consequence, a new formation that rejoins the events in such a way that there are new conditions and circumstances in action. To freeze events as 'independent' and 'dependent' variables is to crystallize the complex dynamics of social life and to impose a sense of stability, directionality, and necessity where such assumptions are problematic.

The emergent and residual tendencies discussed earlier maintain assumptions of a critical attitude. To adopt either is to be, at points, marginal to traditional cultural interests, willing to step aside from the ongoing patterns of social conduct. Yet, to maintain a skeptical attitude is difficult. The human tendency is to reify existence and to create dogma under the canopy of inquiry. Money, prestige, and status are often closely tied to the traditional interests. We are witnessing, for example, the growing importance of contract research in determining priorities and direction of scientific communities. With this has occurred a subtle shift in the reward system of tenure or employment in universities in which grants obtained are made a criterion of promotion. The reward structures thus lessen those efforts which seek to make problematic the agenda established in the political process.

To assume a critical stance towards existing and alternative programs is not, however, to accept Mannheim's notion of a free-floating intellectual. Science involves a paradox of detachment and engagement. A researcher must assume a stance that steps aside from ongoing interactions in society. The purpose is to make a radical critique of society and its institutions, focusing upon barriers to the full realization of an individual's spirit and societal potential. To form this detachment, however, requires an engagement in which ultimate values are defined to guide study. The point of reference of values provides a comparison for the world described. To criticize society is to attack the actual bearers of values as exemplifying or detracting from the realization of those ultimate values.

A critical stance does not disregard the cognitive interests of the empirical-analytic and symbolic sciences. The questions of these paradigms do have importance. The argument here is to place these paradigms within broader social and institutional contexts and to recognize that our inquiries should be part of a general historical skepticism and social philosophical awareness. This awareness is found, for example, in the works of empirical-analytic researchers, such as Easton (1971) and Simon (1981). Their research contains a breadth of understanding, a recognition of history, and a detail that directs attention to the complexity of our social and psychological conditions. The difficulty of much contemporary empirical-analytic and symbolic research, however, is the foregoing of skepticism, history and social philosophical awareness. The application of correct procedures of data collection is defined *as* science.

We should not confuse the formulation of rules and data collection procedures as the work of science. The value of statistics, questionnaires, or field observations is in their contribution to answering questions that are deemed important. Methods of science are more than techniques of data collection. They are inventions that enable us to respond to our curiosities and doubts. There is a strategic interplay of questions, concepts, and procedures. Too often, however, a different definition is given to method. Research questions are formed in relation to a pre-existing technique of data collection: what type of questions can be answered about learning through a multivariate statistical analysis or a field observation. This situation reduces methods to a set of predetermined rules. Formalized tasks outline what one is to do without reference to questions that might be asked and concepts invented. The doctoral thesis, for example, is often defined as having a predefined order and format: there is a statement of problem and hypotheses, review of literature, design and procedure, findings and conclusions. While elements of this order are found in most research, the reconstructed logic of science crystallizes the practice of inquiry and denudes it of its creative potential.

The Relation of Theory to Practice: The Problem of Praxis

One of the most perplexing elements in this exploration is the relation of theory to practice. At root is a rejection of social inquiry as a detached, apolitical endeavor. Throughout I have argued that theory responds to the practical affairs of our life in a number of ways: theories maintain cognitive interests, give direction to will and possibility; and emerge out of the contradictions we confront, the social movements that engage us, and the paths that we define for our contemporary salvation. To recognize the social location and cultural circumstances of theorizing leaves us with a remaining question of the role of theory in social formations and transformations.

One response to the relation of theory to practice is an instrumental view of knowledge (Fay, 1977). Theory is deemed useful because of the power it confers on those who learn its truth. That power is rooted in the capacity of people to control their social environment by being able either to produce a particular event or to prevent its occurrence. Theory is thought of as a tool of manipulation and a basis for social engineering by which one can rationally control objective processes through the manipulation of independent variables. The instrumental view presupposes that those with knowledge are in a position of power to alter social conditions and to control social and psychological processes.

An instrumental view of theory needs rejection. To assume an instrumental quality to theory is to define humanity as an inert objectivity and to deny self-reflection as an element in social conduct. Practice involves strategic choices in political negotiations. These choices involve a dynamic relation among human intentionality, situational and historical constraints and an interplay of multiple social interests. No theory can eliminate the ambiguities and the contigencies of human practice.

Theory is useful to the extent that it informs people about how a particular way of life frustrates their needs and causes suffering. The goal of such theory is to enlighten people about how they can change their lives and arrive at a new self-understanding that illuminates the relations of objective and subjective conditions. 'Social theories are the means by which people can liberate themselves from the particular causal processes that victimize them precisely because they are ignorant of who they are' (Fay, 1977, p. 204).

The relation of theory to social practice, movement, and change has been called *praxis*. The Greeks made a distinction which is helpful in understanding this idea. The distinction was between *praxis* and *poiesis*. Praxis is *doing* and is a self-contained activity in which there is no direct means to an end. Poiesis, in contrast, referred to *making* in which there is an end-product. Poiesis (making) is concerned with completion and its meaning subsists in the work that it leaves behind. Acting in daily life does not have such a particular end. Praxis or doing is that mode of conduct that contains its meaning in itself and whose completion therefore consists of its satisfactory accomplishment. The right action is something that is related to the concrete situation in which no knowledge can comprehend its entirety. Praxis involves acting in the polis and it is never finished. Not every direction for action can be deduced from theory and theory should not be related to production.

In contemporary critical science, praxis assumes a more specific meaning. Praxis involves a revolutionary form for our actions and theorizing. It is argued that we are part of the world that is studied and that involvement entails commitment and transformation. Praxis introduces a radical moment in practice.

> The man of praxis is revolutionary, the practical man takes the given social order as permanent.... To learn from praxis is to develop a revolutionary doctrine which will enable one to understand the basic forces in history and the possibilities for developing a revolutionary movement so that men may again gain control over their lives (Hoffman, 1975, p. 17).

Theory is seen as an element in the creation and transformation of the social world. The alienation, loss of self-identity and control that many believe typify our contemporary conditions are to be overcome through the dialectics of theory and practice. Praxis is to unite the object and subject through an interplay of theory and practice.

No matter how appealing the rhetoric of politics and freedom, the problem of praxis involves ambiguities that are not easily resolved. A belief in a causal efficacy of ideas is inadequate, for one must recognize that 'particular social forces not only presuppose a kind of ignorance but also give rise to it in the first place and sustain it as long as a person participates in this form' (Fay, 1977, p. 204). Ideas are a function of social conditions and play a causal role in creating and sustaining particular social structures. The dilemma is that while ideas are also to guide action, ideas are located in and a product of historical actions in which certain interests are favored and handicapped.

A different type of dilemma is posed in the meaning and relation between theory and practice. Ottmann (1982) posed the dilemma as the theory problem and the praxis problem. To look to theory as the practical freeing of people from particular ideologies and power structures undermines reason's claim to universality. The praxis problem is to historically relativize theory and therefore to be unable to legitimate a universally binding praxis.

The relation of theory to practice remains clear yet a dilemma. Theory responds to and is a part of our social condition and its possibility. The working out of that relationship, however, involves contingencies, human agency, and strategic actions. To take praxis seriously is to consider our social affairs as one of accomplishments not completions. The role of theory in practice is a part of our history, not of prediction and manipulation. We cannot take for granted the promises of freedom or emancipation that are offered by science but must retain a skepticism to our contemporary routes to salvation.

A Concluding Remark

The arguments of the preceding chapters used a method of critique to focus inwardly upon a community's history, structure, and conduct. To study institutions such as schools requires that we also study and maintain a skepticism towards those who do the studying. This skepticism is posed by considering educational science as an occupational community. That community involves internal debates about its nature and character. But it also involves forms of work that have relation to larger issues of social structure, cultural reproduction, and transformation. The analysis of theory, method, and techniques in social science continually points to problems of interest, control, and reification. These horizons of scientific communities and social/ cultural context are important for understanding the possibilities and pathologies of disciplined work.

These notes of caution, pathology, and possibility, however, contain both humility and trepidation. There is a regretfulness in the partial transformation of the intellectual into a professional, with the narrower function of the intelligentsia to use knowledge to manipulate social affairs. The expert-to-policy-maker has limited the horizon of inquiry and introduced bureaucratic elements. Much of current work in educational science is denuded of creativity and inspiration. Yet to argue from a perspective of critique is to realize that there can be no clearcut solution to the conflict of value or a straightforward alternative to what passes as scientific knowledge. The struggles which are played out in our sciences are often those of our society and therefore important as debates about what is an appropriate world. The call for prescription is both to limit the debate and to alter the character of the struggle. Further, those who offer prescriptions seem to offer only new (or old) banalities and introduce glibness. At best, what can be offered is an argument by example. The appropriateness of what is offered is judged by what is provided.

Perhaps the most perplexing aspect of the argument and one which requires the greatest humility is the problem of praxis. It is clear that there is a relation of theory and practice. The history of social science in America has been concerned with strategies of social reform and amelioration that entail elements of praxis, although not always in its revolutionary meaning. While this relationship can be noted, the actual dynamic cannot be stipulated. The history of 'ideas' in social contexts is not straightforward. As ideas pass into the realm of practice, there are essential modifications in both ideas and situation. These modifications involve unanticipated and sometimes unwilled consequences. This 'limitation' requires a self-critical quality that enables researchers to scrutinize the assumptions, implications, and consequences of their work.

The social predicaments of researchers require that I return to an issue raised in the preface. The patterns of socialization in disciplines often obscure the complex and profound quality of research. If one looks at graduate research programs, the novice is initiated in research courses of design, statistics, or data collection techniques such as interviewing or observing. Association conventions and journals also give emphasis to the procedural logic and technological elements of inquiry. This emphasis is often labeled 'methods' or 'methodology'. The defining of procedures of data collection as 'methods' creates a specific set of meanings for the conduct of research. The interplay of social, philosophical, political, and communal elements with technique is lost. Statistics or 'case study' stand as independent of the intellectual traditions in which questions are generated and findings considered. The vital and creative quality of science is not in technical proficiencies *per se*, but in a playfulness and imagination that combines with a detailed attention to the empirical. To ignore the intellectual, social, and historical roots of science is to create what the philosopher Feyerabend calls 'professionalized incompetence'.

Notes

1 This issue is discussed in different ways. See, for example, Bensman and Lilienfeld, 1973; Gramsci, 1971; Gouldner, 1979; Karabel, 1976; Williams, 1977; Konrad and Szelenyi, 1979; Szelenyi, 1982; Mannheim, 1936.
2 Williams (1977) discusses these tendencies of alternative and oppositional. Also see Chapter 2 for a discussion of residual and emergent critical sciences.
3 The interaction among paradigms needs to be interrelated with internal developments of a paradigm to understand the development of science. An internal development might be the invention or refinement of a new technique for data collection or a new concept.
4 One can consider educational debates at the turn of century related to these more general issues of the different locations of the intellectual in a changing society. Eliot's suggestions for reform of the secondary school, for example, reflected certain dominant cultural ideas about mental training. These ideas can be contrasted to residual and emergent themes found in the work of Dewey, Snedden, and Bobbitt. Dewey wanted to use science and technology in ways that captured and reinforced traditional values of community and craft. Snedden and Bobbitt, in contrast, rejected traditional cultural values, which, at that time, were associated with the gentry and *laissez-faire* capitalism. These educators sought to combine the emergent cultural interests of science with the new corporate interests. The task of social amelioration was to control social and natural phenomena through administration and efficiency. As conditions changed, the emergent interest of the 1900s became dominant, tied to traditional interests. Social efficiency and human engineering are part of the hegemony and concerned with maintaining consensus and stability.
5 To recognize science as one form of knowledege is also to recognize that science complements other ways of knowing, such as those found in art, literature, and poetry.

References

APPLE, M. (1982) *Education and Power*, Boston, Mass., Routledge and Kegan Paul.

BENSMAN, J. and LILIENFELD, R. (1973) *Craft and Consciousness, Occupational Technique and the Development of World Images*, New York, John Wiley and Son.

BERGER, P. (1976) *Pyramids of Sacrifice, Political Ethics and Social Change*, New York, Anchor-Doubleday.

BLEDSTEIN, B. (1976) *The Culture of Professionalism: The Middle Class and the Development of Higher Education in America*, New York, W.W. Norton Co.

DONZELOT, J. (1979) *The Policing of Families*, R. Hurley (Trans), New York, Pantheon Books.

EASTON, D. (1971) *The Political System: An Inquiry into the State of Political Science*, New York, Knopf.

EDELMAN, M. (1977) *Political Language, Words That Succeed and Policies That Fail*, New York, Academic Press.

FAY, B. (1977) 'How people change themselves: The relationship between critical theory and its audience', in BALL, T. (Ed.), *Political Theory and Praxis: New Perspectives*, Minneapolis, Minn., University of Minnesota Press, pp. 200–36.

GIROUX, H. (1983) *Theory and Resistance in Education: A Pedagogy for the Opposition*, Hadley, Mass., Bergin and Garvey.

GOULDNER, A. (1979) *The Future of Intellectuals and the Rise of the New Class*, New York, Seabury Press.

GRAMSCI, A. (1971) *Selections from the Prison Notebooks*, Q. Hoare and G. Smith (Eds and Trans), New York, International Publishers.

HABERMAS, J. (1968) *Knowledge and Human Interests*, J. Shapiro (Ed.), Boston, Mass., Beacon Press.

HOFFMAN, J. (1975) *Marxism and the Theory of Praxis: A Critique of Some New Versions of Old Fallacies*, London, Lawrence and Wishart.

KARABEL, J. (1976) 'Revolutionary contradictions: Antonio Gramsci and the problem of intellectuals', *Politics and Society*, 6, 2, pp. 123–73.

KONRAD, G. and SZELENYI, I. (1979) *The Intellectuals on the Road to Class Power: A Sociological Study of the Role of the Intelligentsia in Socialism*, A. Arato and R. Allen (Trans), New York, Harcourt, Brace, Jovanovich.

LASCH, C. (1977) *Haven in a Heartless World, the Family Besieged*, New York, Basic Books.

MANNHEIM, K. (1936) *Ideology and Utopia: An Introduction to the Sociology of Knowledge*, New York, Harcourt, Brace and World.

OTTMANN, H. (1982) 'Cognitive interest and self-reflection', in THOMPSON, J. and HELD, D. (Eds), *Habermas: Critical Debates*, Cambridge, Mass., MIT Press, pp. 79–97.

POPKEWITZ, T. (1983) 'Methods of teacher education and cultural codes', in BEN-PERETZ, M. *et al.* (Eds), *Preservice and Inservice Education of Science Teachers*, Rehovot, Israel, Balaban Publishers.

POPKEWITZ, T. *et al.* (1978) 'Dulling the senses: Research in teacher education', *Journal of Teacher Education*, 33, 5, pp. 52–60.

SIMON, H. (1981) *The Sciences of the Artificial*, Cambridge Mass., MIT Press.

SZELÈNYI, I. (1982) 'Gouldner's theory of intellectuals as a flawed universal class', *Theory and Society*, 11, pp. 779–98.

WHITTY, G. (1981) 'Left policy and the practice and sociology of education', Paper presented at Fourth Annual Sociology of Education Conference, Birmingham, England, January 1981.

WILLIAMS, R. (1977) *Marxism and Literature*, New York, Oxford University Press.

WRIGHT, E. (1978) *Class, Crisis and the State*, London, New Left Books.

Author Index

Author Index

Subject Index